Janis Fehr

Local Invariant Features for 3D Image Analysis

AF137009

Janis Fehr

Local Invariant Features for 3D Image Analysis

Dissertation

Südwestdeutscher Verlag für Hochschulschriften

Impressum/Imprint (nur für Deutschland/ only for Germany)
Bibliografische Information der Deutschen Nationalbibliothek: Die Deutsche Nationalbibliothek verzeichnet diese Publikation in der Deutschen Nationalbibliografie; detaillierte bibliografische Daten sind im Internet über http://dnb.d-nb.de abrufbar.
Alle in diesem Buch genannten Marken und Produktnamen unterliegen warenzeichen-, marken- oder patentrechtlichem Schutz bzw. sind Warenzeichen oder eingetragene Warenzeichen der jeweiligen Inhaber. Die Wiedergabe von Marken, Produktnamen, Gebrauchsnamen, Handelsnamen, Warenbezeichnungen u.s.w. in diesem Werk berechtigt auch ohne besondere Kennzeichnung nicht zu der Annahme, dass solche Namen im Sinne der Warenzeichen- und Markenschutzgesetzgebung als frei zu betrachten wären und daher von jedermann benutzt werden dürften.

Verlag: Südwestdeutscher Verlag für Hochschulschriften Aktiengesellschaft & Co. KG
Dudweiler Landstr. 99, 66123 Saarbrücken, Deutschland
Telefon +49 681 37 20 271-1, Telefax +49 681 37 20 271-0, Email: info@svh-verlag.de
Zugl.: Freiburg, Albert-Ludwigs-universität, Diss., 2009

Herstellung in Deutschland:
Schaltungsdienst Lange o.H.G., Berlin
Books on Demand GmbH, Norderstedt
Reha GmbH, Saarbrücken
Amazon Distribution GmbH, Leipzig
ISBN: 978-3-8381-1083-7

Imprint (only for USA, GB)
Bibliographic information published by the Deutsche Nationalbibliothek: The Deutsche Nationalbibliothek lists this publication in the Deutsche Nationalbibliografie; detailed bibliographic data are available in the Internet at http://dnb.d-nb.de.
Any brand names and product names mentioned in this book are subject to trademark, brand or patent protection and are trademarks or registered trademarks of their respective holders. The use of brand names, product names, common names, trade names, product descriptions etc. even without a particular marking in this works is in no way to be construed to mean that such names may be regarded as unrestricted in respect of trademark and brand protection legislation and could thus be used by anyone.

Publisher:
Südwestdeutscher Verlag für Hochschulschriften Aktiengesellschaft & Co. KG
Dudweiler Landstr. 99, 66123 Saarbrücken, Germany
Phone +49 681 37 20 271-1, Fax +49 681 37 20 271-0, Email: info@svh-verlag.de

Copyright © 2009 by the author and Südwestdeutscher Verlag für Hochschulschriften Aktiengesellschaft & Co. KG and licensors
All rights reserved. Saarbrücken 2009

Printed in the U.S.A.
Printed in the U.K. by (see last page)
ISBN: 978-3-8381-1083-7

Abstract

The automatic analysis of 3D volume data is an emerging topic. The recent development towards increasingly cheaper, faster and better 3D imaging devices, such as CT, MRI and especially confocal microscopy results in huge amounts of 3D data which eventually have to be analyzed and evaluated. In most cases, the evaluation is still accomplished by very tedious and resource consuming manual work. This rises the demand for (semi)-automatic algorithms, which not only allow a qualitative high throughput evaluation of the recorded data, but also provide reliable and reproducible quantitative measures for further statistical analysis or mathematical modelling of complex systems.
Typical tasks of 3D image analysis usually include the detection, segmentation and classification of objects and (sub)-structures, counting and localizing, as well as the quantitative description of textures, shapes and positions.

While there has been very intense research in the area of 3D medical image analysis over the last decades, most of the methods developed in this context tend to fail on recently emerging biological 3D image analysis problems. The main reasons can be seen in the more difficult imaging properties, smaller target structures and higher intra class variations within the biological data. Also, other new research areas in demand for 3D evaluation methods, like the analysis of protein structures or 3D object retrieval, hardly benefit from existing medical image processing results.
This motivated us to try to address the problem of 3D image analysis in a more general way - moving away from very specialized "one Ph.D. per problem" solutions and towards highly generic, multi purpose methods which can easily be adapted to new problems. It is obvious that this is a very ambiguous goal, but we were able to show that the methods and ideas which we derive throughout this thesis cover a wide range of different operations (detection, segmentation, classification, etc.) on quite different types of 3D volume data from different sources.

In this thesis, we present a novel *framework* **which provides generic methods for the automatic analysis of 3D volume data**. We combine **local invariant feature** descriptors with **learning techniques** to infer mathematical models describing 3D objects (structures) in dense and cluttered data. Using annotated training examples, our overall *framework* is able to adapt to a wide range of different problems by learning local formations of shape and texture properties.

Local feature descriptors play the key role in our concept. Due to the often times high intra class variations and anisotropic nature of the data, we derive features that are invariant towards the most common data transformations, including rotation, gray-scale changes and for some applications also scaling and translation. Throughout this thesis, we provide as many as 14 different local 3D features: from general texture and shape features to very specific and highly specialized detectors.
The derived features operate either on gray-scale and scalar multi-channel volume data or on 3D vector fields (which usually are obtained from the gradient information of scalar input data).
Besides an in-depth theoretical investigation of the mathematical background and the actual, highly optimized implementation of invariant features for 3D volume data, we also provide learning methods for the selection and data driven construction of the features.

The second key contribution to our *framework* are supervised and partially interactive learning methods using the input of the local features to detect, segment and classify given objects or structures. While we are mostly relying on "standard" algorithms such as Support Vector Machines (SVM) and Markov Random Fields (MRF) to train our *framework*, we derived several algorithms to speedup the classification of huge 3D volume datasets:
We introduce a novel fast linear approximation of non-linear SMVs and also derive two new algorithms for the fast inference of MRFs via "Generalized Belief Propagation".

Besides the evaluation of individual parts of the *framework*, such as the features or the classifiers, on standardized benchmarks, we show the performance and generality of our approach for three quite different applications:

Spine Detection: Neuronal spines play an important role in many neuro-physiological processes. We applied our *framework* to automatically detect and count spines in 3D volume data recorded by a confocal laser scanning microscope (LSM). For this application, our approach is able to achieve a detection performance of over 80%, which is close to the rate at which two human experts agree.

Cell Classification: We apply our *framework* to automatically segment and classify different cell types in dense 3D LSM tissue recordings. The goal of this application is to establish a quantitative high-throughput analysis of tissue samples in order to gain statistics on the cooccurrence of certain cell types during physiological processes.

Depending on the cell types, we reach segmentation and classification rates of 80%-95%.

3D Shape Retrieval: Finally, we apply our *framework* to 3D shape retrieval, which is a common problem when searching in large databases of 3D objects like protein databases or other 3D object collections.

We evaluated our novel approach of local 3D shape descriptors, which is motivated by the "Bag of Features" approach form 2D image retrieval, on the "Princeton Shape Benchmark".

Acknowledgments

The completion of this thesis required quite a lot of dedication from my side, but most certainly would not have been possible without the support and inspiration of many people.

My interest in pattern recognition has been largely inspired by Prof. Burkhardt's enthusiasm for his field and his "hands on" teaching style in his seminars and lab sessions. Starting as an undergraduate student teaching assistant, I spent the last six and a half years at the LMB: from student projects, to the master thesis and the dissertation. I'm very thankful for Prof. Burkhardt's support during this time, for his confidence in me and the backing of some of my less common activities like my research stay in Oulu, my "Sommercampus" activities and other projects.

I thank Prof. Flusser for the co-examination of my thesis and the good discussions during my visit in Prague. One highlight in the last years have been the winter months of my research stay in Oulu, Finland. I thank Prof. Heikkilä for the invitation and Esa Rahtu for the cooperation and local guidance.

Large parts of the thesis rely on the practical application of my theories and algorithms to real world biological image analysis problems. Hence, I thank my biological collaborators, especially Prof. Kurz, for their ongoing supply with data, fruitful discussions, helpful feedback and the patience to wait for useful results.

One of the most important aspects of my daily work during the last years has been the great support and friendly atmosphere provided by my colleagues at the LMB. Special thanks to Olaf Ronneberger, who appears to be an unlimited source of inspiration and always tried (not very successfully) to teach me some of his perfectionism, and Marco Reisert, who has been a great discussion partner and guidance when ever I tried to squeeze my ideas into mathematically sound formulations.
I thank Janina Schulz for helping me to survive the teaching duties, Alexandra Teynor for the very helpful feedback on my thesis and our exciting conference trips to Tokyo and Florida, the "code masters" Thorsten Schmidt and Mario Emmenlauer for their enthusiasm to take care of obscurest C++ problems, Henrik Skibbe for his nice volume renderer, Stefan Teister and all other members of the LMB their support and efforts.
I also thank Cynthia Findlay taking on the daily fight with bureaucracy and her always cheerful and supportive nature.

I further thank my students: Karina Zapien, Catharina Sauer, Christian Ott, Julia Eckert, Ruben Schilling, Philip Schroll, Kersten Petersen, Matthias Asaal and Alexander Streicher who did their student project or master thesis with me. I'm proud that quite many results of our projects have found their way into publications and are reflected as parts of this thesis.

Finally, my greatest thanks belong to Margret, who has become the most important person in my life.

Janis Fehr

"... mein Werk bestehe aus zwei Teilen, aus dem, der hier vorliegt, und aus alledem, was ich *nicht* geschrieben habe. Und gerade dieser zweite Teil ist der Wichtige."

L. Wittgenstein, *Der Tractatus*

Contents

1 Introduction

In this thesis, we address the general problem of automatic analysis of 3D volume images. Recent advances in the area of 3D imaging techniques led to a wide range of novel, more accurate, faster and cheaper imaging devices, such as 3D microscopes for the recording of biological structures or CT and MRT scanners for medical and industrial applications. A direct consequence of this development is a massive increase in the number and size of recorded 3D volume data sets which eventually need to be analyzed and evaluated. Since in most cases, these tasks still have to be performed manually, it is not surprising that the demand for (semi)-automatic analysis methods is rising.

The focus of potential automatic methods lies on the replacement of many tedious and resource consuming manual tasks which are typically occurring in the context of quantitative evaluations, including the detection, segmentation and classification of objects and (sub)-structures, counting and localizing, as well as the quantitative description of textures, shapes and positions.
An automation of these tasks generally is anything but trivial. The greatest challenges towards automatic methods are high intra class variations combined with often unknown transformations, the sometimes still poor imaging quality and last but not least the computational complexity of problems in large 3D volume data sets.
Another key problem is the issue of reusability of the automatic analysis methods. Many current approaches are highly specialized and are strongly bound to problem specific models. These models might solve a given problem, but are usually inflexible in terms of changes in the problem setting. This results in many specialized solutions which cannot be easily adapted to new problem
Our approach towards an automatic and generic analysis of 3D volume data is based on a combination of local invariant features combined with learning techniques.

1.1 Motivation of our Approach

The use of invariant feature descriptors has a long tradition in pattern recognition. For many complex recognitions problems, which practically cannot be solved by "brute force" combinatoric matching, the extraction of invariant features provides adequate and elegant solutions. Classical examples for such feature based solutions are the Fourier Descriptors (Arbter et al., 1990) and object moments (Flusser, 1998) for the affine invariant description of 2D shapes or Local Binary Pattern (LBP) (Mäenpää and Pietikäinen, 2005) and Haar-Integration Features (Schulz-Mirbach, 1995b) for 2D texture description and defect detection.

A key inspiration for the methodology of our approach has been derived from recent advances in 2D image retrieval, where complex objects in cluttered scenes are modeled as a collection of local image patches. The patches, mostly small rectangular image regions, are represented by local (invariant) descriptors. The most prominent example is the SIFT feature (Lowe, 2004).

However, given this inspiration, an extension of existing 2D feature methods to 3D volume data is not straight forward and in most cases quite difficult. One indicator for these difficulties is the fact that

13

only few invariant volume features have been published so far. As one of the main contributions of this thesis, we close this gap by the introduction of several novel rotation and gray-scale invariant local features for 3D volume data and 3D vector fields.

There are several major problems we have to solve on our way to a suitable feature representation. General problems, which are even more evident in 3D data, are high intra class variations and partially unknown transformations within object equivalence classes. We engage these problems by embedding learning techniques into our feature methods. The applied learning approaches are twofold: First, we try to design very flexible and generic feature models that can be adapted to a wide range of problems. This is achieved by the use of annotated training samples which provide implicit information on the given problem. We use learning methods to infer data driven features from this information. The second learning aspect is that we use the same annotations to infer the combination of the local feature information into a problem specific global model.

1.2 Our *Framework*: Combining Local Invariant 3D Features with Learning

Let us give a brief sketch of our basic approach. In the following, we refer to this setup (and derivations of it) as our local feature *framework*. Figure 1.1 gives an overview of the principle training and test pipelines. Details of the algorithmic process may be varying from application to application (see part III). The technical details of the local 3D features and the applied learning techniques are discussed in-depth in parts I and II. At this point, we simply give a rough overview of the *framework* and the interaction of its interrelated parts and properties:

Annotated training data. Our entire approach relies on (at least weakly) labeled training samples. The given annotation may be sparse, and for many applications we suggest an interactive training procedure which iteratively provides intermediate training results that can be corrected by a human expert. This way, our approach gains a supervised labeling of the training set which needs only little human interaction in order to converge to a stable model.

Constructing data driven features. A key property of our *framework* is that we do not simply apply "off the shelf features", but try to infer the local characteristics of object classes from the annotated training samples and use this information to automatically generate highly discriminative features. Because of this property, we refer to these methods as *data driven features*.
We also use the labeled training data to automatically select the most discriminative combination of the generated features.

Learning data models. Finally, based on the collection of local descriptors, we try to infer a global model of the given problem, which is potentially capable of solving segmentation, classification or detection problems. A key aspect of this global model is that we are considering the local interaction of neighboring of the descriptors. This is done in a Markovian approach.

1.3 Main Contributions

The scientific and technical contributions in this thesis are manifold. In order to establish our central idea to solve complex 3D image analysis problems via the generic combination of local invariant 3D features and learning methods, we have to address several, quite diverse topics: we give an in-depth investigation of the mathematical background on the local representation of 3D data in the frequency domain, use the advantages of this representation to derive as many as 14 different invariant local features for 3D volume data, introduce new speed-up techniques for the classification and inference of very large datasets and finally, show how all these parts are combined to solve very different problems from 3D biological image analysis to 3D shape retrieval.

Mathematical Background: Most of the 3D invariant features we introduce throughout the thesis are based on mathematical foundations and tools which allow us to effectively perform computations on local spherical neighborhoods in the harmonic domain. In the first chapters of the thesis, we adapt, analyze and extend this mathematical foundation which has been well established over decades in quantum physics (angular momentum theory) and theoretical chemistry. We give an in-depth review of the theoretic background and show how these established methods can be transfered to be used for image analysis problems. Further, we introduce some effective algorithmic implementations for these methods. Finally, we extend the existing theory by some very effective novel methods, like the fast and accurate correlation of signals in the harmonic domain or an extension of the entire theoretical framework from scalar to vectorial data (Fehr et al., 2008a).

Local Features for 3D Volume Data: The central contribution of this thesis is the theoretic derivation and highly optimized implementation of local rotation and gray-scale invariant features for 3D volume data. Based on the mathematical models and tools for the representation of local 3D data in the harmonic domain, we introduce several different invariant features which encode local 3D textures, shapes or vector fields.
We adopt and extend existing feature methods to 3D, like Haar-Features (Ronneberger and Fehr, 2005) (Ronneberger et al., 2005) (Fehr et al., 2008) or Local Binary Pattern (Fehr, 2007a) (Fehr and Burkhardt, 2008) and also introduce novel approaches for invariants on 3D gray-scale data and 3D vector fields (Fehr and Burkhardt, 2006) (Fehr et al., 2008).

Fast Classification and Inference on large Datasets: The combination of our local 3D features with learning methods raises the problem that we have to apply classification and inference algorithms on very large problems. Since most common learning techniques turn out to be too slow for most of our applications, we introduce several novel speed-up algorithms for Support Vector Machine classification (Zapién et al., 2006) (Fehr et al., 2007) (Fehr and Zapién, 2007) (Zapien, 2005) (Fehr and Burkhardt, 2007a) a and inference of Markov Random Fields via "Generalized Belief Propagation" (Petersen et al., 2008) (Petersen, 2008).

Applications: Finally, we combine our local features and learning methods to form our generic 3D image analysis *framework*. We apply this *framework* to several 3D biomedical image analysis problems such as the segmentation and classification of cell nuclei in dense tissue samples (Kurz et al., 2008) (Fehr et al., 2005) (Ronneberger et al., 2005) (Fehr et al., 2006) (Schilling, 2007) (Schilling et al., 2007) (Wicklein, 2006) (Kurz et al., 2007) (Kurz et al., 2006) (Sauer et al., 2006) (Kurz et al., 2005a) (Kurz et al., 2005b) (Fehr, 2005) (Fehr, 2007b) (Fehr and Burkhardt, 2007a) or the detection and counting of neural spines (Asal, 2008). Additionally, we apply our *framework* to 3D shape retrieval (Fehr and Burkhardt, 2007b) (Streicher, 2008).

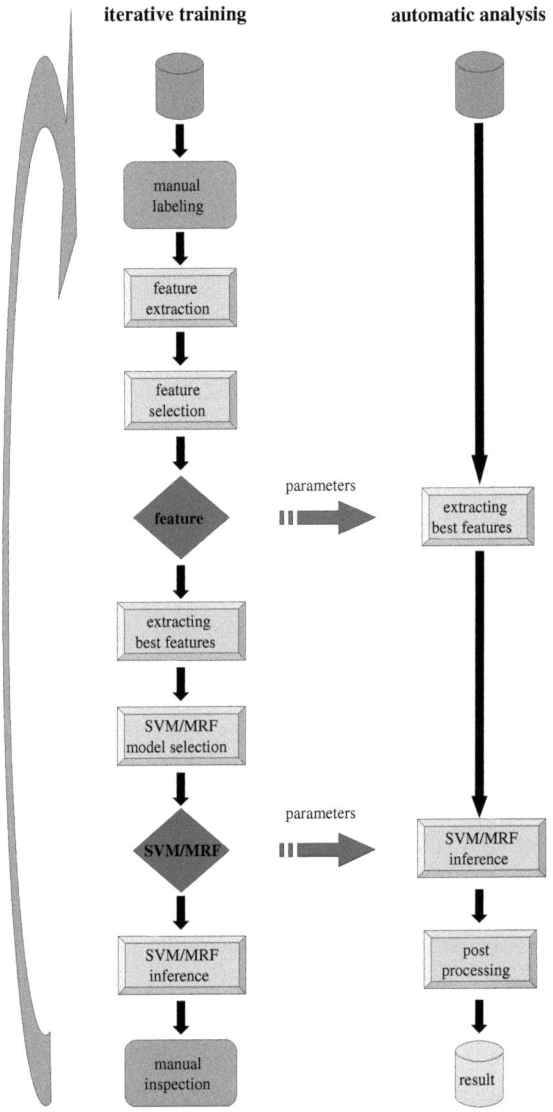

Figure 1.1: Overview of our "Local Invariant 3D Features and Learning" *framework*. **Iterative train-ing** procedure: the interactive annotation cycle is repeated until the model converges to a stable result. The blue arrows indicate the feature and SVM/MRF **parameters** which we infer during the training phase and then pass on for the **automatic evaluation** of unknown data.

Own Publications Contributing To This Thesis

M. Asal. *Segmentierung und Klassifikation von Dendritischen Spines in 3D Volumendaten.* University of Freiburg, Masterthesis, supervised by J. Fehr and H. Burkhardt., 2008.

J. Fehr. Rotational invariant uniform local binary patterns for full 3d volume booktitleure analysis. In *Proc. FinSig 2007*, 2007a.

J. Fehr. Selbstlernende segmentierung und klassifikation von zellkernen in 3d volumendaten basierend auf grauwertinvarianten. In *Workshop "Quantitative Bildanalyse", FH Darmstadt.*, 2005.

J. Fehr. Lernen im kontext der bildanalyse. In *Workshop "Quantitative Bildanalyse", FH Darmstadt.*, 2007b.

J. Fehr and H. Burkhardt. Rotational invariant uniform local binary patterns for full 3d volume booktitleure analysis. In *Proc. ICPR 2008 (to apear)*, 2008.

J. Fehr and H. Burkhardt. Fast implementation of classification algorithms on the gpu. In *Proceedings of the GfKl 2007, Freiburg March 7-11*, 2007a.

J. Fehr and H. Burkhardt. Invariant local features for 3d biomedical image analysis. In *Proceedings of the Workshop on Image Analysis and in Vivo Pharmachology (IAVP), 12-14 April 2007,Roskilde, Denmark*, 2007b.

J. Fehr and H. Burkhardt. Harmonic shape histograms for 3d shape classification and retrieval. In *IAPR Workshop on Machine Vision Applications (MVA2007)*, Tokyo, Japan, 2007c.

J. Fehr and H. Burkhardt. Phase based 3d booktitleure features. In *Proceedings of the DAGM 2006, Springer LNCS 4174, pp 263-272*, 2006.

J. Fehr and K. Zapién. Fast support vector machine classification of very largedatasets. Internal report 2/07, IIF-LMB, University Freiburg, march 2007.

J. Fehr, O. Ronneberger, H. Kurz, and H. Burkhardt. Self-learning segmentation and classification of cell-nuclei in 3d volumetric data using voxel-wise gray scale invariants. *Proceedings of the 27th DAGM Symposium, in number 3663 LNCS, Springer, Vienna, Austria, 30.8 - 2.9. 2005.*, 2005.

J. Fehr, H. Kurz, C. Sauer, O. Ronneberger, and H. Burkhardt. Identifikation von zellen in intaktem gewebe - selbst-lernende segmentierung und klassifikation von zellkernen in 3d volumendaten mittels voxel-weiser grauwertinvarianten. In *Handels H. Ehrhardt J. Editors, Informatik Aktuell, Bildverarbeitung für die Medizin 2006, Hamburg 19. - 21.3.06*, pages 368–373. Springer-Verlag, 2006.

J. Fehr, K. Z. Arreola, and H. Burkhardt. Fast support vector machine classification of very large-datasets. In *submitted to GfKl 2007 post proceedings*, 2007.

J. Fehr, M. Reisert, and H. Burkhardt. Fast and accurate rotation estimation on the 2-sphere without correspondences. In *Proceedings of the ECCV 2008, LNCS 5303*, page 239 ff., 2008a.

J. Fehr, O. Ronneberger, J. Schulz, T. Schmidt, M. Reisert, and H. Burkhardt. Invariance via group-integration: A feature framework for 3d biomedical image analysis. In *proceeding of the special session on Invariance And Robustness at the International Conference on Computer Graphics and Imaging (CGIM 2008), Innsbruck, Austria*, 2008b.

H. Kurz, J. Fehr, S. Winnik, M. Moser, O. Ronneberger, and H. Burkhardt. Dynamics of vascular cells in their social conbooktitle: quantitative 3-d-analysis of vascular growth and remodeling and new insights into mechanisms of angiogenesis. In *Proceedings of the Jahrestagung der AnatoInProceedingshen Gesellschaft, Freiburg, 7 - 10 April*, 2005a.

H. Kurz, O. Ronneberger, J. Fehr, R. Baumgartner, J. Korn, and H. Burkhardt. Automatic classification of cell nuclei and cells during embryonic vascular development. *Ann Anat*, 187:130ff, 2005b.

H. Kurz, C. Sauer, J. Fehr, O. Ronneberger, and H. Burkhardt. Automated identification of large numbers of cells in intact tissues as a highthroughput approach in morphology. In *Proceedings of the Jahrestagung der AnatoInProceedingshen Gesellschaft, Freiburg, 7 - 10 April*, 2006.

H. Kurz, J. Fehr, R. Nitschke, and H. Burkhardt. Two types of perivascular cells in the chorioallantoic membrane capillary plexus. In *Proceedings of the 24. Arbeitstagung Anat Ges, Sept 26-28, Würzburg*, 2007.

H. Kurz, J. Fehr, R. Nitschke, and H. Burkhardt. Pericytes in the mature chorioallantoic membrane capillary plexus contain desmin and alpha-smooth muscle actin: relevance for non-sprouting angiogenesis. *Journal of Histochemistry and Cell Biology*, 2008.

K. Petersen. *Efficient Generalized Belief Propagation for Image Segmentation*. University of Freiburg, Masterthesis, supervised by J. Fehr and H. Burkhardt., 2008.

K. Petersen, J. Fehr, and H. Burkhardt. Fast general belief propagation for map estimation on 2d and 3d grid-like markov random fields. In *Proceedings of the DAGM 2008*, pages 41–50, München, Germany, 2008. LNCS, Springer.

O. Ronneberger and J. Fehr. Voxel-wise gray scale invariants for simultaneous segmentation and classification. In *Proceedings of the 27th DAGM Symposium, in number 3663 LNCS, Springer, Vienna, Austria,*, 2005.

O. Ronneberger, J. Fehr, and H. Burkhardt. Voxel-wise gray scale invariants for simultaneous segmentation and classification – theory and application to cell-nuclei in 3d volumetric data. Internal report 2/05, IIF-LMB, University Freiburg, april 2005.

C. Sauer, J. Fehr, O. Ronneberger, H. Burkhardt, K. Sandau, and H. Kurz. Automated identification of large cell numbers in intact tissues - self-learning segmentation, classification, and quantification of cell nuclei in 3-d volume data via voxel-based gray scale invariants. In *Proceedings of the Jahrestagung der AnatoInProceedingshen Gesellschaft, Freiburg, 7 - 10 April*, 2006.

R. Schilling. *Elastische Registrierung in 3D Volumen Daten*. University of Freiburg, Masterthesis, supervised by J. Fehr and H. Burkhardt., 2007.

R. Schilling, J. Fehr, R. Spörle, H. Burkhardt, B. Herrmann, M. Vingron, and A. Schliep. Comparison of whole mouse embryos by non-linear image registration. In *Proceedings of the German Conference on Bioinformatics, Potsdam, September 26-28*, 2007.

A. Streicher. *3D Shape Retrieval mit lokalen Merkmalen.* University of Freiburg, Masterthesis, supervised by J. Fehr and H. Burkhardt., 2008.

J. Wicklein. *Segmentierung biologischer Strukturen in 3D Volumen Daten mit assoziativen Markov-Netzwerken.* University of Freiburg, Masterthesis, supervised by J. Fehr and H. Burkhardt., 2006.

K. Zapien. *Fast Support Vector Machine Classification using linear SVM Decision Trees.* University of Freiburg, Masterthesis, supervised by J. Fehr and H. Burkhardt., 2005.

K. Zapién, J. Fehr, and H. Burkhardt. Support vector machine classification using linear svms. In *ICPR Hong Kong*, pages 366–369, 2006.

1.4 Structure of the Thesis

This thesis is organized in tree main parts. **Part I** covers the theory of 3D feature design, extraction and selection. We review general aspects of feature design (section 2.1) and motivate the use of local (section 2.2) and invariant (section 2.1.2) features.
After deriving essential mathematical tools in chapter 3, we introduce our local 3D invariant features in chapters 5 to 9. In chapter 10 we discuss existing and new automatic selection methods for our features, before we evaluate our features and methods in terms of accuracy and complexity in chapter 11.

Part II of the thesis covers the learning aspects of our work. We review the two standard algorithms used throughout our work: Support Vector Machines (SVM) (see chapter 13) and Markov Random Fields (MRF) (see chapter 15) and introduce novel speed-up techniques to enhance the classification complexity of SVMs via a linear approximation of non linear kernels (see chapter 14) and fast MRF inference via Generalized Belief Propagation in chapter 16.

In **part III**, we then combine our feature and learning methods to solve different "real world" applications. In chapter 19, we introduce a set of algorithms which uses an iterative training procedure to learn from a human expert to automatically segment and classify cell nuclei in dense 3D tissue samples. The same method with sightly different features is used in chapter 20 to automatically detect and count neuronal spines. Finally, we apply our local 3D features to a 3D shape retrieval task, extending the well established "bag of features" approach to 3D (see chapter 21).

The **appendix** contains samples from the databases used for the various evaluations and applications.

1.5 Related Work

Even though the content of this thesis strictly follows a general goal, which is the combination of local invariant 3D features and learning algorithms to solve difficult 3D image analysis problems, the individual parts and sub-topics are quite diverse. Hence, we review and discuss related work part by part in a decentralized manner: we provide the related work for the local features, the feature selection, the SVM and MRF speed-up as well as for the applications directly in the regarding chapters and sections.
To our knowledge, there has not been any approach that would describe a generalized *framework* for the combination of 3D features and learning as we propose with this thesis.

1.6 Mathematical Notation

$x \in \mathbb{R}, x \in \mathbb{C}$	real or complex scalar value
$\Re(x)$	real part of a complex value
$\Im(x)$	imaginary part of a complex value
$\bar{x}$	complex conjugate
$\mathbf{x} \in \mathbb{R}^n, \mathbf{x} \in \mathbb{C}^n$	n-dimensional position or vector
$X : \mathbb{R}^n \to \mathbb{R}, X : \mathbb{Z}^n \to \mathbb{R}$	image function representing a nD scalar image
$X[c_i] : \mathbb{R}^n \to \mathbb{R}$	i-th channel of a m-channel nD continuous scalar image
$\mathbf{X} : \mathbb{R}^n \to \mathbb{R}^m$	image function representing a nD field of mD vectors
$X(\mathbf{x}) \in \mathbb{R}$	scalar value at position $\mathbf{x}$
$\mathbf{X}(\mathbf{x}) \in \mathbb{R}^n$	vectorial value at position $\mathbf{x}$
$\kappa(x)$	non-linear kernel function $\kappa : \mathbb{R} \to \mathbb{R}$
$T[X]$ and $T[\mathbf{X}]$	voxel-wise feature extraction
$\mathcal{S}[r](\mathbf{x}) := \{\mathbf{x_i} \in \mathbb{R}^n \mid \|\mathbf{x} - \mathbf{x_i}\| = r\}$	spherical neighborhood around $\mathbf{x}$
$\mathcal{F}(\cdot)$	Fourier transform
$\mathcal{SH}\left(X\vert_{\mathcal{S}[r](\mathbf{x})}\right)$	Spherical Harmonic transform of a local neighborhood
$\mathcal{SH}[r](X)$	element-wise Spherical Harmonic transform with radius r
$\mathcal{VH}\left(\mathbf{X}\vert_{\mathcal{S}[r](\mathbf{x})}\right)$	Vectorial Harmonic transform of a local neighborhood
$\mathcal{VH}[r](\mathbf{X})$	element-wise Vectorial Harmonic with radius r
$\widehat{X} := \mathcal{F}(X)$ or $\widehat{X} := \mathcal{SH}[r](X)$	X transformed into frequency domain
$A \cdot B$	scalar or voxel-wise multiplication
$\mathcal{R}_{(\phi,\theta,\psi)}$ or just $\mathcal{R}$	rotation matrix
$A * B$	convolution in $\mathbb{R}^n$ or S^2
$A \# B$	correlation in $\mathbb{R}^n$ or S^2
$\mathcal{C}^*$	convolution matrix
$\mathcal{C}^\#$	correlation matrix
$\mathcal{G}$	mathematical group
$g \in \mathcal{G}$	group element
$\mathcal{SO}(3)$	rotation group in $\mathbb{R}^3$
ϕ, θ, ψ	parameterization angles of $\mathcal{SO}(3)$
S^2	sphere
Φ, Θ	parameterization angles of S^2
$\nabla \mathbf{X}$	vector field containing gradients of scalar field $\mathbf{X}$
$\nabla \mathbf{X}(\mathbf{x})$	gradient at position $\mathbf{x}$

Table 1.1: Overview of the mathematical notation used throughout the thesis.

Part I

Local Invariant Features

2 Introduction

The construction and selection of suitable local features is the crucial step in our approach. The overall *framework* (see section 1.2) heavily depends on a distinctive feature encoding of the local data to feed the learning algorithms. Hence, this first part of the presented thesis introduces most of our key contributions to the *framework* : algorithms for the extraction of local invariant features and data-driven feature selection.

Structure of Part I: This part of this thesis is structured as follows: in this introductory chapter we review the aspects of feature design in general (section 2.1), take a closer look at local (section 2.2) and invariant features (section 2.1.2) and summarize our contributions to the feature extraction part of this thesis.

In chapter 3 we introduce the essential mathematical basics and derive further mathematical techniques needed for the formulation of our features.

Chapter 4 discusses basic implementation issues like sampling problems or parallelization and fills the gap between the continuous mathematical theory and discrete implementation: for each of the following features, we first derive the theoretic foundation in a continuous setting, and then give details on the actual discrete implementation based on these methods.

Central to this part are the chapters which introduce several different classes of features and their feature extraction algorithms: chapter 5 introduces the class of $\mathcal{SH}$-Features, chapter 6 extends the class of "Local Binary Patterns" (LBP) to 3D, chapter 7 derives new features based on Haar-Integration and finally the chapters 8 and 9 show how we can compute different features on 3D vector fields. An overview of all features which are covered in this thesis can be found in table 2.1.

In chapter 10 we tackle the problem of automatic and data-driven feature selection from (weakly) labeled training data.

Finally, we evaluate and compare the introduced features on an artificial benchmark (chapter 11).

2.1 General Feature Design

Most pattern recognition tasks can be derived from a very general and basic problem setting: given an arbitrary set of patterns $\{X_i | X_i \in \mathcal{X}\}$, we are looking for some function $\Gamma : X_i \to y_i$ which denotes each pattern with a semantic label $y_i \in Y$ from the category space $Y \subset \mathbb{Z}$.

In general, $\mathcal{X}$ contains all possible patterns, which are usually defined as the digitalized signals obtained from a sensor capturing the "real world" (see figure 2.1). Y holds the semantic meaning (categorization) of the real world, where each category y_i defines an equivalence class.

The actual task of assigning the label y_i is called classification and Γ is often referred as decision function or classifier which should hold:

$$X_1 \sim_y X_2 \Leftrightarrow \Gamma(X_1) = \Gamma(X_2). \tag{2.1}$$

The most crucial step towards a suitable Γ is to find an adequate equality measure on X. Since the notion of equivalence of real world objects is given by the human perception and is often highly

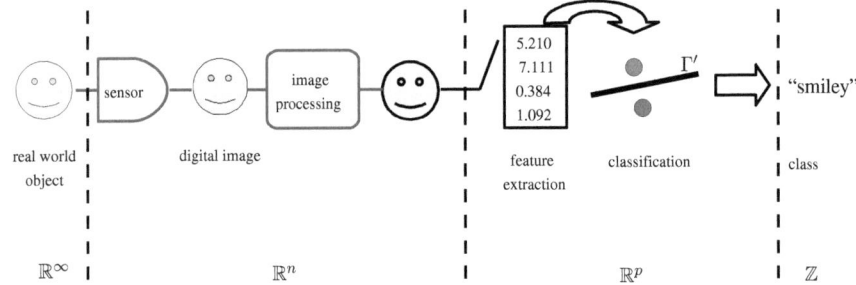

Figure 2.1: Idealized pattern recognition pipeline on images: in general, we try to reduce the problem complexity from continuous real world data to an 1D categorization space. The semantic match of real world objects to such categories is given by definitions based the human perception and thinking.

semantic, it is usually very hard to construct a measure which fulfills (2.1).

In practice, there are two strategies to tackle this problem: learning and feature extraction - which are usually combined.

The first approach tries to learn Γ from a set of training examples - we discuss this method in depth in part II of this thesis. However, most practical problems are too complex to construct or learn Γ directly by raw "pattern matching". Such a "pattern matching" is usually too expensive in terms of computational complexity, or even completely intractable in cases with a large intra class variance, e.g. if patterns of the same equivalence class are allowed to have strong variations in their appearance.

The second approach tries to solve the problem by simplifying the original problem: the goal is to find a reduced representation $\widetilde{X}$ of the original pattern X which still preserves the distinctive properties of X. A commonly used analogy for the feature concept is the notion of "fingerprints" which are extracted from patterns to help to find a simpler classifier Γ' which holds:

$$X_1 \sim_y X_2 \Leftrightarrow \Gamma(X_1) = \Gamma(X_2) \Leftrightarrow \Gamma'(\widetilde{X_1}) = \Gamma'(\widetilde{X_2}). \tag{2.2}$$

Either a perfect feature extraction or a perfect classifier would solve the problem completely, but in practice we have to combine both methods to obtain reasonable results: We use features to reduce the problem and then learn Γ' (see figure 2.2).

2.1.1 Feature Extraction

We formalize the feature extraction in form of some function $T(X_i)$ which maps all input signals X_i into the so-called feature space $\widetilde{\mathcal{X}}$:

$$\widetilde{X_i} =: T(X_i). \tag{2.3}$$

For the theoretical case of a "perfect" feature, $T(X_i)$ maps all input signals X_i belonging to the same semantic class with label y_i onto one point $\widetilde{X_i}$ in this features space:

$$X_1 \sim_y X_2 \Leftrightarrow T(X_1) = T(X_2). \tag{2.4}$$

As mentioned before, the nature of practical problems includes that there are intra class variations which make things more complicated. We model these intra class variations by transformations $h_i \in$

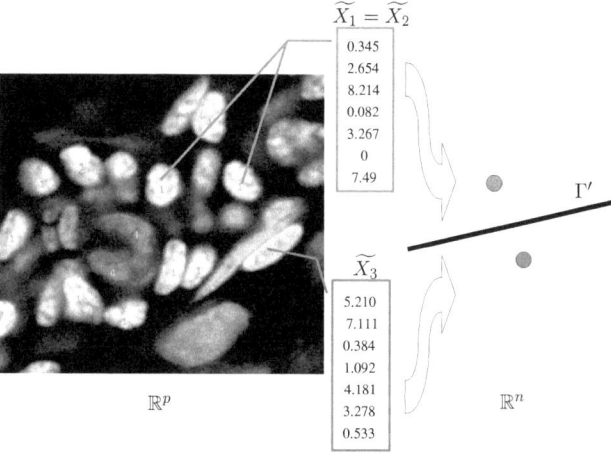

Figure 2.2: Feature extraction duality: instead of trying to solve the difficult problem in the original $\mathbb{R}^p$ space, we extract "mathematical fingerprints" (features) and try to find a dual classifier Γ' in the simpler $\mathbb{R}^n$ space, where $n \ll p$

H_y, where H_y is the set of all possible transformations, which do not change the label y of the ideal class template X_y:

$$X_i := h_i X_y. \tag{2.5}$$

If it is impossible to construct the "perfect" feature for a practical application, the goal is to find feature mappings $T(hX_y)$ which at least fulfill the following properties:

- **(I) size:** the feature space should be much smaller than the pattern space: $n <<< p$ with $\widetilde{\mathcal{X}} \subset \mathbb{R}^n, \mathcal{X} \subset \mathbb{R}^p$.

- **(II) continuity:** small changes in the input pattern X_i should have only small effects in feature space $\widetilde{\mathcal{X}}$

- **(III) cluster preservation:** local neighborhoods should be transfered from input to feature space

If the extracted feature $\widetilde{X}_i$ adheres to these properties, $\widetilde{\mathcal{X}}$ provides several advantages for the further construction or learning of Γ: first, (I) drastically reduces the computational complexity and second, (II) and (III) make it possible to introduce a meaningful similarity measure on $\widetilde{\mathcal{X}}$ (like a simple Euclidean-Norm), which is an essential precondition to the application of learning algorithms (see part II).

Still, the question remains how to construct features which hold the properties I-III. While size property (I) is rather easy to meet, continuity (II) and cluster preservation (III) are more difficult to obtain. This leads us to the notions of invariance and robustness of features, which are central to the methods presented in this thesis.

2.1.2 Invariance

Feature extraction methods are strongly interlaced with the concept of invariance. The basic idea of invariant features is to construct $T(X)$ in such a way that the effect of those transformations $h_i \in H_y$

(2.5) which are not affecting the semantic class label y of X, e.g. $X \sim_y h_i X$, is canceled out by T:

$$T(h_i X_y) = \widetilde{X_y}, \forall h_i \in H_y. \tag{2.6}$$

For two signals X_1 and X_2 which are considered to be equivalent under a certain transformation $h_i \in H_y$, $X_1 \overset{h_i}{\sim} X_2$, the **necessary condition** (Burkhardt, 1979) for invariance against h_i is:

$$X_1 \overset{h_i}{\sim} X_2 \Rightarrow T(X_1) = \widetilde{X_1} = \widetilde{X_2} = T(X_2). \tag{2.7}$$

In order to achieve **completeness** (Burkhardt, 1979), T has to hold:

$$T(X_1) = T(X_2) \Rightarrow X_1 \overset{h_i}{\sim} X_2. \tag{2.8}$$

In most cases the mathematical completeness condition is too strict, since it is not practicable to have a distinct mapping for every theoretically possible pattern X_i. However, with only little a priori knowledge, one can determine a sufficient subset of likely patterns $\mathcal{X}'$. If (2.8) holds for all $X_i, X_j \in \mathcal{X}'$, **separability** (Burkhardt, 1979) can be guaranteed for the likely patterns.

It is straightforward to see that a feature which holds the necessary condition (2.7) and achieves at least separability meets the properties II and III.

Group Transformations

The construction of an invariant feature requires that we are able to model the allowed transformations $h_i \in H_y$ of the equivalence class with label y. In general this is a hard and sometimes infeasible task, e.g. just think of arbitrary deformations. However, for the subset of transformations $G_y \subset H_y$, where G_y forms a compact mathematical group, we have sophisticated mathematical tools to model the individual transformations $g_i \in G_y$.

Luckily, many practically relevant transformations like rotations are groups or can easily be transformed to groups, e.g. translations if we consider cyclic translations. Overall, we can formulate translations, rotations, shrinking, shearing and even affine mappings as group operations (Burkhardt and Siggelkow, 2001).

General Techniques For The Construction Of Invariant Features

In general, there are three generic ways of constructing invariant features: by normalization, derivation and integration (Burkhardt and Siggelkow, 2001). For allowed transformations H_y, the individual transformations $h \in H_y$ differ only by their associated set of parameters λ, which cover the degrees of freedom under H_y. The most popular method for invariant feature construction is to eliminate the influence of λ via normalization of the class members $X_i := h_\lambda X_y$ with a class template X_y.

We apply normalization techniques in the following features: $\mathcal{SH}_{abs}$ (chapter 5.1), $\mathcal{SH}_{phase}$ (chapter 5.2), $\mathcal{SH}_{bispectrum}$ (chapter 5.4), fuLBP (chapter 6.2), the rotation invariance of the fLBP (chapter 6.5) and $\mathcal{VH}_{abs}$ (chapter 8.1)

However, it should be noted that normalization techniques in general tend to suffer in cases of noisy or partially corrupted data and are often totally infeasible for complex data where no normalized template can be found.

A second possibility is the elimination of λ via derivation:

$$\frac{\partial T(g_\lambda X_i)}{\partial \lambda} \equiv 0. \tag{2.9}$$

The resulting differential equations can be solved using Lie-Theory (Lenz, 1990) approaches, but in practice it is often very difficult to obtain solutions to the differential equations. The only example where we used a differential approach to obtain invariance is in the case of the gray-scale invariance of the fLBP (chapter 6.5), where the differentiation is exceptionally simple.

Finally, the approach which has been proposed by (Schulz-Mirbach, 1995b) can be applied on the subset of group transformations: It generates invariant features via Haar-Integration over all degrees of freedom of the transformation group G. We take an in-depth look at the Haar-Integration approach in chapter 7 and apply it in several of our features: 2p-Haar (chapter 7.1), 3p-Haar (chapter 7.2), np-Haar (chapter 7.3), 1v-Haar (chapter 9.1), 2v-Haar (chapter 9.2) and nv-Haar (chapter 9.3).

For many practical applications invariance can be achieved by the combination of several different approaches: we can split transformations h into a combination of several independent transformations $h := h_1 \circ h_2 \circ \dots$, where h_1 might be a group transformation like i.e. rotation and h_2 a non-group transformation like gray-scale changes. An example of such a combination is the fLBP-Feature (chapter 6.5), where we obtain rotation invariance via normalization and gray-scale invariance by differentiation.

The concept of invariance provides us with a powerful tool for the construction of features which is suitable for a wide range of problems. However, there are still many practically relevant cases where some of the underlying transformations h_i cannot be sufficiently modelled, or are even partially unknown. Then it becomes very hard or impossible to construct invariant features. In these cases we have to fall back to the sub-optimal strategy to construct robust instead of invariant features.

2.1.3 Robustness

Robustness is a weaker version of invariance: if we are not able to cancel out the effect of the transformations h_i like in (2.7), we can at least try to minimize the impact of these intra class variations. Given $X_1 \overset{h}{\sim} X_2, X_1, X_2 \in \mathcal{X}$, we are looking for a feature T which maps X_1, X_2 in such a way that the intra class variance in $\widetilde{\mathcal{X}}$ is smaller than the extra class distances given some distance measure d in $\widetilde{\mathcal{X}}$:

$$X_1 \overset{h_i}{\sim} X_2 \Rightarrow d\Big(T(X_1), T(X_2)\Big) < d\Big(T(X_{1,2}), T(X')\Big), \quad \forall X' \in \mathcal{X} : X' \neg \overset{h_i}{\sim} X_{1,2}. \tag{2.10}$$

It is obvious that the robustness property (2.10) directly realizes the feature properties II and III. In practice, robustness is often achieved by simplified approximations of complex intraclass variations, e.g. linear approximations of actually non-linear transformations h_i. In theses cases, we often use an even weaker definition of robustness and demand that (2.10) has only to hold for most but not all $X' \in \mathcal{X}$.

2.1.4 Equivariance

For some applications it is desirable to explicitly transfer the variations to the feature space:

$$X_1 \overset{h_i}{\sim} X_2 \Rightarrow T(X_1) = h_i T(X_2). \tag{2.11}$$

These features are called equivariant, and are often used to compute the parameters of known transformations h_i.

2.2 Local Features

The feature definition in the last section (2.1.1) considered only the extraction of so-called "global" features, i.e. features are extracted as descriptors $\widetilde{X}_i = T(X_i)$ (or "Fingerprints") of the entire pattern

X_i. This global approach is suitable for many pattern recognition problems, especially when the patterns are taken from prior segmented objects (see part III). In other cases, it can be favorable to describe a global pattern as an ensemble of locally constrained sub-patterns. Such a local approach is suitable for object retrieval, object detection in unsegmented data, or data segmentation itself (see part III).

2.2.1 Local Features on 3D Volume Data

Throughout the rest of this thesis we deal with 3D volume data or 3D vector fields. In general we derive the theoretical background of the local features in settings of continuous 3D volumes, which we define as functions $X : \mathbb{R}^3 \rightarrow \mathbb{R}^m$ with values $X(\mathbf{x}) \in \mathbb{R}^m$ at evaluation coordinates $\mathbf{x} \in \mathbb{R}^3$. We then transfer the feature algorithms to operate on the practical relevant discrete 3D volume grids: $X : \mathbb{Z}^3 \rightarrow \mathbb{R}^m$, where we often refer to the position $\mathbf{x}$ as a "**voxel**".

Given 3D volume data, we capture the locality of the features extracted from X in terms of a spatial constraining of the underlying sub-pattern. More precisely, we define a sub-pattern as "local neighborhood" around a data point at $\mathbf{x}$ with the associated local feature $\widetilde{X(\mathbf{x})}$.

Further, we parameterize the local "neighborhood" in concentric spheres with radii r around $\mathbf{x}$. This has several advantages over a rectangular definition of the "local neighborhood":

First, we can easily define the elements of the sub-pattern by a single parameter r using the following notation for the sub-pattern around $\mathbf{x}$:

$$\mathcal{S}[r](\mathbf{x}) := \{\mathbf{x}_i \in \mathbb{R}^3 \| \|\mathbf{x} - \mathbf{x}_i\|_2 = r\}. \tag{2.12}$$

Second, we can address all points in $\mathcal{S}[r](\mathbf{x})$ via the parameterization in radius r and the spherical coordinates (Φ, Θ) - see section 3.2 for more details on the parameterization. And finally, we can rely on a well known and sound mathematical theory to handle signals (patterns) in spherical coordinates which provides us with very useful tools to handle common transformations such as rotations.

We give an in-depth introduction and further extensions to this mathematical basis for our local features in chapter 3.

Gray-Scale Data

In cases where the 3D volume data is scalar $X : \mathbb{R}^3 \rightarrow \mathbb{R}$, we can directly apply the locality definition (2.12). Note, that we usually refer to scalar data as "gray-scale" data, this term is derived from the usual data visualization as gray-scale images - even though the scalar values might encode arbitrary information. Analogous to this, we denote intensity changes as gray-scale changes.

For many pattern recognition tasks on scalar 3D volume data we like to obtain gray-scale and rotation invariant local features in order to cancel out the dominant transformations which act locally. Other transformations of the data do not act locally, like translations, or are very hard to model like arbitrary deformations. In these cases we try to obtain local robustness, which is usually easier to obtain than global robustness since the local affect of complex global transformations is limited in most cases.

Multi-Channel Data

In many cases we face volumes with data which holds more than a single scalar value at each position $\mathbf{x}$. Then we define $X : \mathbb{R}^3 \rightarrow \mathbb{R}^m$ for data with m scalar values per position. The classic example could be a RGB color coding at each voxel, but we might also have other multi-modal data with an arbitrary number of scalar values.

We refer to these volumes as multi-channel data, where we address the individual channels c_i by $X[c_i](\mathbf{x}) \in \mathbb{R}$. Figure 2.3 shows an example of such multi-channel data.

It is obvious that we also need features which operate on multiple channels - this is an important aspect we have to take into account for the feature design.

Figure 2.3: Example of multi-channel volume data: xy-slice of volume data recorded by a Laser Scanning Microscope (LSM): **Left:** channel with *YoPro* staining. **Center:** channel with *SMA* staining. **Right:** pseudo coloration of the combined channels.

2.2.2 Local Features on 3D Vector Fields

Besides local features for scalar gray-scale and multi-channel scalar volumes, we further investigate and derive features which operate on 3D vector fields $\mathbf{X} : \mathbb{R}^3 \to \mathbb{R}^3$. Usually these vector fields are directly obtained by the extraction of gradient information from scalar volumes (see figure 2.4).
In contrast to multi-channel data, the elements of the vectors in the field are not independent and change according to transformations, e.g. under rotation. This makes the feature design a lot more complicated.

Figure 2.4: Example of vectorial data: xy-slice of the thresholded gradient vector field of volume data recorded by a Laser Scanning Microscope (LSM): **Left:** pseudo coloring of the gradient directions. **Right:** 3D vector field reconstruction of the same data.

2.3 Related Work

The number of publications on feature extraction methods and their applications is countless. Hence, we restrict our review of related work to methods which provide local rotation invariant features for 3D volume data or 3D vector fields. This restriction reduces the number of methods we have to consider to a manageable size. Since we provide an in-depth discussion of most of the suitable methods in the next chapters (see table 2.1), we are left with those few methods we are aware of, but which are not further considered throughout the rest of this thesis:

The first class of rotational invariant features which operate on spherical signals are based on the so-called "Spherical Wavelets" (Schröder and Sweldens, 1995) which form the analog to standard wavelets on the 2-sphere. These methods have mostly been used for 3D shape analysis, but also for the characterization of 3D textures (Schröder and Sweldens, 1995).

Second, we have to mention methods based on 3D Zernike moments. For shape retrieval (also see Part III), 3D Zernike moments have been successfully applied as 3D shape descriptors, i.e. by (Saupe and Vranic, 2001b) and (Novotni, 2003). In both cases, only the absolute value of the Zernike coefficients were used to obtain rotation invariance which leads to rather weakly discriminative features just as in the case of the $\mathcal{SH}_{abs}$ features 5.1.
(Canterakis, 1999) introduced a set of complete affine invariant 3D Zernike moments which overcome these problems. However, just as for the $\mathcal{SH}_{bispectrum}$ features 5.4, the completeness comes at the price of very high complexity.

Finally, we were not able to find much significant prior work on rotation invariant features operating on 3D vector fields. Mentionable is the work in (Schulz et al., 2006), which uses a generalized Hough approach (Hough, 1962) to detect spherical structures in a 3D gradient vector field. This method is closely related to our 1v-Haar feature 9.1.

2.4 Schematic Overview of all Features

We introduce and derive a large number of different local features in the next chapters. Table 2.1 gives an overview of these features and their invariance properties. Some features operate on scalar (multi-channel) gray-scale volumes, while others are extracted from 3D vector fields. Some features return a single scalar value, while others return vector valued responses.

Feature		Invariance	Input domain	Output domain
$\mathcal{SH}_{abs}$	5.1	**r** invariance & **g** robustness	scalar	band-wise scalar
$\mathcal{SH}_{phase}$	5.2	**r** invariance & **g** invariance	scalar	band-wise scalar
$\mathcal{SH}_{corr}$	5.3	**r** invariance & **g** invariance	scalar	scalar
$\mathcal{SH}_{bispectrum}$	5.4	**r** invariance & **g** robustness	scalar	sub-band-wise scalar
fuLBP	6.2	**r** invariance & **g** invariance	scalar	scalar
fLBP	6.5	**r** invariance & **g** invariance	scalar	scalar
2p-Haar	7.1	**r** invariance & **g** robustness	scalar	scalar
3p-Haar	7.2	**r** invariance & **g** robustness	scalar	scalar
np-Haar	7.3	**r** invariance & **g** invariance	scalar	scalar
$\mathcal{VH}_{abs}$	8.1	**r** invariance & **g** invariance	vectorial	band-wise scalar
$\mathcal{VH}_{autocorr}$	8.2	**r** invariance & **g** invariance	vectorial	scalar
1v-Haar	9.1	**r** invariance & **g** invariance	vectorial	scalar
2v-Haar	9.2	**r** invariance & **g** invariance	vectorial	scalar
nv-Haar	9.3	**r** invariance & **g** invariance	vectorial	scalar

Table 2.1: Schematic overview of all features with their invariance properties and input/output domains (**r** = rotation, **g** = gray-scale).

2.5 Contributions

Our original contributions in this part are manifold: we have introduced and derived all of the features (see table 2.1) with the exception of $\mathcal{SH}_{abs}$ (which is our reference feature) and $\mathcal{SH}_{bispectrum}$, which has been used before for 2D feature extraction - but not for 3D volume data.

We have also introduced the np- and vp-Feature selection algorithm (section 10) and several novel mathematical operations in the Spherical Harmonic domain (e.g. the fast correlation (section 3.4) and convolution (section 3.5)).

Finally, we have provided the benchmark with a 3D texture generation method for the evaluation of the local 3D feature methods (section 11).

3 Mathematical Background

In this chapter we introduce and review the mathematical background of important methods we use later on. First we exploit and formulate the basics of mathematical operations on the 2-sphere, which are essential to derive our features. The theoretical foundation of these methods has been adapted for our purposes from angular momentum theory (Brink and Satchler, 1968), which plays an important role in Quantum Mechanics. Hence, we can rely on a well established and sound theoretical basis when we extend existing and derive novel operations in the second part of this chapter.

The reader may refer to (Brink and Satchler, 1968)(Rose, 1957)(Tinkham, 1992) and (Groemer, 1996) for a detailed introduction to angular momentum theory.

3.1 Spherical Harmonics

Spherical Harmonics ($\mathcal{SH}$) (Groemer, 1996) form an orthonormal base on the 2-sphere S^2. Analogical to the Fourier Transform, any given real or complex valued, integrable function f in some Hilbert space on a sphere with its parameterization over the angles $\Theta \in [0, \pi[$ and $\Phi \in [0, 2\pi[$ (latitude and longitude of the sphere) can be represented by an expansion in its harmonic coefficients by:

$$f(\Phi, \Theta) = \sum_{l=0}^{\infty} \sum_{m=-l}^{m=l} \widehat{f}_m^l Y_m^l(\Phi, \Theta), \tag{3.1}$$

where l denotes the band of expansion, m the order for the l-th band and $\widehat{f}_m^l$ the harmonic coefficients. The harmonic base functions $Y_m^l(\Theta, \Phi)$ are calculated (using the standard normalized (Brink and Satchler, 1968) formalization) as follows:

$$Y_m^l(\Phi, \Theta) = \sqrt{\frac{2l+1}{4\pi} \frac{(l-m)!}{(l+m)!}} \cdot P_m^l(\cos\Theta) e^{im\Phi}, \tag{3.2}$$

where P_m^l is the associated Legendre polynomial (see 3.1.1). Fig. 3.2 illustrates the Y_m^l base functions of the first few bands.

The harmonic expansion of a function f will be denoted by $\widehat{f}$ with corresponding coefficients $\widehat{f}_m^l$. We define the forward Spherical Harmonic transformation as:

$$\mathcal{SH}(f) := \widehat{f}, \quad \text{with} \quad \widehat{f}_m^l = \int\limits_{\Phi,\Theta} \overline{Y_m^l}(\Phi, \Theta) f(\Phi, \Theta) \sin\Theta d\Phi d\Theta, \tag{3.3}$$

where $\widehat{x}$ denotes the complex conjugate, and the backward transformation accordingly:

$$\mathcal{SH}^{-1}(\widehat{f})(\Phi, \Theta) := \sum_{l=0}^{\infty} \sum_{m=-l}^{m=l} \widehat{f}_m^l Y_m^l(\Phi, \Theta). \tag{3.4}$$

3.1.1 Associated Legendre Polynomials

Associated Legendre polynomials $P_m^l(x)$ are derived as the canonical solution of the General Legendre differential equation (Brink and Satchler, 1968):

$$\left((1-x^2)y'\right) + \left(l(l+1) - \frac{(m^2)}{1-x^2}\right)y = 0, \tag{3.5}$$

which plays an important role for the solution of many well known problems such as the Laplace equation (Brink and Satchler, 1968) in our case. For integer values of $-l \leq m \leq l$,

$$P_m^l(x) = \frac{(-1)^m}{2^l l!}(1-x^2)^{m/2}\frac{d^{l+m}}{dx^{l+m}}(x^2-1)^l \tag{3.6}$$

has non-singular solutions in $[-1, 1]$. The Associated Legendre polynomials are linked to the General Legendre polynomials by:

$$P_m^l(x) = (-1)^m(1-x^2)^{m/2}\frac{d^m}{dx^m}(P^l(x)), \tag{3.7}$$

which implies that $P_0^l(x) = P^l(x)$ - as shown in Fig. 3.1.

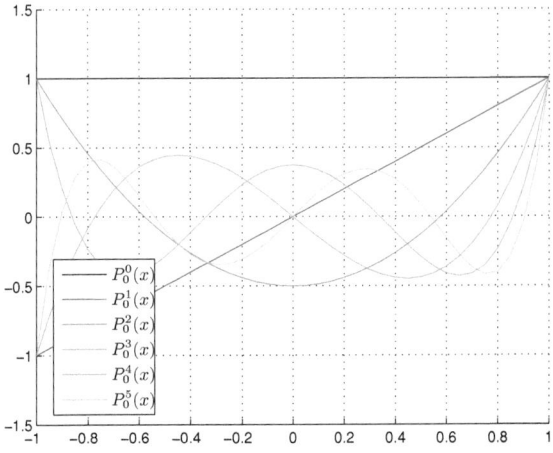

Figure 3.1: A few sample Associated Legendre polynomials of the 0th order which are equal to the General Legendre polynomials.

Properties: Two main properties of the Associated Legendre polynomials in context of this work are the orthogonality of the $P_m^l(x)$ (Brink and Satchler, 1968) as well as the symmetry property:

$$P_{-m}^l = (-1)^m\frac{(l-m)!)}{(l+m)!}P_m^l. \tag{3.8}$$

Another notable fact is that in contrast to its name, the $P_m^l(x)$ are actually only polynomials if m has a even integer value.

3.1.2 Deriving Spherical Harmonics

We give a brief sketch of how Spherical Harmonics have been derived in literature (Brink and Satchler, 1968)(Groemer, 1996) focusing on some aspects which are useful for our purposes. For more details please refer to (Brink and Satchler, 1968) or (Groemer, 1996).

Given a function f parameterized in Φ, Θ on S^2, its Laplacian is:

$$\nabla^2 \Phi = \frac{\partial^2 f}{\partial \Theta^2} + \cot \Theta \frac{\partial f}{\partial \Theta} + \csc^2 \Theta \frac{\partial^2 f}{\partial \Phi^2}. \tag{3.9}$$

A solution to the partial differential equation

$$\frac{\partial^2 f}{\partial \Theta^2} + \cot \Theta \frac{\partial f}{\partial \Theta} + \csc^2 \Theta \frac{\partial^2 f}{\partial \Phi^2} + \lambda f = 0 \tag{3.10}$$

can be obtained (Groemer, 1996) by separation into Φ-dependent parts

$$
\begin{aligned}
\sin(m\Phi) && \text{for} && m < 0 \\
\cos(m\Phi) && \text{else} &&
\end{aligned} \tag{3.11}
$$

and Θ-dependent parts

$$\frac{d^2 y}{d\Theta^2} + \cot \Theta \frac{dy}{d\Theta} + \left(\lambda - \frac{m^2}{\sin^2 \Theta} \right) y = 0, \tag{3.12}$$

with solutions given by $P_m^l(\cos(\Theta))$ (section 3.1.1) for the integer valued $m \geq 0$ and $\lambda = l(l+1)$. Rewriting the Φ-dependent parts in exponential notation and adding the normalization to $\sum |Y_m^l|^2 = 1$ (Brink and Satchler, 1968), we obtain the Spherical Harmonics:

$$Y_m^l(\Phi, \Theta) := \sqrt{\frac{2l+1}{4\pi} \frac{(l-m)!}{(l+m)!}} \cdot P_m^l(\cos \Theta) \mathrm{e}^{im\Phi}. \tag{3.13}$$

3.1.3 Useful Properties of Spherical Harmonics

We give some of the useful properties of Spherical Harmonics which we exploit later. All presented properties are valid for the use of normalized base functions.

Orthonormality: As mentioned before, the key property is that the base functions Y_m^l are orthonormal:

$$\int_{\Theta \Phi} Y_m^l \overline{Y_{m'}^{l'}} \sin \Theta d\Theta d\Phi = \delta_{ll'} \delta_{mm'}, \tag{3.14}$$

with the Kronecker symbol δ.

Symmetry: Symmetry of the Spherical Harmonic base functions can be nicely observed in Fig. 3.3 and is given by:

$$\overline{Y_m^l} = (-1)^m Y_{-m}^l. \tag{3.15}$$

$$\tag{3.16}$$

---

[1]Thanks to O. Ronneberger for the MATLAB visualization

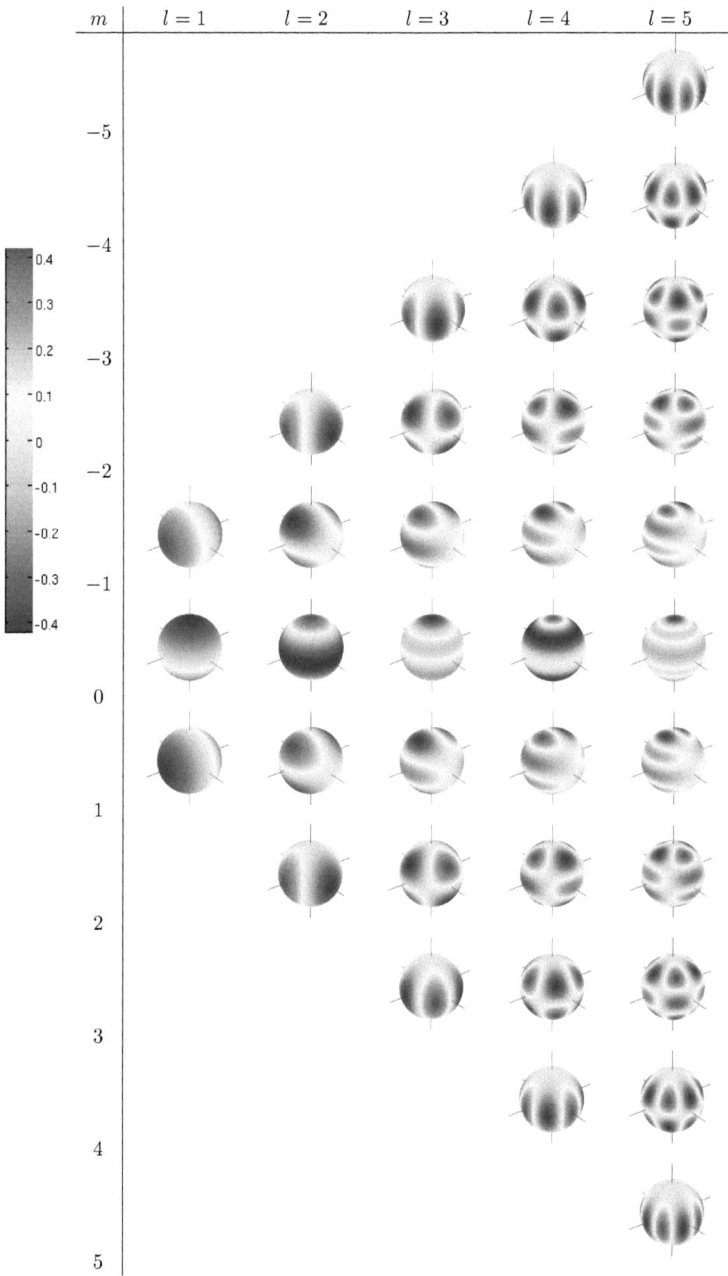

Figure 3.2: Real part of the first 5 bands of the complex Spherical Harmonic base functions[1].

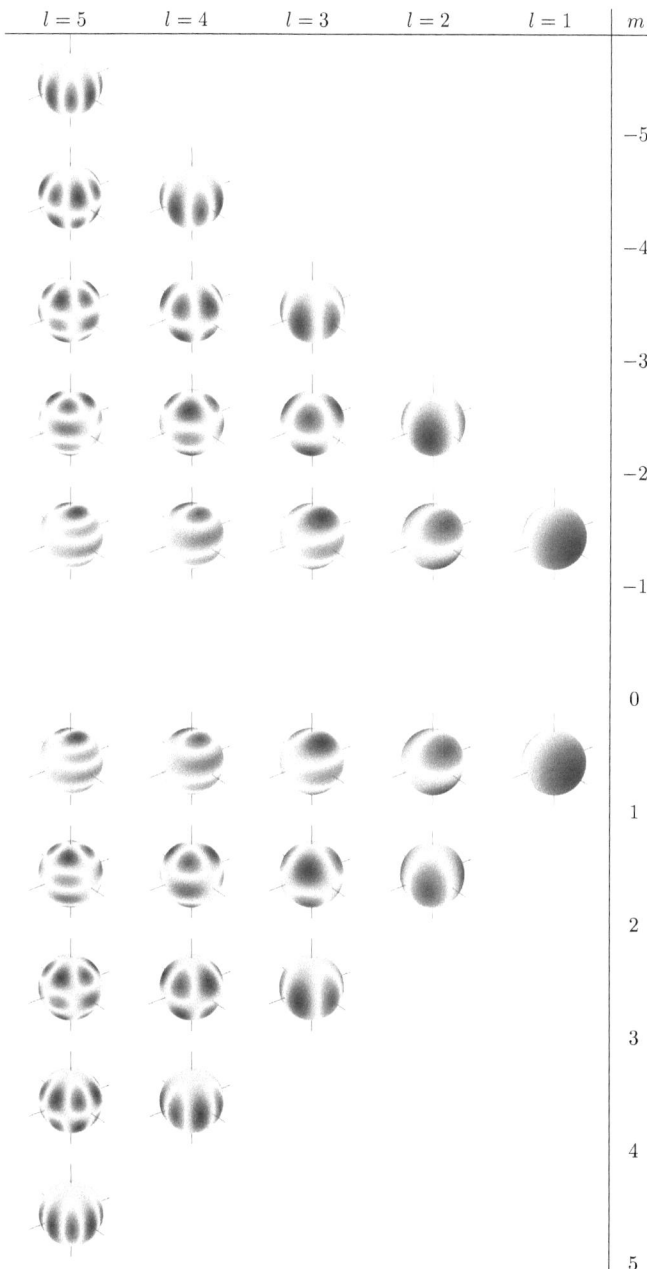

$l = 5$	$l = 4$	$l = 3$	$l = 2$	$l = 1$	m
					-5
					-4
					-3
					-2
					-1
					0
					1
					2
					3
					4
					5

Figure 3.3: Complex part of the first 5 bands of the complex Spherical Harmonic base functions. Note that all Y_0^l are only real-valued.

Addition Theorem: For γ given by

$$\cos(\gamma) = \cos(\Theta)\cos(\Theta') + \sin(\Theta)\sin(\Theta')\cos(\Phi - \Phi')$$

the Addition Theorem (Brink and Satchler, 1968) states that $P^l(\cos(\gamma))$ can be obtained by:

$$P^l(\cos(\gamma)) = \frac{4\pi}{2l+1}\sum_m \overline{Y_m^l}(\Theta, \Phi)Y_m^l(\Theta', \Phi'), \tag{3.17}$$

which also implies the property (Brink and Satchler, 1968)

$$Y_0^l = \left(\frac{2l+1}{4\pi}\right)^{1/2}P^l(\cos(\Theta)). \tag{3.18}$$

3.2 Rotations in $\mathcal{SH}$

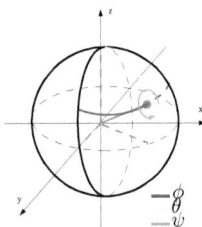

Figure 3.4: Rotations in Euler angles using the zyz' convention. First we rotate ϕ around the z-Axis, then θ around y and finally ψ around the new z-Axis z'.

Throughout the rest of this thesis we will use the Euler notation in zyz'-convention (see Fig. 3.4) denoted by the angles ϕ, θ, ψ with $\phi, \psi \in [0, 2\pi[$ and $\theta \in [0, \pi[$ to parameterize the rotations $\mathcal{R} \in \mathcal{SO}(3)$ (abbreviated for $\mathcal{R}(\phi, \theta, \psi) \in \mathcal{SO}(3)$).
Rotations $\mathcal{R}(\phi, \theta, \psi)$ in the Euclidean space find their equivalent representation in the harmonic domain in terms of the so called Wigner D-Matrices, which form an irreducible representation of the rotation group $\mathcal{SO}(3)$ (Brink and Satchler, 1968). For each band l, $D^l(\phi, \theta, \psi)$ (or abbreviated $D^l(\mathcal{R})$) defines a band-wise rotation in the $\mathcal{SH}$ coefficients. A rotation of f by $\mathcal{R}$ in the Euclidean space can be computed in the harmonic domain by:

$$\mathcal{R}f = \sum_{l=0}^{\infty}\sum_{m=-l}^{l}\sum_{n=-l}^{l}D_{mn}^l(\mathcal{R})\widehat{f}_m^l Y_n^l. \tag{3.19}$$

Hence, we rotate $\widehat{f}_m^l$ by $\mathcal{R}(\phi, \theta, \psi)$ via band-wise multiplications:

$$f' = \mathcal{R}(\phi, \theta, \psi)f \Rightarrow \widehat{f'}_m^l = \sum_{n=-l}^{l}D_{mn}^l(\phi, \theta, \psi)\widehat{f}_m^l. \tag{3.20}$$

Due to the use of the zyz'-convention, we have to handle inverse rotations with some care:

$$f' = \mathcal{R}^{-1}(\phi, \theta, \psi)f \Rightarrow \widehat{f'}_m^l = \sum_{n=-l}^{l}D_{mn}^l(-\psi, -\theta, -\phi)\widehat{f}_m^l. \tag{3.21}$$

3.2.1 Computation of Wigner d-Matrices

The actual computation of the Wigner d-Matrices is a bit tricky. In a direct approach, the d-Matrices can be computed by the sum

$$
d_{mn}^l(\theta) = \sum_t (-1)^t \frac{\sqrt{(l+m)!(l-m)!(l+n)!(l-n)!}}{(l+m-t)!(l-n-t)!t!(t+n-m)!}
$$
$$
\cdot \cos(\theta/2)^{2l+m-n-2t} \cdot \sin(\theta/2)^{2t+n-m} \tag{3.22}
$$

over all t which lead to non-negative factorials (Brink and Satchler, 1968). It is easy to see that the constraints on t are causing the computational complexity to grow with the band of expansion. To overcome this problem, (Trapani and Navaza, 2006) introduced a recursive method for the d-Matrix computation. We are applying a closely related approach inspired by (Reisert and Burkhardt, 2006), where we retrieve d-Matrices from recursively computed D-Matrices.

Recursive Computation of Wigner D-Matrices

Given D^l for the first two bands $l = 0$ and $l = 1$,

$$
D^0(\phi, \theta, \psi) := 1
$$

$$
D^1(\phi, \theta, \psi) := \begin{pmatrix} e^{-i\psi} \frac{1+\cos(\theta)}{2} e^{-i\phi} & \frac{-\sin(\theta)}{\sqrt{2}} e^{-i\phi} & e^{i\psi} \frac{1-\cos(\theta)}{2} e^{-i\phi} \\ e^{-i\psi} \frac{\sin(\theta)}{\sqrt{2}} & \cos(\theta) & -e^{i\psi} \frac{\sin(\theta)}{\sqrt{2}} \\ e^{-i\psi} \frac{1-\cos(\theta)}{2} e^{i\phi} & \frac{\sin(\theta)}{\sqrt{2}} e^{i\phi} & e^{i\psi} \frac{1+\cos(\theta)}{2} e^{i\phi} \end{pmatrix}
$$

we can compute D^l via band-wise recursion:

$$
D_{mn}^l = \sum_{m,m',n,n'=-l}^{l} D_{m'n'}^1 D_{(m-m')(n-n')}^{l-1}
$$
$$
\cdot \langle (l-1)m | 1m', l(m-m') \rangle
$$
$$
\cdot \langle (l-1)n | 1n', l(n-n') \rangle \tag{3.23}
$$

where $\langle lm | l'm', l''m'' \rangle$ denotes Clebsch-Gordan coefficients (see section 3.3) known from angular momentum theory. Using (3.42), we finally obtain:

$$
d_{mn}^l(\theta) = D_{mn}^l(0, \theta, 0). \tag{3.24}
$$

3.2.2 Properties of Wigner Matrices

Orthogonality: The Wigner D-matrix elements form a complete set of orthogonal functions over the Euler angles (Rose, 1957):

$$
\int_{\phi,\theta,\psi} D_{mn}^l(\phi, \theta, \psi) \overline{D_{m'n'}^{l'}}(\phi, \theta, \psi) \sin \Theta d\phi d\theta d\psi = \frac{8\pi^2}{2l+1} \delta_{ll'} \delta_{mm'} \delta_{nn'}, \tag{3.25}
$$

with Kronecker symbol δ.

Symmetry:

$$
D_{mn}^l(\phi, \theta, \psi) = \overline{D_{-m-n}^l}(\phi, \theta, \psi). \tag{3.26}
$$

Relations to Spherical Harmonics: The D-Matrix elements with second index equal to zero, are proportional to Spherical Harmonic base functions (Tinkham, 1992):

$$\overline{D_{m0}^l}(\phi, \theta, \psi) = \sqrt{\frac{4\pi}{2l+1}} Y_m^l(\phi, \theta). \tag{3.27}$$

Relations to Legendre Polynomials: The Wigner small d-Matrix elements with both indices set to zero are related to Legendre polynomials (Rose, 1957):

$$d_{00}^l(\theta) = P^l(\cos(\theta)). \tag{3.28}$$

3.3 Clebsch-Gordan Coefficients

Clebsch-Gordan Coefficients (CG) of the form

$$\langle lm|l_1 m_1, l_2 m_2 \rangle$$

are commonly used for the representation of direct sum decompositions of $\mathcal{SO}(3)$ tensor couplings (Brink and Satchler, 1968). The CG define the selection criteria for couplings and are by definition only unequal to zero if the constraints

$$m = m_1 + m_2 \text{ and } |l_1 - l_2| \le l \le l_1 + l_2$$

hold. In most cases non-zero Clebsch-Gordan Coefficients are not directly evaluated, we rather utilize their orthogonality and symmetry properties to reduce and simplify coupling formulations. The quite complex closed form for the computation of CG can be found in (Rose, 1957).

3.3.1 Properties of Clebsch-Gordan Coefficients

Some useful properties of Clebsch-Gordan Coefficients (Brink and Satchler, 1968):

Exceptions: For $l = 0$ the CG are:

$$\langle 00|l_1 m_1, l_2 m_2 \rangle = \delta_{l_1, l_2} \delta_{m_1, -m_2} \frac{(-1)^{l_1 - m_1}}{\sqrt{2l_2 + 1}} \tag{3.29}$$

and for $l = (l_1 + l_2)$ and $m_1 = l_1, m_2 = l_2$:

$$\langle (l_1 + l_2)(l_1 + l_2)|l_1 l_1, l_2 l_2 \rangle = 1. \tag{3.30}$$

Orthogonality:

$$\sum_{l=|l_1-l_2|}^{l_1+l_2} \sum_{m=-l}^{l} \langle lm|l_1 m_1, l_2 m_2 \rangle \langle lm|l_1 m_1', l_2 m_2' \rangle = \delta_{m_1, m_1'} \delta_{m_2, m_2'} \tag{3.31}$$

$$\sum_{m_1 m_2} \langle lm|l_1 m_1, l_2 m_2 \rangle \langle l'm'|l_1 m_1, l_2 m_2 \rangle = \delta_{l, l'} \delta_{m, m'}. \tag{3.32}$$

Symmetry: Some symmetry properties of CG. There are even more symmetries (Rose, 1957), but we only provide those which we will use later on:

$$
\begin{aligned}
\langle lm|l_1m_1, l_2m_2\rangle &= (-1)^{l_1+l_2-l}\langle l(-m)|l_1(-m_1), l_2(-m_2)\rangle & (3.33)\\
&= (-1)^{l_1+l_2-l}\langle lm|l_2m_2, l_1m_1\rangle & (3.34)\\
&= (-1)^{l_1-m_1}\sqrt{\frac{2l+1}{2l_2+1}}\langle l_2(-m_2)|l_1m_1, lm\rangle & (3.35)\\
&= (-1)^{l_2+m_2}\sqrt{\frac{2l+1}{2l_1+1}}\langle l_1(-m_1)|l(-m), l_2m_2\rangle. & (3.36)
\end{aligned}
$$

3.4 Fast and Accurate Correlation in $\mathcal{SH}$

So far we have introduced many basic properties of the Spherical Harmonic domain, which we are using now to derive more complex operations. In analogy to the Fourier domain, where the Convolution Theorem enables us to compute a fast convolution and correlation of signals in the frequency domain, we now derive fast convolution and correlation for the Spherical Harmonic domain which we introduced in (Fehr et al., 2008a).

Since some important features and feature selection methods have been derived from the key ideas of this approach, we review this method in detail:

Correlation on the 2-Sphere: The full correlation function $\mathcal{C}^\# : \mathcal{SO}(3) \to \mathbb{R}$ of two signals f and g under the rotation $\mathcal{R} \in \mathcal{SO}(3)$ on a 2-sphere is given as:

$$
\mathcal{SH}_{corr}(\mathcal{R}) := \int_{S^2} f(\mathcal{R}g) \quad \sin\Theta d\Phi d\Theta. \tag{3.37}
$$

Obviously, the computational cost of a direct evaluation approach - over all possible rotations $\mathcal{R}$ - is way too high. Especially when we are considering arbitrary resolutions of the rotation parameters. To cope with this problem, we derive a fast but accurate method for the computation of the correlation in the harmonic domain.

Besides the obvious usage of the (cross)-correlation as similarity measure, the correlation on the 2-sphere can also be used to perform a rotation estimation of similar signals on a sphere.

Rotation Estimation: given any two real valued signals f_1 and f_2 on a 2-sphere which are considered to be equal or at least similar under some rotational invariant measure ($\sim_\mathcal{R}$):

$$
f_1 \sim_\mathcal{R} f_2, \mathcal{R} \in SO(3), \tag{3.38}
$$

the goal is to estimate the parameters of an arbitrary rotation $\mathcal{R}$ as accurate as possible without any additional information other than f_1, f_2 and considering arbitrary resolutions of the rotation parameters.

Related Approaches: Recently, there have been proposals for several different methods which try to overcome the direct matching problem. Here, we are only considering methods which provide full rotational estimates (there are many methods covering only rotations around the z-axis without correspondences.

A direct nonlinear estimation (DNE) which is able to retrieve the parameters for small rotations via iterative minimization techniques was introduced in (Makadia et al., 2004). However, this method fails for larger rotations and was proposed only for "fine tuning" of pre-aligned rotations. Most other methods use representations in the Spherical Harmonic domain to solve the problem.

The possibility to recover the rotation parameters utilizing the spherical harmonic shift theorem (SHIFT) (Brink and Satchler, 1968) has been shown in (Burel and Henoco, 1995). This approach also uses an iterative minimization and was later refined by (Makadia and Daniilidis, 2003). Again, the estimation accuracy is limited to small rotations.

Rotation Estimation via Correlation: The basis of our method was first suggested by (Crowther, 1972), presenting a fast correlation in two angles followed by a correlation in the third Euler angle in an iterative way (known as FCOR). This method was later extended to a full correlation in all three angles by (Kovacs and Wriggers, 2002). This approach allows the direct computation of the correlation from the harmonic coefficients via FFT, but was actually not intended to be used to recover the rotation parameters. Its angular resolution directly depends on the range of the harmonic expansion - making high angular resolutions rather expensive. But FCOR was used by (Makadia et al., 2004) to initialize the DNE and SHIFT "fine tuning" algorithms. The same authors used a variation of FCOR (using inverse Spherical Fourier Transform (D. Healy Jr. and Moore, 2003) in stead of FFT) in combination with SHIFT (Makadia and Daniilidis, 2006) to recover robot positions from omni-directional images via rotation parameter estimation.

3.4.1 Basic $\mathcal{SH}$-Correlation Algorithm

Starting from the full correlation function (3.37) we use the Convolution Theorem and substitute f and g with their $\mathcal{SH}$ expansions (3.19, 3.1) , which leads to

$$\mathcal{SH}_{corr}(\mathcal{R}) = \sum_{l=0}^{\infty} \sum_{m=-l}^{l} \sum_{n=-l}^{l} \overline{D_{mn}^l(\mathcal{R})} \hat{f}_m^l \overline{\hat{g}_n^l}. \tag{3.39}$$

The actual "trick" to obtain the fast correlation is to factorize the original rotation $\mathcal{R}(\phi, \theta, \psi)$ into $\mathcal{R} = \mathcal{R}_1 \cdot \mathcal{R}_2$, choosing $\mathcal{R}_1(\xi, \pi/2, 0)$ and $\mathcal{R}_2(\eta, \pi/2, \omega)$ with $\xi = \phi - \pi/2, \eta = \pi - \theta, \omega = \psi - \pi/2$.

Using the fact that

$$D_{mn}^l(\phi, \theta, \psi) = \mathrm{e}^{-im\phi} d_{mn}^l(\theta) \mathrm{e}^{-in\psi}, \tag{3.40}$$

where d^l is a real valued "Wigner (small) d-matrix" (see (3.2.1)), and

$$D_{mn}^l(\mathcal{R}_1 \cdot \mathcal{R}_2) = \sum_{h=-l}^{l} D_{nh}^l(\mathcal{R}_1) D_{hm}^l(\mathcal{R}_2), \tag{3.41}$$

we can rewrite

$$D_{mn}^l(\mathcal{R}) = \sum_{h=-l}^{l} d_{nh}^l(\pi/2) d_{hm}^l(\pi/2) \mathrm{e}^{-i(n\xi + h\eta + m\omega)}. \tag{3.42}$$

Substituting (3.42) into (3.39) provides the final formulation for the correlation function regarding the new angles ξ, η and ω:

$$\mathcal{SH}_{corr}(\xi, \eta, \omega) = \sum_{l=0}^{\infty} \sum_{m=-l}^{l} \sum_{h=-l}^{l} \sum_{m'=-l}^{l} d_{mh}^l(\pi/2) d_{hm'}^l(\pi/2) \hat{f}_m^l \overline{\hat{g}_{m'}^l} \mathrm{e}^{-i(m\xi + h\eta + m'\omega)}. \tag{3.43}$$

The direct evaluation of this correlation function is of course not possible - but it is rather straightforward to obtain the Fourier transform of (3.43), hence eliminating the missing angle parameters:

$$\widehat{\mathcal{SH}_{corr}}(m, h, m') = \sum_{l=0}^{\infty} d_{mh}^l(\pi/2) d_{hm'}^l(\pi/2) \hat{f}_m^l \overline{\hat{g}_{m'}^l}. \tag{3.44}$$

Finally, the correlation $\mathcal{SH}_{corr}(\xi, \eta, \omega)$ can be retrieved via inverse Fourier transform of $\widehat{\mathcal{SH}_{corr}}$,

$$\mathcal{SH}_{corr}(\xi, \eta, \omega) = \mathcal{F}^{-1}(\widehat{\mathcal{SH}_{corr}}(m, h, m')), \tag{3.45}$$

revealing the correlation values in a three dimensional $\mathcal{C}^{\#}(\xi, \eta, \omega)$-space.

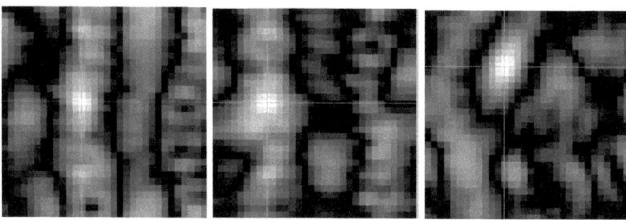

Figure 3.5: Orthoview of a resulting 3D correlation grid in the $\mathcal{C}^{\#}(\xi, \eta, \omega)$ -space with a maximum spherical harmonic expansion to the 16th band, $\phi = \pi/4, \theta = \pi/8, \psi = \pi/2$. From left to right: xy-plane, zy-plane, xz-plane.

3.4.2 Euler Ambiguities

The final obstacle towards the recovery of the rotation parameters inherits from the Euler parameterization used in the correlation function. Unfortunately, Euler angle formulations cause various ambiguities and cyclic shift problems.

One minor problem is caused by the fact that our parameter grid range is from $0, \dots, 2\pi$ in all dimensions, while the angle θ is only defined $\theta \in [0, \pi[$. This causes two correlation peaks at $\theta = \beta$ and $\theta = 2\pi - \beta$ for an actual rotation of $\theta = \beta$. We avoid this problem by restricting the maximum search to $\theta \in [0, \pi[$, hence neglecting half of the correlation space.

The formulation of the correlation function also causes further cyclic shifts in the grid representation of the Euler angles. This way, the zero rotation $\mathcal{R}(\phi = 0, \theta = 0, \psi = 0)$ does not have its peak at the zero position $C^{\#}(0, 0, 0)$ of the parameter grid as one would expect. For a more intuitive handling of the parameter extraction from the grid, such that the $(0, 0, 0)$ position in the grid corresponds to no rotation, we extend the original formulation of (3.44) and use a shift in the frequency space in order to normalize the mapping of $\mathcal{R}(\pi, 0, \pi)$ to $C^{\#}(0, 0, 0)$:

$$\widehat{C^{\#}}(m, h, m') = \sum_{l=0}^{\infty} d_{mh}^{l}(\pi/2)d_{hm'}^{l}(\pi/2)\widehat{f_{lm}}\overline{\widehat{g_{lm'}}} \cdot i^{m+2h+m'}. \tag{3.46}$$

3.4.3 Increasing the Angular Resolution

For real world applications, where the harmonic expansion is limited to some maximum expansion band $b_{\max}$:

$$\widehat{C^{\#}}(m, h, m') = \sum_{l=0}^{b_{\max}} d_{mh}^{l}(\pi/2)d_{hm'}^{l}(\pi/2)\widehat{f_{m}^{l}}\overline{\widehat{g_{m'}^{l}}} \cdot i^{m+2h+m'}, \tag{3.47}$$

the resulting (ξ, η, ω) space turns into a sparse and discrete space. Unfortunately, this directly affects the angular resolution of the correlation. Let us take a closer look at figure (3.5): first of all, it appears (and our experiments in section 11.1) clearly support this assumption) that the fast correlation function has a clear and stable maximum in a point on the grid. This is a very nice property, and we could simply recover the corresponding rotation parameters which are associated with this maximum position. But there are still some major problems: The image in Figure (3.5) appears to be quite coarse - and in fact, the parameter grids for expansions up to the 16th band ($b_{max} = 16$) have the size of $33 \times 33 \times 33$ since the parameters m, m', h in (3.44) are running from $-b_{max}, \ldots, b_{max}$. Given rotations up to $360°$, this leaves us in the worst case with an overall estimation accuracy of less than $15°$.

In general, even if our fast correlation function (3.45) would perfectly estimate the maximum position in all cases, we would have to expect a worst case accuracy of

$$Err_{corr} = 2 \cdot \frac{180°}{2b_{max}} + \frac{90°}{2b_{max}}, \tag{3.48}$$

accumulated over all three angles. Hence, if we would like to achieve an accuracy of $1°$, we would have to take the harmonic expansion roughly beyond the 180th band. This would be computationally expensive. Even worse, since we are considering discrete data, the signals on the sphere are band-limited. So for smaller radii, higher bands of the expansion are actually not carrying any valuable information. Due to this resolution problem, the fast correlation has so far only been used to initialize iterative algorithms (Makadia and Daniilidis, 2006)(Makadia et al., 2004).

Sinc Interpolation.

Now, instead of increasing the sampling rate of our input signal by expanding the harmonic transform, we have found an alternative way to increase the correlation accuracy: interpolation in the frequency domain.

In general, considering the Sampling Theorem and given appropriate discrete samples a_n with step size Δ_x of some continuous 1D signal $a(x)$, we can reconstruct the original signal via sinc interpolation (Yaroslavsky, 2003):

$$a(x) = \sum_{n=-\infty}^{\infty} a_n \mathrm{sinc}(\pi(x/\Delta_x - n)), \tag{3.49}$$

with

$$\mathrm{sinc}(x) = \frac{\sin(x)}{x}. \tag{3.50}$$

For a finite number of samples, (3.49) changes to:

$$a(x) = \sum_{k=0}^{N} a_k \frac{\sin(\pi(x/\Delta_x - k))}{N \sin(\pi(x/\Delta_x - k)/N)}. \tag{3.51}$$

This sinc interpolation features two nice properties (Yaroslavsky, 2003): it entirely avoids aliasing errors and it can easily be applied in the discrete Fourier space. Given the DFT coefficients $\alpha_n, n = 0, 1, \ldots, N - 1$ of the discrete signal $a_n, n = 0, 1, \ldots, N - 1$, the sinc interpolation is implemented by adding a zero padding between $\alpha_{(N/2)-1}$ and $\alpha_{(N/2)}$.

Returning to our original correlation problem, it is easy to see that the (m, h, m')-space in (3.44) is actually nothing else but a discrete 3D Fourier spectrum. So we can directly apply the 3D extension of (3.51) and add a zero padding into the (m, h, m')-space. This way, we are able to drastically increase the resolution of our correlation function at very low additional cost for implementation issues as well as suitable pad sizes). Figure (3.6) shows the effect of the interpolation on the correlation matrix for different pad sizes p.

It has to be noted that even though the sinc interpolation implies some smoothing characteristics to the correlation matrix, the maxima remain fixed to singular positions in the grid.

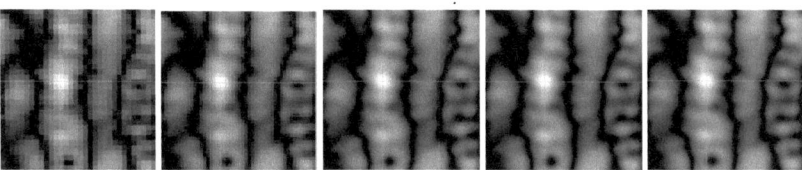

Figure 3.6: Same experiment as in Fig. (3.5) but with increasing size of the sinc interpolation padding. From left to right: $p = 0, p = 16, p = 64, p = 128, p = 256$

Theoretically, we are now finally able to reduce the worst case accuracy to arbitrarily small angles for any given band:

$$Err_{corr}^{pad} = 2 \cdot \frac{180°}{2b_{\max} + p} + \frac{90°}{2b_{\max} + p}. \tag{3.52}$$

Of course, the padding approach has practical limitations - inverse FFTs are becoming computationally expensive at some point. But as our experiments in 11.1 show, resolutions below one degree are possible even for very low expansions.

Implementation: The implementation of the inverse FFT in (3.45) combined with the frequency space padding requires some care: we need an inverse complex to real FFT with an in-place mapping (the grid in the frequency space has the same size as the resulting grid in $\mathbb{R}^3$). Most FFT implementations are not providing such an operation. Due to the symmetries in the frequency space not all complex coefficients need to be stored, hence most implementations are using reduced grid sizes. We can avoid the tedious construction of such a reduced grid from $\widehat{C\#}$ by using an inverse complex to complex FFT and taking only the real part of the result. In this case, we only have to shuffle the coefficients of $\widehat{C\#}$, which can be done via simple modulo operations while simultaneously applying the padding. We rewrite (3.46) to:

$$\widehat{C\#}(a, b, c) = \sum_{l=0}^{b_{\max}} d_{mh}^l(\pi/2) d_{hm'}^l(\pi/2) \widehat{f_{lm}} \overline{\widehat{g_{lm'}}} \cdot i^{m+2h+m'}, \tag{3.53}$$

where

$$s := 2bp, \quad a := (m + s + 1) \bmod s, \quad b := (h + s + 1) \bmod s, \quad c := (m' + s + 1) \bmod s.$$

Concerning the pad size: due to the nature of the FFT, most implementations achieve notable speed-ups for certain grid sizes. So it is very useful to choose the padding in such a way that the overall grid size has, e.g., prime factor decompositions of mostly small primes (Frigo and Johnson, 2005).

3.4.4 Rotation Parameters

Finally, we are able to retrieve the original rotation parameters. For a given correlation peak at the grid position $c(x, y, z)$, with maximum harmonic expansion b and padding p the rotation angles are:

$$\phi = \begin{cases} \pi + (2\pi - x\Delta) & \text{for } x\Delta > \pi \\ \pi - x\Delta & \text{otherwise} \end{cases} \tag{3.54}$$

$$\theta = \begin{cases} (2\pi - y\Delta) & \text{for } y\Delta > \pi \\ y\Delta & \text{otherwise} \end{cases} \tag{3.55}$$

$$\psi = \begin{cases} \pi + (2\pi - z\Delta) & \text{for } z\Delta > \pi \\ \pi - z\Delta & \text{otherwise} \end{cases} \tag{3.56}$$

with $\quad \Delta = 2\pi/(b + p)$.

The resulting rotation estimates return very precise and unique parameter sets. Only one ambiguous

Figure 3.7: $\phi\psi$-plane for of the correlation matrix with $\theta = 0$.

setting has to be noted: for $\theta = 0, \pi$ all zyz'-Euler formulations which hold $\phi + \psi = 2\pi$ encode the very same rotation (see Figure (3.7)). This is actually not a problem for our rotation estimation task, but it might be quite confusing especially in the case of numerical evaluation of the estimation accuracy.

3.4.5 Normalized Cross-Correlation

In many cases, especially when one tries to estimate the rotation parameters between non-identical objects, it is favorable to normalize the (cross-)correlation results. We follow an approach which is widely known from the normalized cross-correlation of 2D images: First, we subtract the mean from both functions prior to the correlation and then divide the results by the variances:

$$\mathcal{SH}_{corr-norm}(\mathcal{R}) := \int\limits_{S^2} \frac{(f - \overline{f})(\mathcal{R}(g - \overline{g}))}{\sigma_f \sigma_g} \quad \sin\Theta d\Phi d\Theta. \tag{3.57}$$

Analogous to Fourier transform, we obtain the expected values $\overline{f}$ and $\overline{g}$ directly from the 0th $\mathcal{SH}$ coefficient. The variances σ_f and σ_g can be estimated from the band-wise energies:

$$\sigma_f \approx \sqrt{\sum_l |\widehat{f}_l|^2}. \tag{3.58}$$

3.4.6 Simultaneous Correlation of Signals on Concentric Spheres

In many applications we consider local signals which are spread over the surfaces of several concentric spheres with different radii. Instead of computing the correlation for each surface separately, we can simply extend (3.45) to compute the correlation over all signals at once.

This can be achieved by the use of a single correlation matrix $C^{\#}$. We simply add the $\widehat{\mathcal{SH}_{corr}}(m, h, m')$ (3.44) for all radii and retrieve the combined correlation matrix $C^{\#}$ via inverse FFT as before.

3.4.7 Complexity

Following the implementation given in section 4, we obtain the harmonic expansion to band b_{max} at each point of a volume with m voxels in $O(m(b_{max})^2 + (m \log m))$. Building the correlation matrix $\widehat{C^{\#}}$ at each point takes $O((2b_{max})^4)$ plus the inverse FFT in $O((b_{max} + p)^3 \log(b_{max} + p)^3)$.

Parallelization: Further speed-up can be achieved by parallelization (see section 4): the transformation into the harmonic domain can be parallelized as well as the point-wise computation of $\widehat{C^{\#}}$.

3.5 Convolution in $\mathcal{SH}$

After the fast correlation has been introduced, it is obvious to also take a look at the convolution in the harmonic domain. If we are only interested in the result of the convolution of two signals at a given fixed rotation, we can apply the so-called "left"-convolution.

3.5.1 "Left"-Convolution

We define the "left"-convolution of two spherical functions f and g in the harmonic domain as $\widehat{f} * \widehat{g}$. Following the Convolution Theorem this convolution is given as:

$$\left(\widehat{f} * \widehat{g}\right)_m^l = 2\pi \sqrt{\frac{4\pi}{2l + 1}} \widehat{f}_m^l \cdot \widehat{g}_0^l. \tag{3.59}$$

Note that this definition is asymmetric and performs an averaging over the translations (rotations) of the "left" signal.

The "left"-convolution is quite useful, but for our methods we typically encounter situations like in the case of the fast correlation, where we need to evaluate the convolution at all possible rotations of two spherical functions.

3.5.2 Fast Convolution over all Angles

Following the approach used for the fast correlation, we introduce a method for the fast computation of full convolutions over all angles on the sphere in a very similar way:

Again, the full convolution function $\mathcal{SH}_{conv} : SO(3) \to \mathbb{R}$ of two signals f and g under the rotation $\mathcal{R} \in SO(3)$ on a 2-sphere is given as:

$$\mathcal{SH}_{conv}(\mathcal{R}) := \int_{S^2} f(\mathcal{R}\bar{g}) \sin \Theta d\Phi d\Theta. \tag{3.60}$$

Applying the same steps as in the case of the correlation, we obtain a convolution matrix:

$$\widehat{C^*}(m, h, m') = \sum_{l=0}^{\infty} d_{mh}^l(\pi/2) d_{hm'}^l(\pi/2) \widehat{f}_m^l \widehat{g}_{m'}^l. \tag{3.61}$$

Analog to equation (3.45),

$$C^*(\xi, \eta, \omega) = \mathcal{F}^{-1}(\widehat{C^*}), \tag{3.62}$$

49

an inverse Fourier transform reveals the convolution $f * g$ for each possible rotation in the three dimensional $C^*(\xi, \eta, \omega)$-space.

Regarding computational complexity and angular resolution, this convolution method shares all the properties of the fast correlation (see sections 3.4.3 to 11.1).

3.6 Vectorial Harmonics

So far, we have exploited and utilized the nice properties of the harmonic expansion of scalar valued functions on S^2 in Spherical Harmonics to derive powerful methods like the fast correlation. These methods can be operated on single scalar input in form of gray-scale volumes, which is one of the most common data types in 3D image analysis. But there are two equally important data types: multi-channel scalar input (e.g. RGB colored volumes) and 3D vector fields (e.g. from gradient data).

In the first case, a harmonic expansion of multi-channel scalar input is straightforward: since the channels are not affected independently, one can simply combine the Spherical Harmonic expansions of each individual channel (e.g. see section 5).

For 3D vector fields, the harmonic expansion turns out to be less trivial, i.e. if we rotate the field, we are not only changing the position of the individual vectors, but we also have to change the vector values accordingly. This dependency can be modeled by the use of Vectorial Harmonics ($\mathcal{VH}$).

Given a vector valued function $\mathbf{f} : S^2 \rightarrow \mathbb{R}^3$ with three vectorial components $[x, y, z] = \mathbf{f}(\Phi, \Theta)$ and parameterized in Euler angles (Fig. 3.4) ϕ, θ, ψ, we can expand $\mathbf{f}$ in Vectorial Harmonics:

$$\mathbf{f}(\Phi, \Theta) = \sum_{l=0}^{\infty} \sum_{k=-1}^{1} \sum_{m=-(l+k)}^{(l+k)} \widehat{\mathbf{f}_{km}^l} \mathbf{Z}_{km}^l(\Phi, \Theta), \tag{3.63}$$

with scalar harmonic coefficients $\widehat{\mathbf{f}_{km}^l}$ and the orthonormal base functions:

$$\mathbf{Z}_{\mathbf{km}}^l = \begin{pmatrix} \langle 1\ 1 & |l+k\ m, l\ 1-m \rangle & Y_{1-m}^l \\ \langle 1\ 0 & |l+k\ m, l\ -m \rangle & Y_{-m}^l \\ \langle 1\ -1 & |l+k\ m, l\ -1-m \rangle & Y_{-1-m}^l \end{pmatrix}^{\mathbf{T}}. \tag{3.64}$$

Figure 3.8 visualizes the first two bands of these base functions as vector fields on a sphere. We define the forward Vectorial Harmonic transformation as

$$\mathcal{VH}(\mathbf{f}) := \widehat{\mathbf{f}}, \quad \text{with} \quad \widehat{\mathbf{f}_{km}^l} = \int_{\Phi, \Theta} \overline{\mathbf{Z}}_{(-1)m}^l(\Phi, \Theta) \mathbf{f}[-1](\Phi, \Theta) \sin \Theta d\Phi d\Theta$$

$$+ \int_{\Phi, \Theta} \overline{\mathbf{Z}}_{(0)m}^l(\Phi, \Theta) \mathbf{f}[0](\Phi, \Theta) \sin \Theta d\Phi d\Theta$$

$$+ \int_{\Phi, \Theta} \overline{\mathbf{Z}}_{(1)m}^l(\Phi, \Theta) \mathbf{f}[1](\Phi, \Theta) \sin \Theta d\Phi d\Theta, \tag{3.65}$$

where $\mathbf{f}[-1]$ returns the scalar function on S^2 which is defined by the complex transformation (3.67) of the z component of the vector-valued $\mathbf{f}$. The backward transformation in is defined as:

$$\mathcal{VH}^{-1}\left(\widehat{\mathbf{f}}(\Phi, \Theta)\right) := \sum_{l=0}^{\infty} \sum_{k=-1}^{1} \sum_{m=(l+k)}^{(l+k)} \widehat{\mathbf{f}_{km}^l} \mathbf{Z}_{km}^l(\Phi, \Theta). \tag{3.66}$$

In our case, the Vectorial Harmonics are defined to operate on vector fields with complex vector coordinates. For fields of real valued vectors $\mathbf{r}(x, y, z) \in \mathbb{R}^3$, we need to transform the vector coordinates to $\mathbb{C}^3$ according to the Spherical Harmonic relation:

$$\mathbf{u} \in \mathbb{C}^3 : \mathbf{u} := \begin{pmatrix} \frac{x-iy}{\sqrt{2}} \\ z \\ \frac{x+iy}{\sqrt{2}} \end{pmatrix}. \tag{3.67}$$

3.6.1 Deriving Vectorial Harmonics

There have been several different approaches towards Vectorial Harmonics, like (Hill, 1954) or (Barrera et al., 1985). All use a slightly different setting and notation. For our purposes, we derive our methods from a very general theory of Tensorial Harmonics (Reisert and Burkhardt, 2008), which provides expansions for arbitrary real valued tensor functions $\mathbf{f}$ on the 2-sphere:

$$\mathbf{f}(\Phi, \Theta) := \sum_{l=0}^{\infty} \sum_{k=-d}^{d} \sum_{m=-(l+k)}^{(l+k)} \widehat{\mathbf{f}^l_{km}} \mathbf{Z}^l_{km}(\Phi, \Theta), \tag{3.68}$$

where $\widehat{\mathbf{f}^l_{km}}$ is the expansion coefficient of the l-th band of tensor order d and harmonic order m. The orthonormal Tensorial Harmonic base functions $\mathbf{Z}^l_{km}$ are given as:

$$\mathbf{Z}^l_{km} := \mathbf{e}^{(l+k)}_m \circ_1 Y^l, \tag{3.69}$$

with the Spherical Harmonic bands Y^l. The $\mathbf{e}^l_m$ are elements of the standard Euclidean base of $\mathbb{C}^{2d+1}$, and $\circ_l$ denotes a bilinear form connecting tensors V_{l_1} and V_{l_2} of different ranks:

$$\circ_d : V_{l_1} \times V_{l_2} \rightarrow \mathbb{C}^{2d+1}, \tag{3.70}$$

where $l_1, l_2 \in \mathbb{N}$ have to hold $|l_1 - l_2| \le l \le l_1 + l_2$. $\circ_l$ is computed as follows:

$$(\mathbf{e}^l_m)^T (\mathbf{v} \circ_l \mathbf{u}) := \sum_{m=m_1+m_2} \langle lm | l_1 m_1, l_2 m_2 \rangle v_{m_1} u_{m_2}. \tag{3.71}$$

See (Reisert, 2008) for details and proofs.

If we limit the general form to tensors of order one ($d := 1$) and use 3.71 for the computation of the base functions 3.69, we directly obtain Vectorial Harmonic expansions as in 3.63.

3.6.2 Useful Properties of Vectorial Harmonics

Vectorial Harmonics inherit most of the favorable properties of the underlying Spherical Harmonics, such as orthonormality.

Orthonormality:

$$\int\limits_{\Phi, \Theta} \left(\mathbf{Z}^l_{km}(\Phi, \Theta) \right)^T \mathbf{Z}^{l'}_{k'm'}(\Phi, \Theta) \sin \Theta d\Phi d\Theta = \frac{4\pi}{(1/3)(2l+1)(2(l+k)+1)} \delta_{l,l'} \delta_{k,k'} \delta_{m,m'}. \tag{3.72}$$

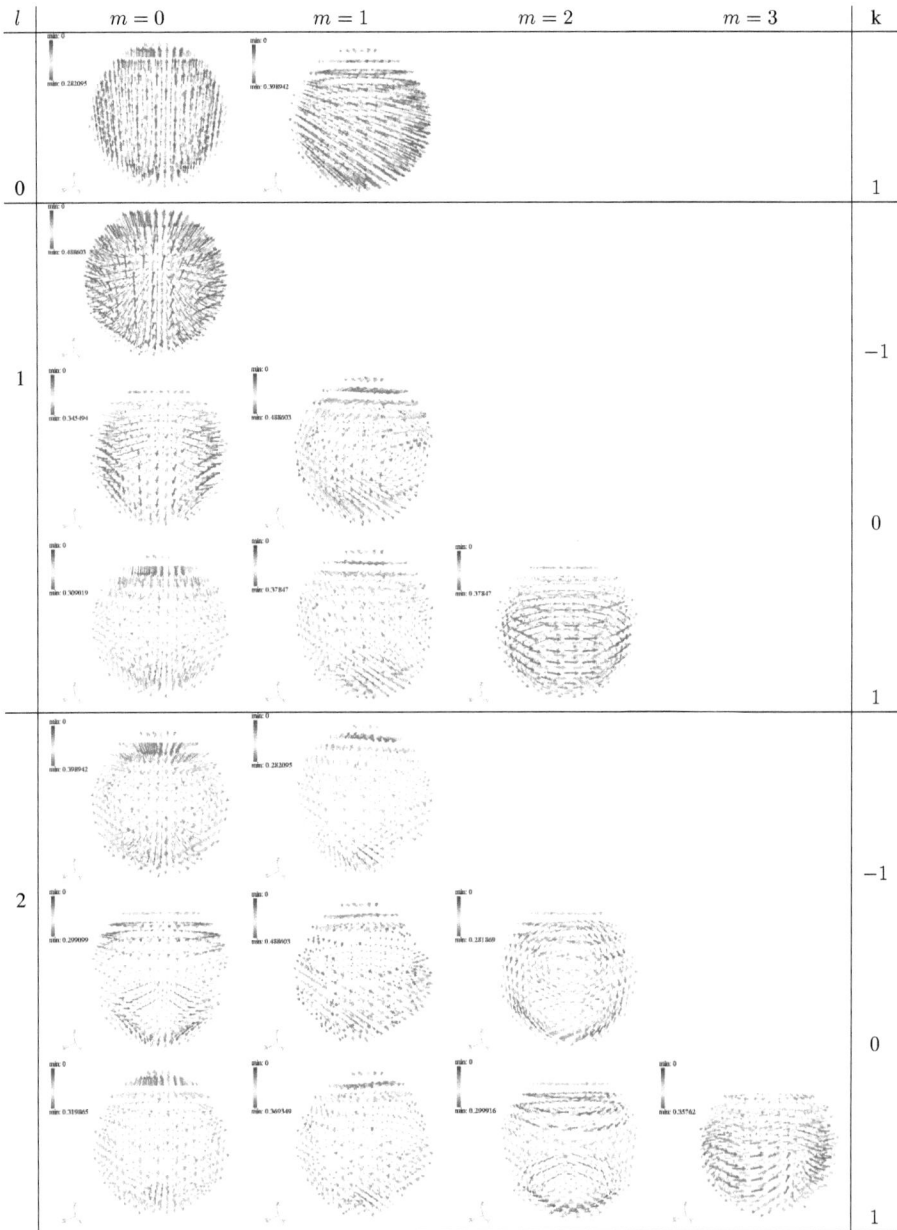

Figure 3.8: The first Vectorial Harmonic base functions to $l = 2$. Due to space limitations we only visualize functions with $0 \leq m \leq l + k$ instead of the actual $-(l + k) \leq m \leq l + k$.

3.7 Rotations in Vectorial Harmonics

The analogy of Vectorial Harmonics to Spherical Harmonics continues also in the case of rotation in the harmonic domain. Complex 3D vector valued signals $\mathbf{f}$ with Vectorial Harmonic coefficients $\widehat{\mathbf{f}}$ are rotated (Reisert and Burkhardt, 2008) by:

$$\mathcal{R}\mathbf{f} = \sum_{l=0}^{\infty} \sum_{k=-1}^{k=1} \sum_{m=-(l+k)}^{l+k} \sum_{n=-(l+k)}^{l+k} D_{mn}^{l+k}(\mathcal{R})\widehat{\mathbf{f}}_{km}^{l}\mathbf{Z}_{kn}^{l}, \tag{3.73}$$

which is a straightforward extension of (3.19). One notable aspect is that we need to combine Wigner-D matrices of the upper $l+1$ and lower $l-1$ bands in order to compute the still band-wise rotation of $\widehat{\mathbf{f}}_{km}^{l}$. Hence, we rotate $\widehat{\mathbf{f}}_{km}^{l}$ by $\mathcal{R}(\phi, \theta, \psi)$ via band-wise multiplications:

$$\mathbf{f}' = \mathcal{R}(\phi, \theta, \psi)\mathbf{f} \Rightarrow \widehat{\mathbf{f}}'^{l}_{km} = \sum_{n=-(l+k)}^{l+k} D_{mn}^{l+k}(\phi, \theta, \psi)\widehat{\mathbf{f}}_{km}^{l}. \tag{3.74}$$

Due to the use of the zyz'-convention, we have to handle inverse rotations with some care:

$$\mathbf{f}' = \mathcal{R}^{-1}(\phi, \theta, \psi)\mathbf{f} \Rightarrow \widehat{\mathbf{f}}'^{l}_{km} = \sum_{n=-(l+k)}^{l+k} D_{mn}^{l+k}(-\psi, -\theta, -\phi)\widehat{\mathbf{f}}_{km}^{l}. \tag{3.75}$$

3.8 Fast Correlation in Vectorial Harmonics

We use local dot-products of vectors to define the correlation under a given rotation $\mathcal{R}$ in Euler angles ϕ, θ, ψ as:

$$(\mathbf{f}\#\mathbf{g})(\mathcal{R}) := \int_{\Phi, \Theta} \langle \mathbf{f}(\Phi, \Theta), \mathcal{R}\mathbf{g}(\Phi, \Theta) \rangle \quad \sin\Theta d\Phi d\Theta. \tag{3.76}$$

Using the rotational properties (3.73) of the Vectorial Harmonics, we can extend the fast correlation approach (see section 3.4) from $\mathcal{SH}$ to $\mathcal{VH}$. Starting from (3.37) we insert (3.73) into (3.39) and obtain:

$$\mathcal{VH}_{corr}(\mathcal{R}) = \sum_{l=0}^{l=\infty} \sum_{k=-1}^{k=1} \sum_{m,n=-(l+k)}^{(l+k)} \overline{D_{mn}^{l+k}(\mathcal{R})\widehat{\mathbf{f}}_{km}^{l}}\,\overline{\widehat{\mathbf{g}}_{kn}^{l}}. \tag{3.77}$$

Analogous to (3.43), substituting (3.42) into (3.77) provides the final formulation for the correlation function regarding the new angles ξ, η and ω:

$$\mathcal{VH}_{corr}(\xi, \eta, \omega) = \sum_{l=0}^{l=\infty} \sum_{k=-1}^{k=1} \sum_{m,h,m'=-(l+k)}^{m,h,m'=(l+k)} d_{mh}^{l+k}(\pi/2)d_{hm'}^{l+k}(\pi/2)\widehat{\mathbf{f}}_{km}^{l}\overline{\widehat{\mathbf{g}}_{km'}^{l}}e^{-i(m\xi+h\eta+m'\omega)}. \tag{3.78}$$

Following (3.44) we obtain the Fourier transform of the correlation matrix $\mathcal{C}^{\#}$ (3.78) to eliminate the missing angle parameters:

$$\widehat{\mathcal{C}^{\#}}(m, h, m') = \sum_{l=0}^{l=\infty} \sum_{k=-1}^{k=1} d_{mh}^{l+k}(\pi/2)d_{hm'}^{l+k}(\pi/2)\widehat{\mathbf{f}}_{km}^{l}\overline{\widehat{\mathbf{g}}_{km'}^{l}}. \tag{3.79}$$

Again, the correlation matrix $\mathcal{C}^{\#}(\xi, \eta, \omega)$ can be retrieved via inverse Fourier transform of $\widehat{\mathcal{C}^{\#}}$:

$$\mathcal{C}^{\#}(\xi, \eta, \omega) = \mathcal{F}^{-1}(\widehat{\mathcal{C}^{\#}}(m, h, m')), \tag{3.80}$$

revealing the correlation values in a three dimensional (ξ, η, ω)-space.

3.9 Fast Convolution in Vectorial Harmonics

The fast convolution $\mathcal{C}^*$ in Vectorial Harmonics can be directly derived from sections 3.8 and 3.5:

$$\widehat{\mathcal{C}^*}(m, h, m') = \sum_{l=0}^{\infty} \sum_{-1}^{k=1} d_{mh}^{l+k}(\pi/2) d_{hm'}^{l+k}(\pi/2) \widehat{\mathbf{f}}_{km}^l \widehat{\mathbf{g}}_{km'}^l. \tag{3.81}$$

Analog to equ. (3.80), we reconstruct $\mathcal{C}^*(\xi, \eta, \omega)$ from (3.81) via inverse Fourier transform:

$$\mathcal{C}^*(\xi, \eta, \omega) = \mathcal{F}^{-1}(\widehat{\mathcal{C}^*}(m, h, m')). \tag{3.82}$$

4 Implementation

So far, we derived the mathematical foundations for the computation of local features with a parameterization on the 2-sphere (see chapter 3) in a setting with strong continuous preconditions: the input data in form of functions on 3D volumes $X : \mathbb{R}^3 \rightarrow \mathbb{R}$ is continuous, and the harmonic frequency spaces of the transformed neighborhoods $\mathcal{S}[r](\mathbf{x})$ are infinitely large because we assume to have no band limitations. This setting enables us to nicely derive sound and easy to handle methods, however, it is obvious that these preconditions cannot be met in the case of real world applications where we have to deal with discrete input data on a sparse volume grid $(X : \mathbb{Z}^3 \rightarrow \mathbb{R})$ and we have to limit the harmonic transformations to an upper frequency (band-limitation to $b_{\max}$). Hence, we some how have to close this gap, when applying the theoretically derived feature algorithms to real problems.

In general, we try to make this transition to the continuous setting as early as possible so that we can avoid discrete operations which are usually causing additional problems, i.e. the need to interpolate. Since we derive all of our feature algorithms (chapters 5.1 - 9) in the locally expanded harmonic domain, we actually only have to worry about the the transition of the local neighborhoods $\mathcal{S}[r](\mathbf{x})$ in X by $\mathcal{SH}\left(X|_{\mathcal{S}[r](\mathbf{x})}\right)$ (see section 3.1) and $\mathcal{VH}\left(\mathbf{X}|_{\mathcal{S}[r](\mathbf{x})}\right)$ (see section 3.6).
Hence, we need sound Spherical and Vectorial Harmonic transformations for discrete input data which handle the arising sampling problems and the needed band limitation. We derive these transformations in the next sections 4.1, 4.2 and discuss some relevant properties like complexity.

Another issue we frequently have to face in the context of an actual implementation of algorithms is the question of parallelization. We tackle the basics of parallelization in section 4.3.

The introduction of the actual features in the next chapters always follows the same structure: first, we derive the theoretic foundation of the feature in a continuous setting, and then we give details on the actual discrete implementation based on the methods we derive in this chapter.

4.1 Discrete Spherical Harmonic Transform

We are looking for discrete version of the Spherical Harmonic transform, e.g. we want to obtain the frequency decomposition of local discrete spherical neighborhoods $\mathcal{S}[r](\mathbf{x})$ (2.12) in $X : \mathbb{Z}^3 \rightarrow \mathbb{R}$.
If we disregard the sampling issues for a moment, the discrete implementation is rather straightforward: first, we pre-compute discrete approximations of the orthonormal harmonic base functions $Y_m^l[r, \mathbf{x}]$ (3.1) which are centered in $\mathbf{x}$. In their discrete version, the Y_m^l are parameterized in Euclidean coordinates $\mathbf{x} \in \mathbb{Z}^3$ rather then Euler angles:

$$Y_m^l : \mathbb{Z}^3 \rightarrow \mathbb{C}. \tag{4.1}$$

Next, we obtain the transformation coefficients $\mathcal{SH}\left(X|_{\mathcal{S}[r](\mathbf{x})}\right)_m^l$ via the discrete dot-product:

$$\mathcal{SH}\left(X|_{\mathcal{S}[r](\mathbf{x})}\right)_m^l := \sum_{\mathbf{x_i} \in \mathcal{S}[r](\mathbf{x})} X(\mathbf{x_i}) Y_m^l[r, \mathbf{x}](\mathbf{x_i}). \tag{4.2}$$

For most practical applications we have to compute the harmonic transformation of the neighborhoods around each voxel $\mathbf{x}$, which can be computed very efficiently: since (4.2) is actually determined via convolution, we can apply the standard convolution theorem "trick" and perform a fast convolution via FFT to obtain $\mathcal{SH}_m^l(X) : \mathbb{R}^3 \rightarrow \mathbb{C}^b$ (with $b = b_{\max}(b_{\max} - 1)$):

$$\mathcal{SH}[r] \left(X \right)_m^l = X * Y_m^l[r]. \tag{4.3}$$

This leaves us with the problems to construct correct base function templates $Y_m^l[r]$, which is essentially a sampling issue, and to find an appropriate $b_{\max}$.

4.1.1 Correct Sampling

The key problem of obtaining discrete approximations of continuous signals is to avoid biased results due to false sampling. In the case of the discrete harmonic transformations we have to handle two different sampling steps: first, the discretization of the input data, and second the construction of the base function templates $Y_m^l[r]$. In both cases, we can rely on the Sampling Theorem (Cundy and Rollett, 1961) (Nyquist, 1928) to obtain correct discretizations:

> If a function x(t) contains no frequencies higher than B cycles per second[1], it is completely determined by giving its ordinates at a series of points spaced $1/(2B)$ seconds apart (Nyquist, 1928)

The sampling rate during the discretization of the input data is usually bound by the imaging device. While most modern microscope systems obey the sampling theorem (see part III), other data sources might be more problematic. Hence, we are forced to introduce an artificial band-limitation, i.e. apply a low pass filtering on the input data whenever we face insufficient sampling.

The construction of correct discrete base function templates $Y_m^l[r]$ is more challenging because due to the dot-product nature of the discrete transformation (4.2) the sampling rate is fixed by the resolution of the input data and dominantly by the radius r, e.g. we cannot simply increase the sampling for higher frequency bands l (see figure 4.2)[2].
This results in an insurmountable limitation for our discrete harmonic transformations: the maximum expansion band b_{max} is bound by the radius: given small radii, the regarding spherical neighborhood $S[r]$ only provides a sufficient number of sampling points for low frequent base functions.
Further more, the discretization of convex structures like spheres easily causes aliasing effects we have to avoid. We cope with this problem by a Gaussian smoothing in radial direction. Figure 4.1 shows an example of a discrete base function template.

4.1.2 Band Limitation $b_{\max}$

Assuming that we obey the sampling theorem during the construction of $Y_m^l[r]$ (see previous section), we still have to worry about the effect of the band limitation of the harmonic expansion and reasonable choice of $b_{\max}$ below the theoretic limit.
The good news is that reconstructions from the harmonic domain are strictly band-wise operations (e.g. see (3.4)). Hence, the actual band limitation has no effect on the correctness of the lower frequencies: the band limitation simply acts as low-pass filter on the spherical signal. Figure 4.3[3]shows the effects of the band-limitation in a synthetic example. One should also keep in mind that a limitation of higher frequencies directly affects the angular resolution $\mathcal{SH}_{res}$ of the fast correlation and convolution in the

---

[1]equivalent to modern unit hertz
[2]Thanks to O. Ronneberger for the "Volvim" orthoviewer.
[3]Thanks to H. Skibbe for his volume rendering tool.

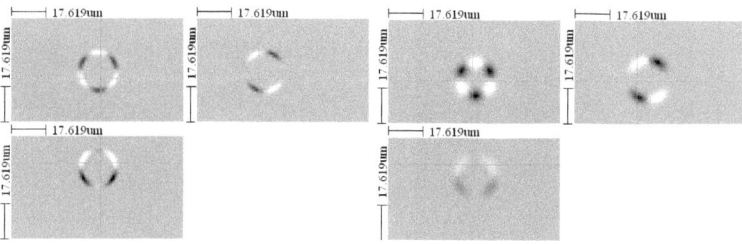

Figure 4.1: Construction of a correct discrete base function template. Orthoview of the example Y_3^4 at $r = 10$ and with an Gaussian smoothing of $\sigma = 2$ (**left**) and $\sigma = 4$ (**right**).

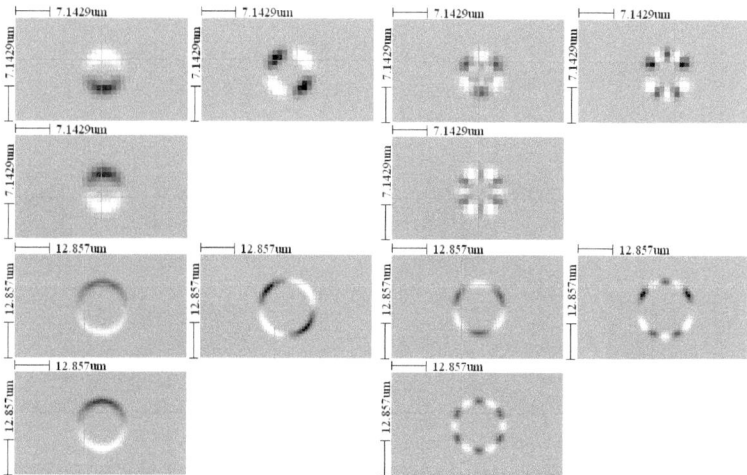

Figure 4.2: Example of sampling problems for small radii: **Top:** $r = 4$ and $b_{max} = 2, 7$. **Bottom:** $r = 10$ and $b_{max} = 2, 7$. The orthoview visualization clearly shows that the small radius does not provide enough sampling points for the higher frequencies in the 7th band.

harmonic domain (see section 3.4).

In the end, the selection of b_{max} is always a tradeoff between computational speed and maximum resolution.

4.1.3 Invariance

Another practical aspect of the harmonic expansion is that we are able to obtain additional invariance or robustness properties directly from the transformation implementation.

Gray-Scale Robustness

The most obvious example is the simple "trick" to become robust against gray-scale changes: As mentioned before in section 3.1, one very convenient property of the spherical harmonic transformations

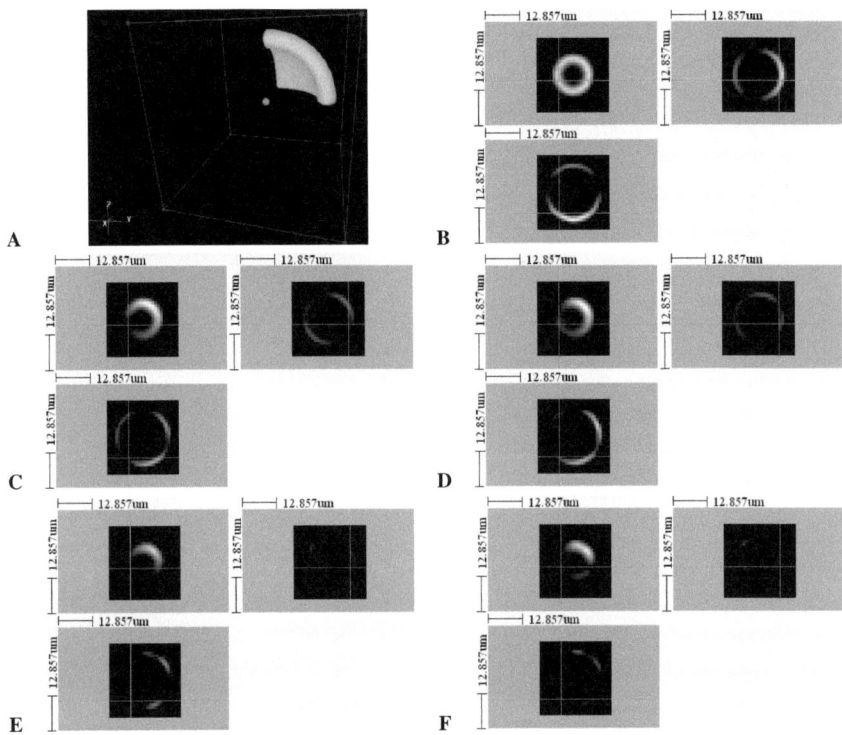

Figure 4.3: Effects of the band-limitation on the reconstruction of a spherical signal: **A**: volume rendering of the original binary signal on a sphere. **B-F**: orthoview of reconstructions with $b_{\mathrm{max}} = 1, 2, 3, 5, 10$.

is that analogous to the Fourier transform, the constant component of the expanded signal is given by the 0th coefficient $\mathcal{SH}[r] \left(X \right)_0^0$. Hence, we can easily achieve invariance towards shift of the mean gray-value in scalar operations if we simply normalize all coefficients by the 0th component.

Usually we denote this invariance only as "gray-scale robustness" since most practical applications include more complex gray-scale changes as this approach can handle.

Scale Normalization

It is also very easy to normalize the $\mathcal{SH}$ coefficients to compensate known changes in the scale of the data. In case we need to compute comparable features for data of different scale, we can normalize the coefficients $\mathcal{SH}[r]$ by the surface of the base functions, which is $4\pi r^2$ in a continuous setting. In the discrete case, we have to take the Gaussian smoothing into account: we simply use the sum over Y_0^0 as normalization coefficient.

Resolution Robustness

A typical problem which arises in the context of "real world" volume data is that we sometimes have to deal with non-cubic voxels, i.e. the input data is the result of a sampling of the real world which has not been equidistant in all spatial directions. This problem is usually caused by the imaging devices, e.g. confocal laser scanning microscopes (LSM) (see section 18.1.3) typically have a lower resolution in z-direction than in x and y.

Such non-cubic voxels cause huge problems when we try to obtain rotation invariant features. Fortunately, we can cope with this problem during the construction of the base function templates $Y_m^l[r]$: as figure 4.4 shows, we simply adapt the voxel resolution of the input data to the templates. Usually, we can obtain the necessary voxel resolution information directly from the imaging device.

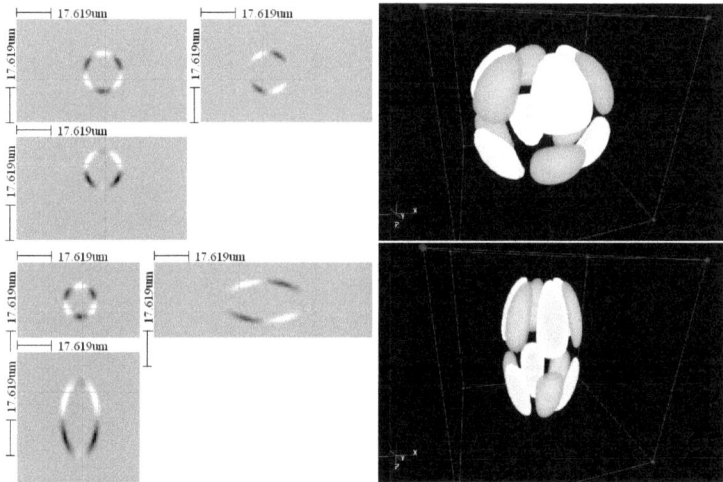

Figure 4.4: Resolution Robustness: **Top:** orthoview and volume rendering of the Y_3^4 base function $(r = 10)$ with the same resolution in all spatial directions. **Bottom:** orthoview and volume rendering of a base function with higher z-resolution.

4.1.4 Complexity

Concerning the voxel-wise local transformation for a single radius $\mathcal{SH}[r]\left(X\right)$ of a 3D volume X with m voxels, we obtain the harmonic expansion to band b_{max} in $O(m(b_{\mathrm{max}})^2 + (m \log m))$ if we follow the fast convolution approach (4.3) and assume the base function templates are given.

Since we have to extract $n = b_{\mathrm{max}}(b_{\mathrm{max}}-1)$ coefficients, the memory consumption lies in $O(m(b_{\mathrm{max}})^2)$.

4.1.5 Parallelization

Further speed-up can be achieved by parallelization (see section 4.3): the data can be transformed into the harmonic domain by parallel computation of the coefficients. For $\mathcal{C}$ CPU cores with $\mathcal{C} \leq (b_{\mathrm{max}})^2$ and $\mathcal{C} \leq m$ we obtain: $O(\frac{m(b_{\mathrm{max}})^2}{\mathcal{C}}) + O(\frac{(m \log m)}{\mathcal{C}})$.

4.1.6 Fast Spherical Harmonic Transform

Recently, there has been an approach towards a fast Spherical Harmonic transform (fSHT) (Healy et al., 2003) for discrete signals. The fSHT uses a similar approach as in the FFT speed-up of the DFT and performs the computation of the entire inverse transformation in $O(N \log^2 N)$, where N is the number of sampling points.

Since we hardly need the inverse transformation and only a small set of different extraction radii throughout this thesis, we prefer a simple caching of the pre-computed base functions to achieve faster transformations over of the quite complex fSHT method. Additionally, for real valued input data, we can exploit the symmetry properties (3.16):

$$\overline{Y_m^l} = (-1)^m Y_{-m}^l, \tag{4.4}$$

allowing us to actually compute only the positive half of the harmonic coefficients.

4.2 Discrete Vectorial Harmonic Transform

For the extraction of features on 3D vector fields, we need a discrete version of the Vectorial Harmonic transform (see section 3.6), i.e. we need to obtain the frequency decomposition of 3D vectorial signals at discrete positions on the discrete spherical neighborhoods $\mathcal{S}[r](\mathbf{x})$ (2.12) in $\mathbf{X} : \mathbb{Z}^3 \to \mathbb{R}^3$.

As for the discrete Spherical Harmonic transform, we pre-compute discrete approximations of the orthonormal harmonic base functions $\mathbf{Z}_{k,m}^l[r, \mathbf{x}]$ (3.64) which are centered in $\mathbf{x}$. In their discrete version, the $\mathbf{Z}_{k,m}^l$ are parameterized in Euclidean coordinates $\mathbf{x} \in \mathbb{Z}^3$ rather then Euler angles:

$$\mathcal{VH}\left(\mathbf{X}|_{\mathcal{S}[r](\mathbf{x})}\right)_{k,m}^l := \sum_{\mathbf{x_i} \in \mathcal{S}[r](\mathbf{x})} X(\mathbf{x_i}) \mathbf{Z}_{k,m}^l[r, \mathbf{x}](\mathbf{x_i}). \tag{4.5}$$

For most practical applications we have to compute the harmonic transformation of the neighborhoods around each voxel $\mathbf{x}$, which can be computed very efficiently: since (4.6) is actually determined via convolution, we can apply the standard convolution theorem "trick" and perform a fast convolution via FFT to obtain $\mathcal{VH}_{k,m}^l(\mathbf{X}) : \mathbb{R}^3 \to \mathbb{C}^b$:

$$\mathcal{VH}[r]\left(\mathbf{X}\right)_{k,m}^l = \mathbf{X} * \mathbf{Z}_{k,m}^l[r]. \tag{4.6}$$

The sampling and non-cubic voxel problems can be solved in the very same way as for the Spherical

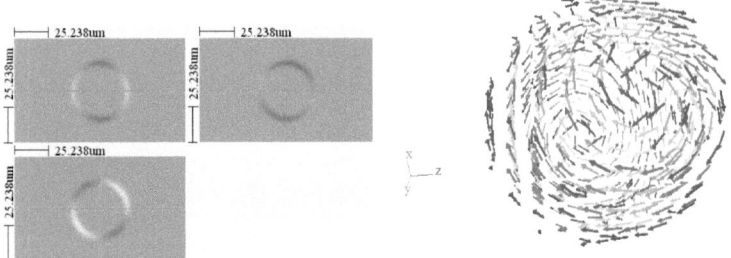

Figure 4.5: **Left:** Color coded orthoview visualization of the $\mathbf{Z}_{1,4}^2$ base function. **Right:** 3D vector visualization of the same base function.

Harmonics. Figure 4.6 shows an artificial reconstruction example.

The complexity of a vectorial transformation grows by factor three compared to the Spherical Harmonics, but we are able to apply the same parallelization techniques.

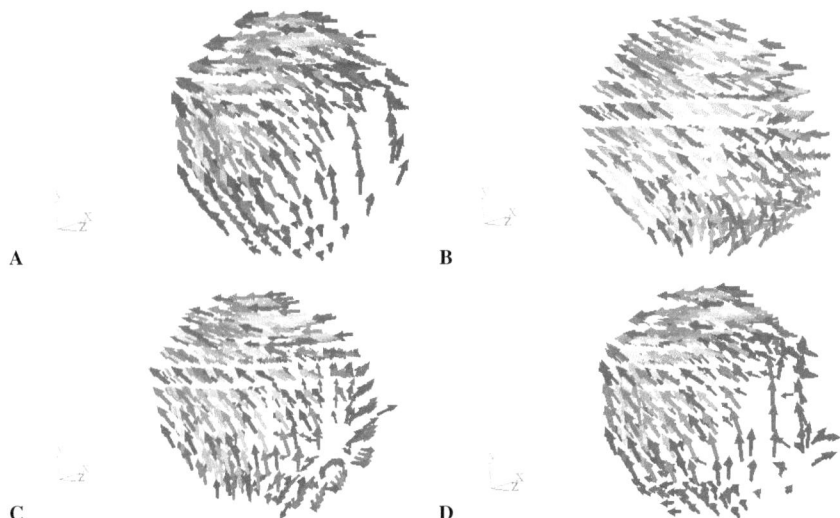

Figure 4.6: Effects of the band-limitation on the reconstruction of a vectorial signal: **A**: original vectorial signal on a sphere. **B-D**: reconstructions with $b_{\max} = 1, 2, 5$.

4.2.1 Gray-Scale Invariance

The notion of gray-scale invariance might appear a bit odd, since vector fields are not directly associated with scalar gray values. But it is common practice to obtain the 3D vector fields by the gradient evaluation of 3D scalar data (see part III). Hence, it is of major interest to know if and how a 3D gradient vector field changes under gray-scale changes of the underlying data.

(Ronneberger, 2008) showed that the gradient direction is in fact invariant under additive and multiplicative gray-scale changes. Therefore, we consider features based on Vectorial Harmonics to be gray-scale invariant - which is an important property for many applications.

4.3 Parallelization

Modern computing architectures come with an increasing number of general computing units: standard PCs have multi-core CPUs and more specialized computing servers combine several of these multi-core CPUs in a single system. This endorses the use of parallel algorithms.

In this thesis, parallel computing is only a little side aspect - but one with great speed-up potential. We restrict ourself to very simple cases of parallelization algorithms: first, we only consider systems with shared memory where all computing units (we refer to them as cores) share the same memory address space of a single system - hence, we explicitly disregard clusters. Second, we only consider algorithmically very simple cases of parallelization where the individual threads run independently, i.e. we avoid scenarios which would require a mutual exclusion handling, while still going beyond simplest cases data parallelization.

We give more details on the actual parallelization at the individual description of each feature implementation.

5 $\mathcal{SH}$-Features

In this chapter, we derive a set of local, rotation invariant features which are directly motivated by the sound mathematical foundation for operations on the 2-sphere introduced in chapter 3. We take advantage of the nice properties of Spherical Harmonics (3.2) which allow us to perform fast feature computations in the frequency domain.

Given scalar 3D volume data X, the transformation $\mathcal{SH}\left(X|_{S[r](\mathbf{x})}\right)$ (4.2) of local data on a sphere with radius r around the center point $\mathbf{x}$ in Spherical Harmonics is nothing more than a change of the base-functions representing the initial data. So the new base might provide us with a nice framework to operate on spheres, but we still have to perform the actual feature construction. Primarily, we want to obtain rotation and possibly gray-scale invariance.

First we introduce a simple method to obtain rotational invariance: In section 5.1 we review $\mathcal{SH}_{abs}$ features, which use the fact that the band-wise energies of a $\mathcal{SH}$ representation does not change under rotation. This method is well known from literature (i.e. (Kazhdan, 2003)), but has its limitations.

To cope with some of the problems with $\mathcal{SH}_{abs}$ features, we introduced a novel rotation and gray-scale invariant feature based on the $\mathcal{SH}$ phase information (Fehr and Burkhardt, 2006). We derive the $\mathcal{SH}_{phase}$ feature in section 5.2.

The third member of the $\mathcal{SH}$-Feature class is a fast and also rotation invariant auto-correlation feature $\mathcal{SH}_{autocorr}$ (section 5.3) which is based on the fast correlation in Spherical Harmonics from section 3.4.

Finally, in section 5.4, we derive a complete local rotation invariant 3D feature from a global 2D image feature introduced in (Kondor, 2007). The $\mathcal{SH}_{bispectrum}$ feature.

5.1 $\mathcal{SH}_{abs}$

The feature we chose to call $\mathcal{SH}_{abs}$ throughout this thesis is also known as "Spherical Harmonic Descriptor" and has been used by several previous publications e.g. for 3D shape retrieval in (Kazhdan, 2003). We use $\mathcal{SH}_{abs}$ as one of our reference features to evaluate the properties and performance of our methods (see chapter 11).

5.1.1 Feature Design

$\mathcal{SH}_{abs}$ achieves rotation invariance by exploiting some basic principals of the Spherical Harmonic (3.2) formulation. Analogous to the Fourier transformation, where we can use the power spectrum as a feature, we use the absolute values of each harmonic expansion band l as power of the l-th frequency in the Spherical Harmonic power spectrum:

$$\left(\mathcal{SH}_{abs}[r](\mathbf{x})\right)^l := \sqrt{\sum_{m=-l}^{l}\left(\left(\mathcal{SH}\left(X|_{S[r](\mathbf{x})}\right)\right)^l_m\right)^2}. \tag{5.1}$$

Rotation Invariance   Rotations $\mathcal{R}(\phi, \theta, \psi) \in \mathcal{SO}(3)$ (see section 3.2) are represented in the harmonic domain in terms of band-wise multiplications of the expansions $\widehat{f}^l$ with the orthonormal Wigner D-Matrices D^l (3.19).
The power spectrum of a signal f in Spherical Harmonics is given as (also see section 5.4 for more details):

$$q(f, l) := \left(\overline{\widehat{f}^l}\right)^T \widehat{f}^l. \tag{5.2}$$

The D^l are orthonormal (3.25), hence it is easy to show the rotation invariance of the band-wise $\mathcal{SH}_{abs}$ entries of the power spectrum:

$$\begin{aligned}
\mathcal{SH}_{abs}\left(D^l(\mathcal{R})\widehat{f}^l\right) &= \left(\overline{D^l(\mathcal{R})\widehat{f}^l}\right)^T D^l(\mathcal{R})\widehat{f}^l \\
&= \left(\overline{\widehat{f}^l}\right)^T \left(\overline{D^l(\mathcal{R})}\right)^T D^l(\mathcal{R})\widehat{f}^l \\
&= \left(\overline{\widehat{f}^l}\right)^T \widehat{f}^l
\end{aligned}$$

So, we note that a rotation has only a band-wise effect on the expansion but does not change the respective absolute values. Hence, the approximation of the original data via harmonic expansion can be cut off at an arbitrary band, encoding just the level of detail needed for the application.

Gray-Scale Robustness: We can obtain invariance towards additive gray-scale changes by normalization by the 0th harmonic coefficient as described in section 4.

5.1.2 Implementation

The implementation of the $\mathcal{SH}_{abs}$ is straightforward. We follow the implementation of the Spherical Harmonic transformation as described in chapter 4.

Multi-Channel Data: $\mathcal{SH}_{abs}$ cannot directly combine data from several channels into a single feature. In case of multi-channel data, we have to separately compute features for each channel.

Complexity

Following the implementation given in section 4, we obtain the harmonic expansion to band b_{max} at each point of a volume with m voxels in $O(m(b_{\mathrm{max}})^2 + (m \log m))$. The computation of the absolute values takes another $O((b_{\mathrm{max}})^3)$.

Parallelization Further speed-up can be achieved by parallelization (see section 4): the data can be transformed into the harmonic domain by parallel computation of the coefficients and the computation of the absolute values can also be split into several threads. For $\mathcal{C}$ CPU cores with $\mathcal{C} \leq (b_{\mathrm{max}})^2$ and $\mathcal{C} \leq m$ we obtain:

$$O(\frac{m(b_{\mathrm{max}})^3}{\mathcal{C}}) + O(\frac{m(b_{\mathrm{max}})^2 + (m \log m)}{\mathcal{C}})$$

5.1.3 Discussion

The $\mathcal{SH}$-Features are a simple and straightforward approach towards local 3D rotation invariant features. They are computationally efficient and easy to implement, however, the discriminative properties are quite limited. The band-wise absolute values only capture the energy of the respective frequencies in the overall spectrum. Hence, we loose all the phase information which leads to strong ambiguities within the feature mappings. In many applications it is possible to reduce these ambiguities by the combination of $\mathcal{SH}$-Features which were extracted at different radii.

$\mathcal{SH}_{abs}$ **Ambiguities:** in theory, there is an infinite number of input patterns which are mapped on the same $\mathcal{SH}$-Feature just as there is an infinite number of possible phase shifts in harmonic expansions. However, one might argue that this does not prevent a practically usage of the $\mathcal{SH}$-Feature since we generally do not need completeness (see section 2.1.2).

But we still need discriminative features, and there are practical relevant problems where $\mathcal{SH}_{abs}$ is not powerful enough, as figure 5.1 shows.

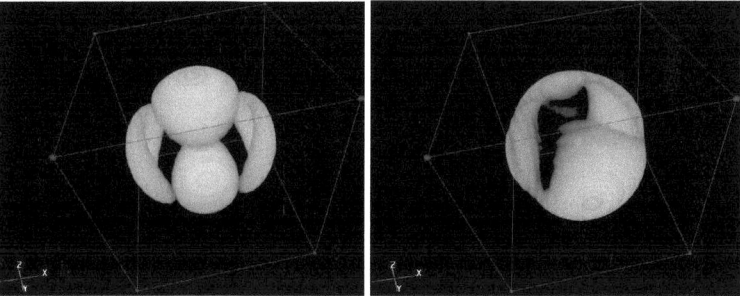

Figure 5.1: 3D volume rendering of two quite different signals on spheres which have exactly the same $\mathcal{SH}_{abs}$ value.

5.2 $\mathcal{SH}_{phase}$

Motivated by the ambiguity problems caused by neglecting the phase information in the $\mathcal{SH}_{abs}$-Features (see discussion in section 5.1.3) we presented an oppositional approach in (Fehr and Burkhardt, 2006). $\mathcal{SH}_{phase}$-Features preserve only the phase information of the Spherical Harmonic representation and disregard the amplitudes. This approach is further motivated by results known from Fourier transform, which showed that the characteristic information is dominant in the phase of a signal's spectrum rather than in the pure magnitude of it's coefficients (Lohmann et al., 1997). Following a phase-only strategy has the nice side-effect that since the overall gray-value intensity is only encoded in the amplitude, the $\mathcal{SH}_{phase}$ method is gray-scale invariant. Like the $\mathcal{SH}_{abs}$-Features (from section 5.1) $\mathcal{SH}_{phase}$-Features are computed band-wise, but instead of a single radius $\mathcal{SH}_{phase}$ combines expansions at different radii r_1, r_2 into a feature.

5.2.1 Feature Design

The phase of a local harmonic expansion in band l at radius r is given by the orientation of the vector $\mathbf{p}^l[r]$, which contains the $2l + 1$ harmonic coefficient components of the band-wise local expansion (5.3). Since the coefficients are changing when the underlying data is rotated, the phase itself is not a rotational invariant feature.

$$\mathbf{p}^l_m[r](\mathbf{x}) := \frac{\left(\mathcal{SH}\left(X|_{S[r](\mathbf{x})}\right)\right)^l_m}{\left(\mathcal{SH}_{abs}[r](\mathbf{x})\right)^l} \tag{5.3}$$

Since we are often interested in encoding the neighborhood at several concentric radii, we can take advantage of this additional information and construct a phase-only rotational invariant feature based on the band-wise relations of phases between the different concentric harmonic series.

Fig. (5.2) illustrates the basic idea: for a fixed band l, the relation (angle) between phases of harmonic expansions at different radii are invariant towards rotation. Phases in the same harmonic band undergo the same changes under rotation of the underlying data (see section 3.2 for details), keeping the angle between the phases of different radii constant. We encode this angle in terms of the dot-product of band-wise Spherical Harmonic expansions at radii r_1, r_2:

$$\left(\mathcal{SH}_{phase}[r_1, r_2](\mathbf{x})\right)^l := \langle \mathbf{p}^l[r_1], \mathbf{p}^l[r_2]\rangle. \tag{5.4}$$

Rotation Invariance: the proof of the rotation invariance is rather straightforward basic linear algebra:

Rotations $\mathcal{R}X$ acting on 5.4: $\langle D^l\mathbf{p}^l[r_1], D^l\mathbf{p}^l[r_2]\rangle$

$$= \left(\overline{D^l\mathbf{p}^l[r_1]}\right)^T (D^l\mathbf{p}^l[r_2]) \qquad \text{rewrite as matrix multiplication}$$

$$= \left(\overline{\mathbf{p}^l[r_1]}\right)^T (\overline{D^l})^T (D^l\mathbf{p}^l[r_2]) \qquad \text{resolve transposition}$$

$$= \left(\overline{\mathbf{p}^l[r_1]}\right)^T \left((\overline{D^l})^T D^l\right)(\mathbf{p}^l[r_2]) \qquad \text{commutativity}$$

$$= \left(\overline{\mathbf{p}^l[r_1]}\right)^T \underbrace{\left((\overline{D^l})^T D^l\right)}_{=I}(\mathbf{p}^l[r_2]) \qquad \text{use orthogonality of } D^l$$

$$= \left((\overline{\mathbf{p}^l[r_1]})^T \mathbf{p}^l[r_2]\right)$$

$$= \langle \mathbf{p}^l[r_1], \mathbf{p}^l[r_2]\rangle$$

The rotation $\mathcal{R}$ of the underlying data can now be expressed in terms of matrix multiplications with the same Wigner-D matrix D^l (3.19). Since the rotational invariance is achieved band-wise, the approximation of the original data via harmonic expansion can be cut off at an arbitrary band, encoding just the level of detail needed for the application.

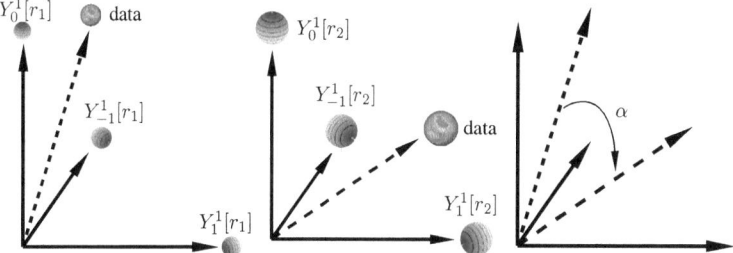

Figure 5.2: Schematic example of the phase based feature calculation. Left: representation of the original data as combination of the 3D base functions of an expansion in the 1st band at radius r_1. Center: representation at radius r_2. Right: the feature is encoding the 1st band phase angle α between the two concentric harmonic expansions.

5.2.2 Implementation

The implementation of the $\mathcal{SH}_{phase}$ is straightforward. We follow the implementation of the Spherical Harmonic transformation as described in section 4 for the two radii r_1 and r_2. The band-wise computation of the phases and the evaluation of the dot-product is also very simple.

Multi-Channel Data: $\mathcal{SH}_{phase}$-Features can also directly combine data from several channels into a single feature: we simply extract the harmonic expansions for the different radii from different data channels.

Complexity

Following the implementation given in section 4, we obtain the harmonic expansion to band b_{max} at each point of a volume with m voxels in $O(m(b_{max})^2 + (m \log m))$. The computation of the dot-products and the phase vectors takes another $O((b_{max})^3)$.

Parallelization Further speed-up can be achieved by parallelization (see section 4.3): the data can be transformed into the harmonic domain by parallel computation of the coefficients and the computation of the absolute values can also be split into several threads. For $\mathcal{C}$ CPU cores with $\mathcal{C} \leq (b_{max})^2$ and $\mathcal{C} \leq m$ we obtain:

$$O(\frac{m(b_{max})^3}{\mathcal{C}}) + O(\frac{m(b_{max})^2 + (m \log m)}{\mathcal{C}})$$

5.2.3 Discussion

Event though the $\mathcal{SH}_{phase}$-Features are not complete either, their discrimination abilities tend to be better than those of the $\mathcal{SH}_{abs}$-Features (see section 5.1). Also, the additional gray-scale invariance is very useful in many applications.

Intuitively, $\mathcal{SH}_{phase}$ encodes local changes between the different radii. This property is especially applicable for texture classification or to find 3D interest points (see part III).

5.3 $\mathcal{SH}_{autocorr}$

The next approach to compute invariant features directly from the harmonic representation is motivated by the introduction of the fast normalized cross-correlation in the harmonic domain (see introduction of chapter 3.4). The cross-correlation $\mathcal{SH}_{corr}(f, g)$ on two signals $f, g \in S^2$ is a binary operation $\mathcal{SH}_{corr} : S^2 \times S^2 \to \mathbb{R}$. Hence, it cannot be used directly as a feature, where we require a mapping of individual local signals $f \in S^2 \to \mathcal{H}$ into some feature space $\mathcal{H} \subseteq \mathbb{R}^n$ (see section 2).

A general and widely known method to obtain features from correlations is to compute the auto-correlation, e.g. (Kangl et al., 2005). In our case, we propose the local $\mathcal{SH}_{autocorr}$-Feature, which performs a fast auto-correlation of $f \in S^2$.

The auto-correlation under a given rotation $\mathcal{R}$ in Euler angles ϕ, θ, ψ is defined as:

$$(f \# f)(\mathcal{R}) := \int_{S^2} f(\mathcal{R}f) \quad \sin \Theta d\Phi d\Theta. \tag{5.5}$$

5.3.1 Feature Design

As for most of our other features, we first expand the local neighborhood f at radius r around the point x in Spherical Harmonics, $\widehat{f} := \mathcal{SH}\left(X|_{S[r](\mathbf{x})}\right)$.

Then we follow the fast correlation method which we introduced in section 3.4 to obtain the full correlation $C^\#$ from equation (3.45).

Invariance: In order to obtain rotation invariant features, we follow the Haar-Integration approach (see chapter 7.0.4) and integrate over the auto-correlations at all possible rotations $\mathcal{R}$. $C^\#$ holds the necessary auto-correlation results in a 3D (ϕ, θ, ψ)-space (3.44), hence we simply integrate over $C^\#$,

$$\mathcal{SH}_{autocorr} := \int_{\phi, \theta, \psi} \kappa \left(C^\#(\phi, \theta, \psi) \right) \sin \theta d\phi d\theta d\psi \tag{5.6}$$

and obtain a scalar feature. Additionally, we insert a non-linear kernel function κ to increase the separability. Usually, very simple non-linear functions, such as $\kappa(x) := x^2, \kappa(x) := x^3$ or $\kappa(x) := \sqrt{x}$, are sufficient.

Like in the case of the $\mathcal{SH}_{abs}$-Features, we can obtain invariance towards additive gray-scale changes by normalization by the 0th harmonic coefficient. If we additionally normalize $C^\#$ as in (3.57), $\mathcal{SH}_{autocorr}$ becomes completely gray-scale invariant.

5.3.2 Implementation

We follow the implementation of the Spherical Harmonic transformation as described in chapter 4 and the implementation of the fast correlation from (3.53).

In practice, where the harmonic expansion is bound by a maximal expansion band $b_{\max}$, the integral (5.6) is reduce to the sum over the then discrete angular space $C^\#$:

$$\mathcal{SH}_{autocorr} = \sum_{\phi, \theta, \psi} \kappa \left(C^\#(\phi, \theta, \psi) \right). \tag{5.7}$$

Multi-Channel Data: It is straightforward to combine the information from several data channels into a single $\mathcal{SH}_{autocorr}$-Feature: We simply use the same approach as described in section 3.4.6, where we correlated the information of several different radii.

Complexity

Following the implementation given in chapter 4, we obtain the harmonic expansion to band b_{max} at each point of a volume with m voxels in $O(m(b_{\text{max}})^2 + (m \log m))$. The complexity of the auto-correlation depends on b_{max} and the padding parameter p (3.53) and can be computed in $O(m(b_{\text{max}} + p)^3 \log(b_{\text{max}} + p)^3))$. The sum over $C^\#$ takes another $O((b_{\text{max}} + p)^3)$ at each point.

Parallelization: Further speed-up can be achieved by parallelization (see section 4): the data can be transformed into the harmonic domain by parallel computation of the coefficients and the computation of the absolute values also be split into several threads. For $\mathcal{C}$ CPU cores with $\mathcal{C} \leq (b_{\text{max}})^2$ and $\mathcal{C} \leq m$ we obtain:

$$O(\frac{m\left((b_{\text{max}} + p)^3 + (b_{\text{max}} + p)^3 \log(b_{\text{max}} + p)^3\right)}{\mathcal{C}}) + O(\frac{m(b_{\text{max}})^2 + (m \log m)}{\mathcal{C}})$$

5.3.3 Discussion

Auto-correlation can be a very effective feature to encode texture properties. The discriminative power of $\mathcal{SH}_{autocorr}$ can be further increased by we combining the correlation a several different radii to a single correlation result $C^\#$, as described in section 3.4.

5.4 $\mathcal{SH}_{bispectrum}$

The final member of the class of features which are directly derived from the Spherical Harmonic representation is the so-called $\mathcal{SH}_{bispectrum}$-Feature. The approach to obtain invariant features via the computation of the bispectrum of the frequency representation is well known (e.g. see (Wenndt and Shamsunder, 1997)), hence, we review the basic concept in a simple 1D setting before we move on to derive it in Spherical Harmonics.

Given a discrete complex 1D signal $f : \{0, 1, \ldots, n-1\} \to \mathbb{C}$ and its DFT $\hat{f}$, the power spectrum $q(f, \omega)$ of f at frequency ω is:

$$q(f, \omega) := \overline{\hat{f}(\omega)} \cdot \hat{f}(\omega). \tag{5.8}$$

The power spectrum is translation invariant since a translation z of f only affects the phases of the Fourier coefficients which are canceled out by $\overline{\hat{f}(\omega)} \cdot \hat{f}(\omega)$:

$$\overline{e^{-i2\pi z\omega/n}\hat{f}(\omega)} \cdot e^{-i2\pi z\omega/n}\hat{f}(\omega) = e^{i2\pi z\omega/n}\overline{\hat{f}(\omega)} \cdot e^{-i2\pi z\omega/n}\hat{f}(\omega) \tag{5.9}$$

$$= \overline{\hat{f}(\omega)} \cdot \hat{f}(\omega). \tag{5.10}$$

We use the same principle to construct the $\mathcal{SH}_{abs}$-Features (see section 5.1). As mentioned in the context of $\mathcal{SH}_{abs}$, neglecting the valuable phase information makes the power spectrum not a very discriminative feature.

The basic idea of the bispectrum is to couple two frequencies ω_1, ω_2 in order to implicitly preserve the phase information:

$$q(f, \omega_1, \omega_2) := \overline{\hat{f}(\omega_1)} \cdot \overline{\hat{f}(\omega_2)} \cdot \hat{f}(\omega_1 + \omega_2). \tag{5.11}$$

While the invariance property is the same as for the power spectrum:

$$e^{i2\pi z\omega_1/n}\overline{\hat{f}(\omega_1)} \cdot e^{i2\pi z\omega_2/n}\overline{\hat{f}(\omega_2)} \cdot e^{-i2\pi z(\omega_1+\omega_2)/n}\hat{f}(\omega_1 + \omega_2) = \overline{\hat{f}(\omega_1)} \cdot \overline{\hat{f}(\omega_2)} \cdot \hat{f}(\omega_1 + \omega_2), \tag{5.12}$$

it has been shown (Wenndt and Shamsunder, 1997) that the phases ω_i can be reconstructed from the bispectra. Hence, the bispectrum is a complete feature if f is band limited and we extract the bispectrum at all frequencies.

Due to the analogy of the Spherical Harmonic and the Fourier domain, it is intuitive that the concept of the bispectrum is portable to signals in S^2. This step was derived by (Kondor, 2007) who constructed a global invariant feature for 2D images by projecting the images on the 2-sphere and then computing features in the harmonic domain. We adapt the methods from (Kondor, 2007) to construct local rotation invariant features for 3D volume data.

5.4.1 Feature Design

In our case, we are interested in the extraction of invariant features of the local neighborhood f at radius r around the point $\mathbf{x}$. Just as in the 1D example, we transform f into the frequency space - i.e. in the Spherical Harmonic domain: $\hat{f} := \mathcal{SH}\left(X|_{S[r](\mathbf{x})}\right)$.

Now, the individual frequencies ω correspond to the harmonic bands $\hat{f}^l$, and (Kondor, 2007) showed that the bispectrum can be computed from the tensor product $(\hat{f})^{l_1} \otimes (\hat{f})^{l_2}$.

Further, we want to obtain invariance towards rotation instead of translation: given rotations $\mathcal{R} \in \mathcal{SO}(3)$, the tensor product is affected by $\mathcal{R}$ in terms of:

$$\mathcal{R}\left((\hat{f})^{l_1} \otimes (\hat{f})^{l_2}\right) = \left(D^{l_1}(\mathcal{R}) \otimes D^{l_2}(\mathcal{R})\right)\left((\hat{f})^{l_1} \otimes (\hat{f})^{l_2}\right), \tag{5.13}$$

71

where D^l is the Wigner-D matrix for the l-th band (see section 3.2).

Just like in the 1D case, (Kondor, 2007) proved that the bispectrum (5.13) will cancel out the impact of the rotation $\mathcal{R}$. So, for the l-th band of expansion we can compute the bispectrum of the l_1-th and l_2-th band with $l_1, l_2 \leq l$ by:

$$\left(\mathcal{SH}_{bispectrum}\right)^{l_1, l_2, l} := \sum_{m=-l}^{l} \sum_{m_1=-l_1}^{l_1} \langle lm | l_1 m_1, l_2 m_2 \rangle \overline{\hat{f}_{m_1}^{l_1}} \cdot \overline{\hat{f}_{(m-m_1)}^{l_2}} \cdot \hat{f}_m^l, \tag{5.14}$$

where the Clebsch-Gordan coefficients (see section 3.3) $\langle lm | l_1 m_1, l_2 m_2 \rangle$ determine the impact of the frequency couplings in the tensor product computing the bispectrum. Refer to (Kondor, 2007) for full proof.

5.4.2 Implementation

As before, we follow the implementation of the Spherical Harmonic transformation as described in chapter 4 and stop the expansion at an arbitrary band $b_{\max}$ (depending on the application) which has no effect on the rotation invariance.

The actual computation of bispectrum from (5.14) can be optimized by removing the $\hat{f}_m^l$ term to the outer iteration and limiting the inner iteration to values which form possible Clebsh-Gordan combinations:

$$\left(\mathcal{SH}_{bispectrum}\right)^{l_1, l_2, l} = \sum_{m=-l}^{l} \hat{f}_m^l \times \sum_{m_1=\max -l_1, (m-l_2)}^{\min l_1, (m+l_2)} \langle lm | l_1 m_1, l_2 m_2 \rangle \overline{\hat{f}_{m_1}^{l_1}} \cdot \overline{\hat{f}_{(m-m_1)}^{l_2}}. \tag{5.15}$$

Multi-Channel Data: It is straightforward to combine the information from two different data channels into a single $\mathcal{SH}_{bispectrum}$-Feature: we can simply choose the coefficients $\hat{f}^{l_1}$ and $\hat{f}^{l_2}$ from two t expansions of the data from two different channels.

Complexity

The computational complexity of a singe $\left(\mathcal{SH}_{bispectrum}\right)^{l_1, l_2, l}$ (**x**) feature lies in $O(l^3)$. To obtain completeness we need all $O(b_{\max}^2)$ features at all m positions of X. The harmonic expansion to band $b_{\max}$ at each point takes another $O(m(b_{\max})^2 + (m \log m))$.

Parallelization

It is straightforward to get further speed-up by parallelization (see chapter 4). Since the computation of each single feature $\left(\mathcal{SH}_{bispectrum}\right)^{l_1, l_2, l}$ (**x**) is independent from all others, we can split the overall process in parallel computations.

5.4.3 Discussion

The basic concept of the $\mathcal{SH}_{bispectrum}$-Features is quite similar to what we did for the $\mathcal{SH}_{phase}$-Features (see section 5.2): we try to obtain a better discrimination performance than $\mathcal{SH}_{abs}$-Features by implicit preservation of the phase information. In case of the $\mathcal{SH}_{phase}$-Features we do this by considering the relation of phases over different radii of the expansion, here we relate different frequencies of the expansion. In theory, the completeness property makes the $\mathcal{SH}_{bispectrum}$ approach very competitive, but this comes at high computational costs.

6 LBP Features

"Local Binary Pattern" (LBP) (Mäenpää and Pietikäinen, 2005) have been established as a standard feature based method for 2D image analysis. LBP have been successfully applied to a wide range of different applications from texture analysis (Mäenpää and Pietikäinen, 2005) to face recognition (Yang and Wang, 2007). Various extensions to the basic LBP algorithms were published in recent years, including rotation invariant binary pattern (rLBP) and computationally efficient "uniform binary pattern" (uLBP) - a comprehensive overview can be found in (Mäenpää and Pietikäinen, 2005).

In this chapter, we extend the original LBP from 2D images to 3D volume data and generalize the rotation invariant rLBP (Fehr and Burkhardt, 2008) and uLBP (Fehr, 2007a), implementing full rotation invariance in 3D.

Related Work: So far, standard LBP have only been applied to 2D images and 2D time series. There are several recent publications on "volume local binary patterns" (vLBP)(Zhao and Pietikäinen, 2007b)(Zhao and Pietikäinen, 2006)(Zhao and Pietikäinen, 2007a), but confusingly these methods deal with dynamic texture analysis on 2D time series and not on full 3D volumetric data. Accordingly, vLBP only provide invariance towards rotations around the z-axis.

6.1 LBP in 2D.

In contrast to most of the other feature methods we discuss in this thesis, "Local Binary Pattern" are defined in a discrete setting and operate directly on a pixel/voxel grid. LBP encode N neighboring points with gray values $u_i, i \in \{0 \ldots N - 1\}$ in relation to the center pixel. In 2D, these neighbors are given as equidistant points on a circle with radius r around a center pixel with gray value c (see Fig. 6.1):

$$\text{LBP}_N^r := \sum_{i=0}^{N} \text{sig}(u_i - c) \cdot 2^i \qquad (6.1)$$

$$\text{with sig}(x) := \begin{cases} 1 & \text{for } x > 0 \\ 0 & \text{otherwise} \end{cases}$$

The center is usually chosen to be located at pixel/voxel positions, while the gray-values of the sampling points are obtained via interpolation.
The binarization of the gray-value relations by $\text{sig}(x)$ makes LBPs invariant towards monotonic grayscale changes and the weighting with powers of two guarantees a unique coding. For more details on 2D LBP refer to (Mäenpää and Pietikäinen, 2005).

6.1.1 Rotation Invariance in 2D

It is easy to realize that the naive implementation (6.1) of LBPs is not rotation invariant. To overcome this drawback, (Mäenpää and Pietikäinen, 2005) introduced a refined version of the initial formulation

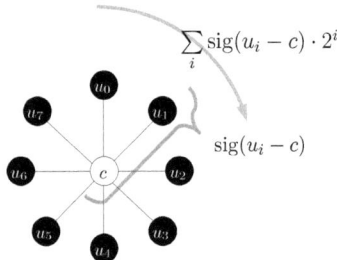

Figure 6.1: Computation of a 2D LBP with $N = 8$ sampling points with gray-values u_i around the center pixel with gray-value c.

which achieves invariance via normalization:

$$\text{rLBP}_N^r := \min\left(\text{ROT}(LBP_N^r, n)\right) \tag{6.2}$$
$$\text{with } n = 0 \dots N - 1,$$

where $\text{ROT}(LBP_N^r, n)$ is a discrete rotation of the assignment of the neighbors u_i to the powers of two 2^{i+n} by n steps. In 2D, this can be implemented via cyclic shifts:

$$\text{rLBP}_N^r := \min\left(\sum_i \text{sig}(u_i - c) \cdot 2^{(i+n) \mod N}\right) \tag{6.3}$$
$$\text{with } n = 0 \dots N - 1,$$

More details on rotation invariant 2D LBP can be found in (Mäenpää and Pietikäinen, 2005).

6.2 Uniform Local Binary Patterns (uLBP) in 2D

One commonly used extension of LBPs are the so called "uniform" LBPs (uLBP), which were introduced in (Mäenpää et al., 2000). The uLBPs form a subset of all theoretically possible patterns, which is restricted to LPBs with a "non-uniformity" measure $U(LBP_N^r) \leq 2$. The "non-uniformity" measure is defined as the number of $0-1$ and $1-0$ transitions in the cyclic sequence $\{\text{sig}(u_i-c)|i = 0, \dots, N\}$. Experiments have shown that up to 90% of all 2D patterns belong to this subset (Mäenpää et al., 2000). Fig. 6.2 shows a set of uLBP templates.

Practically, the uLBP method performs a rotation invariant template matching by simply "counting"

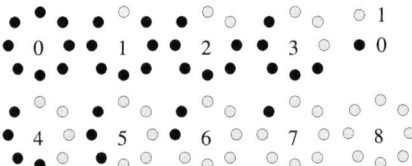

Figure 6.2: Template classes for uniform LBPs using $N = 8$ sampling points around the center c. Black points correspond to the binary value 0, gray to 1.

the number of ones and rejecting input signals with $U(LBP_N^r) > 2$. The number of ones is then used to encode the pattern as uLBP.

Due to this template nature, uLBPs are easier to extend to 3D volume data - an approach we are following in section 6.2, but first, we will discuss the problems of a "naive" LBP implementation in 3D.

6.3 Naive Implementation of LBP in 3D

At a first glimpse, the extension of LBPs to 3D seems to be straightforward: Simply pick a center voxel with gray value c, and sample a fixed number of N equidistant points with gray values $x_0 \ldots x_{N-1}$ on the respective sphere with radius r. Compute $\text{sig}(u_i - c)$ for all u_i and encode the binary pattern as in the usual LBP algorithm.

This appears to be very simple, but one has to face several severe problems following this direct approach: first, equidistant sampling on a sphere is a very hard task which is known as *Fejes Toth's* problem (Cundy and Rollett, 1961). In general, it cannot be solved analytically. Since we need equidistant sampling in order to achieve full rotation invariance, we are limited to the few known point sets where a sampling is known (Cundy and Rollett, 1961) or we have to use rather expensive numerical approximations. Secondly, rotation invariant LBPs require an ordering of the sampled points, which is trivial in 2D - but turns out to be a quite hard problem given three degrees of freedom on a sphere. And last, computational complexity becomes an issue with the vastly rising number of sampling points needed on a sphere.

To cope with these problems we utilize some of the techniques introduced in chapter 3 and 5 to derive methods for the computation of LBPs in the harmonic domain. This way, we are able to avoid the sampling and ordering problems at significantly reduced computational complexity.

First we give a 3D extension for uLBPs (Fehr, 2007a) which has its limitations and should be seen as preliminary work to our later general extension of LBPs for 3D volume data (Fehr and Burkhardt, 2008).

6.4 Fast 3D uLBP (fuLBP)

We presented a first approach towards 3D rotation invariant LBPs in form of a generalization of uniform LBPs (see section 6.2) in (Fehr, 2007a).
This method should be seen as preliminary work to our later general extension of LBPs for 3D volume data (see section 6.5). It demonstrates that it is possible to engage the computation of 3D LBPs in the harmonic domain. Hence, we do not endorse the practical usage of this approach - it should been seen as proof of concept which contributes some important ideas for the methods introduced in section 6.5.

6.4.1 Feature Design

The key idea of the "fast 3D uLBP" (fuLBP) is rather simple: we redefine the uLBP algorithm as simple template matching problem. Given all uniform patterns $\mathbf{uLBP}_i^r$ with radius r, we search for the best match with the underlying data. In the 2D case, this matching is performed by simply counting the "ones" after the binarization step $\mathrm{sig}(x)$ (see section 6.2).
As pointed out in section 6.3, such a direct approach would be too expensive in a 3D application. Therefore we suggest to perform the template matching in the harmonic domain. In order to do so, we need several things: first, we define the uniform pattern templates as $\mathbf{uLBP}_i^r : S^2 \times \{0,1\} \rightarrow \{0,1\}$. Secondly, we compute the Spherical Harmonic expansions (3.1) $\mathcal{SH}\left(X|_{S[r](\mathbf{x})}\right)$ of the local shperical neighborhood of $\mathbf{x}$ in X and $\mathcal{SH}[r](\mathbf{uLBP}_i^r)$ of the "uniform patterns". Thirdly, we need to be able to perform the binarization in the harmonic domain, and finally, we need a similarity measure.

6.4.2 Theory

The first step is trivial: we obtain $\mathcal{SH}\left(X|_{S[r](\mathbf{x})}\right)$ and $\mathcal{SH}[r](\mathbf{uLBP}_i^r)$ directly via the Spherical Harmonic forward transformation (3.3). The binarization step is more difficult:

Binarization: Since it is impossible to perform a local binarization at sampling points u_i after we have transformed the data into frequency space, we reduce the sparse binarization $\mathrm{sig}(u_i - c)$ to the continuous subtraction of c at all points of $\mathcal{SH}[r](X)(\mathbf{x})$. We subtract the value at the center $c = X(\mathbf{x})$ from the signal expanded in $\mathcal{SH}\left(X|_{S[r](\mathbf{x})}\right)$. In the original setting, c is constant for all evaluations of $\mathrm{sig}(u_i - c)$, hence, the subtraction is equal to a shift of the constant component on $\mathcal{SH}\left(X|_{S[r](\mathbf{x})}\right)$ and thus only effects the 0th coefficient:

$$\left(\mathcal{SH}\left(X|_{S[r](\mathbf{x})}\right) - X(\mathbf{x})\right)_0^0 := \left(\mathcal{SH}\left(X|_{S[r](\mathbf{x})}\right)\right)_0^0 - (X(\mathbf{x}) \cdot b_{abs}), \tag{6.4}$$

where b_{abs} is the absolute number of expansion bands. All other coefficients with $l > 0, -l \leq m \leq l$ are not effected:

$$\left(\mathcal{SH}\left(X|_{S[r](\mathbf{x})}\right) - X(\mathbf{x})\right)_m^l := \left(\mathcal{SH}\left(X|_{S[r](\mathbf{x})}\right)\right)_m^l. \tag{6.5}$$

Similarity Measure: Finally, we need a rotation invariant similarity measure for the actual template matching. In (Fehr, 2007a), we suggested to use the $\mathcal{SH}_{abs}$ measure from section 5.1. $\mathcal{SH}_{abs}$ is easy to implement and very fast since we are already operating in the harmonic domain. But, as pointed out in section 5.1, $\mathcal{SH}_{abs}$ is not very discriminative. Hence, we also might use the fast correlation from section 3.4 which provides more discrimination power at the cost of higher computational complexity.

6.4.3 Implementation

The implementation of the fuLBP is straightforward. We follow the implementation of the Spherical Harmonic transformation as described in section 4. Details on the implementation of the similarity measures can be found in section 5.1 and 3.4.3 respectively.

Multi-Channel Data: fuLBPs cannot directly combine data from several channels into a single feature. In case of multi-channel data, we would have to separately compute features for each channel.

Complexity: The main argument for the harmonic approach, besides the fact that we can avoid the equidistant sampling problem, is the better computational complexity. If we assume that we need to extract the features at each of the m voxels of the input volume X, have H "uniform patterns", and take N samples, the naive implementation of $uLBP_N^r$ has a complexity of $O(m \cdot N^2 \cdot H)$, where N samples have to be evaluated at all m points and finding the right pattern takes another $O(N \cdot H)$. The harmonic approach $fuLBP_N^r$ lies in $O\left((m \log m) \cdot b_{\max}^2 + m \cdot H \cdot b_{\max}^2\right)$: $O(m \log m)$ for the Fourier transform of $b_{\max}$ bands plus the cost of finding the right of H possible pattern. Hence, the computation complexity in the harmonic domain does not directly dependent on the number of samples. In 3D, where $N >> b_{\max}$, the additional overhead for the Fourier transform will drastically pay off.

Parallelization: Further speed-up can be achieved by parallelization (see section 4.3): the data can be transformed into the harmonic domain by parallel computation of the coefficients and the computation at each voxel can also be split into several threads. For $\mathcal{C}$ CPU cores with $\mathcal{C} \leq b_{\max}^2$ and $\mathcal{C} \leq m$ we obtain:

$$O((m \log m) \cdot \frac{b_{\max}^2}{\mathcal{C}}) + O(\frac{m}{\mathcal{C}} \cdot H \cdot b_{\max}^2)$$

6.4.4 Discussion

At first glimpse, fuLBPs appear to be quite attractive since the two major problems of a naive implementation are solved sufficiently: the equidistant sampling problem and the complexity. But there is an additional general problem concerning a 3D extension of uLBPs: the definition of 3D "uniform patterns".

It is clear that the 2D definition by $U(LBP_N^r) \leq 2$ (see 6.2) is not applicable in the 3D case with its (Φ, Θ)-coordinate system on the 2-Sphere (see section 3.2). But how should the "uniform patterns" be chosen, regarding the fact that the number of patterns H has a large impact on the complexity?

In (Fehr, 2007a), we suggested to generate a data dependent set of "uniform patterns" via clustering of training data to overcome this problem. Such a "codebook" approach makes sense in cases where the number of codebook entries can be kept small - which strongly depends on the individual problem and is in fact a strong limitation of the entire fuLBP concept.

6.5 Fast 3D LBP (fLBP)

After the introduction of fuLBPs (Fehr, 2007a) (see section 6.4) we presented a general LBP extension to 3D volume data in (Fehr and Burkhardt, 2008), which we named fLBP. Both methods have in common that we are following the key idea of a template formulation (Fehr, 2007a). Hence, we first reformulate the general LBPs as template matching problem. Refere to section 6.1 for the original formulation.

6.5.1 Feature Design

The template approach is based on the pre-computation of so-called "**2-patterns**". A 2-pattern P_N^r is the volume representation (3D grid) of a set of N equidistant points on a sphere with radius r. Each of theses points is weighted in an arbitrary but fixed order with the gray values $p_0 := 2^0, \ldots, p_{N-1} = 2^{N-1}$. All other points in the volume are set to zero.

For each LBP computation at $\mathbf{x}$ in X, we consider the local spherical neighborhood around $\mathbf{x}$ $S[r](\mathbf{x}) := \{\mathbf{x}_i \in \mathbb{R}^n \,|\, \|\mathbf{x} - \mathbf{x}_i\| = r\}$ with radius r. Given a center point with gray value $c = X(\mathbf{x})$, we compute the point-wise threshold T of the entire volume grid:

$$\forall \mathbf{x}_i \in S[r](\mathbf{x}) : \quad T[r, \mathbf{x}](\mathbf{x}_i) := \mathrm{sig}\left(X\Big|_{S[r](\mathbf{x})}(\mathbf{x}_i) - c \right). \tag{6.6}$$

The resulting LBP is then computed via the dot-product of the 2-pattern and the threshold:

$$\mathrm{LBP}_N^r(X, \mathbf{x}) := \langle P_n^r, T[r, \mathbf{x}] \rangle. \tag{6.7}$$

Hence, given an equidistant sampling, the computation of 3D LBP with the template approach is not so difficult - the actual problem is to obtain rotation invariance in 3D.

Rotation Invariance

In the 2D case, where rotations have only one degree of freedom, invariance can be realized via minimum search over all cyclic shifts of the circular 2-pattern in $O(N)$ (6.2). Using our fixed 2-pattern on a sphere, we encounter three degrees of freedom. This makes the 3D case a lot more difficult and computationally expensive.

We engage this problem by revising (6.2): we can reformulate the problem as the computation of the minimum of the full correlation ($\#$) over all angles of the fixed 2-pattern template P_r^N with $T[r, \mathbf{x}]$:

$$\mathrm{rLBP}_N^r := \min(P_N^r \# T[r, \mathbf{x}]). \tag{6.8}$$

Given our fast correlation in the harmonic domain (see section 3.4), we compute the rotation invariant fLBP in three steps: first, generate the 2-pattern P_N^r and compute $T[r, \mathbf{x}]$ using known equidistant samplings (Cundy and Rollett, 1961) with 24 to 124 samples. Then expand both in Spherical Harmonics and obtain the coefficients $\widehat{P_N^r}$ and $\widehat{T[r, \mathbf{x}]}$. Finally, compute the rLBP via the minimum of the fast correlation of $\widehat{P_N^r}$ and $\widehat{T[r, \mathbf{x}]}$ as stated in (6.8).

6.5.2 Implementation

The actual bottleneck of our approach is the complexity of the computation of $T[r, \mathbf{x}]$ which is increasing with the number of sampling points. For full gray-scale invariance we have to compute $\widehat{T[r, \mathbf{x}]}$ correctly, but there is an elegant way to approximate $\widehat{T[r, \mathbf{x}]}$ while preserving a gray-scale robustness: we compute $\widehat{S[r](\mathbf{x})}$ and subtract $c = X(\mathbf{x})$ in the frequency domain, which only affects the 0th coefficient $\widehat{T[r, \mathbf{x}]}$ (6.4). Hence, we no longer have a binary but continuous weighting of the n-pattern.

Multi-Channel Data: fLBPs can only combine data from two different channels into a single feature. We can set the center point to the first channel, and then sample the neighborhood from the second channel.

Complexity

The overall complexity for the evaluation of $fLBP$ at all m voxels of X is:

$$O((m \log m) \cdot b_{\text{max}}^2 + m \cdot (N + (b_{\text{max}}^2 + p) \log(b_{\text{max}}^2 + p)))$$

Where $O((m \log m) \cdot b_{\text{max}}^2)$ is the cost for the Spherical Harmonic transform with b_{max} expansion bands, $O(m \cdot (b_{\text{max}}^2 + p) \log(b_{\text{max}}^2 + p))$ the cost of the fast correlation with padding p (see section 3.4) and $O(N)$ the thresholding for N sampling points.

The dominating cost factor is the number of sampling points N, since $N \gg b_{\text{max}}$. If we use the approximation of the threshold from section 6.5.2, the costs become independent of N:

$$O((m \log m) \cdot b_{\text{max}}^2 + m \cdot ((b_{\text{max}}^2 + p) \log(b_{\text{max}}^2 + p)))$$

Parallelization: Further speed-up can be achieved by parallelization (see section 4). the data can be transformed into the harmonic domain by parallel computation of the coefficients and the computation at each voxel can also be split into several threads. For $\mathcal{C}$ CPU cores with $\mathcal{C} < b_{\text{max}}^2$ and $\mathcal{C} < m$ we obtain:

$$O((m \log m) \cdot \frac{b_{\text{max}}^2}{\mathcal{C}}) + O(\frac{m}{\mathcal{C}} \cdot ((b_{\text{max}}^2 + p) \log(b_{\text{max}}^2 + p)))$$

6.5.3 Discussion

The presented generalization of the LBP feature for 3D volume data preserves all favorable properties of the original 2D formulation at considerable complexity. If we neglect exact thresholding, fLBPs can be computed very fast.

7 Scalar Haar-Features

In this chapter we derive several features operating on scalar data which obtain invariance via Haar-Integration. As discussed in section 2.1.2, one canonical approach to construct invariant features is to perform a Haar-Integration over the transformation group.

Before we turn to the specific feature design, we first review the general framework of Haar-Integration in section 7.0.4 and discuss some aspects of the construction of suitable feature kernels in section 7.0.5. Then we introduce $2p$-Haar features 7.1 and $3p$-Haar features 7.2 which are based on the class of separable kernel functions, before we derive the generalized np-Haar features.

It should be noted that we also use Haar-Integration methods for the computation of the auto-correlation features $\mathcal{SH}_{autocorr}$ (see section 5.3) and $\mathcal{VH}_{autocorr}$ (see section 8.2).

Related Work: Based on the general group-integration framework (7.2) which was introduced by (Schulz-Mirbach, 1995a), (Schulz-Mirbach, 1995b) and (Burkhardt and Siggelkow, 2001), several invariant features were introduced for scalar data in 2D (Schulz-Mirbach, 1995b) and in 3D volumetric data (Schael, 1997) (Ronneberger et al., 2002) (Ronneberger and Fehr, 2005) (Fehr et al., 2008). We will discuss these methods in the next section when we take a closer look at the class of sparse and separable kernels (Ronneberger et al., 2002) (Ronneberger and Fehr, 2005) (Fehr et al., 2008) which form the basis of our features.

7.0.4 Invariance via Group-Integration

Following the general objectives of feature extraction (see 2.1.1) we apply the Haar-Intergration approach to obtain invariant features. This method is generally bound to the sub-class of compact group transformations (see 2.1.2), where for a given transformation group $\mathcal{G}$, the individual transformations $g \in \mathcal{G}$ differ only by their associated set of parameters λ, which cover the degrees of freedom under $\mathcal{G}$.

In this chapter we derive features from the canonical group integration approach (see section 2.1.2) which generates invariant features via Haar-Integration over all degrees of freedom of the transformation group G:

$$T(X) = \int_{\mathcal{G}} (g_{\lambda}X)dg_{\lambda}, \tag{7.1}$$

eliminating the influence of λ. Equation (7.1) is also referred to as the "group-average". For the cause of simplicity, we denote individual transformation g_{λ} just by g.

It has to be noted that even though the Haar-Integration approach (7.1) meets the necessary condition of invariance (2.7), the sufficient condition (2.8) is anything but guaranteed. In fact, a simple group-averaging itself produces incomplete features which often tend to have a weak separability performance. This can be overcome by embedding non-linear kernel functions κ into the integral (Schulz-Mirbach, 1995a): it cannot be stressed enough that the use of such non-linear mappings is essential for any feature design (Burkhardt, 1979) (Schulz-Mirbach, 1995a) (Schulz-Mirbach, 1995b) (Ronneberger et al., 2002) (Fehr et al., 2008), and is the key element of the group-integration framework. The resulting general framework for invariant feature generation via group-integration (7.2) then embeds an arbitrary non-linear kernel function κ.

$$T(X) := \int_G \kappa(gX)dg \tag{7.2}$$

$\mathcal{G}$: transformation group
g : one element of the transformation group
dg : Haar measure
κ : nonlinear kernel function
X : n-dim, multi-channel data set
gX : the transformed n-dim data set

Within this framework, features can be generated for data of arbitrary dimensionality and from multiple input channels. This reduces the key design issue to the selection of appropriate kernel functions.

7.0.5 Local, Sparse and Separable Kernel Functions

Since we are interested in the construction of local features, we restrict the kernel functions κ in the general group-integration approach (7.2) to functions of local support. Further, following the approach

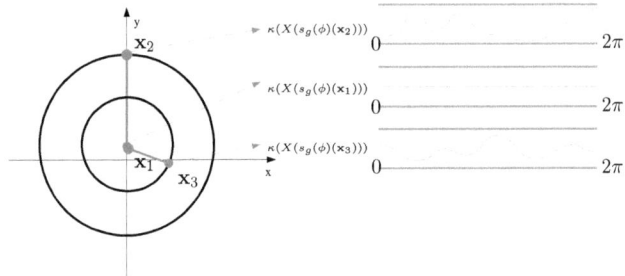

Figure 7.1: Using a local sparse kernel with three points on a continuous 2D image. Regarding the rotation group, this kernel returns the gray values sensed by the kernel points x_1, x_2 and x_3 as one-dimensional functions $X(s_g(\phi)(x_1))$, $X(s_g(\phi)(x_2))$ and $X(s_g(\phi)(x_1))$. Invariant features are computed by combining the kernel points with a nonlinear kernel function κ which is then integrated over all possible rotations (parameterized in ϕ).

in (Ronneberger et al., 2002) (Fehr et al., 2008), we restrict these local kernels to sparse functions which only depend on a few discrete points of the local continuous data. Hence, $\kappa(X)$ can be rewritten as $\kappa\left(X(\mathbf{x}_1), X(\mathbf{x}_2), X(\mathbf{x}_3), \dots\right)$ (Fehr et al., 2008).

This way, we can reformulate (7.2) and perform the group transformation only on the local kernel support, instead of the whole data set X (see Fig. 7.1). This local transformation is denoted as $s_g(\mathbf{x}_i)$ such that

$$(gX)(\mathbf{x}_i) =: X(s_g(\mathbf{x}_i)) \quad \forall g, \mathbf{x}_i. \tag{7.3}$$

For these local kernels, (7.2) can be rewritten as

$$T(X) := \int_G \kappa\left(X(s_g(\mathbf{x}_1)), \ X(s_g(\mathbf{x}_2)), \dots\right) dg. \tag{7.4}$$

Fig. (7.1) shows how a **sparse kernel** with a local support of three discrete points can be applied to "sense" the local continuous data.

For kernels with a larger support it does not make much sense to combine single data points over a certain distance. Instead we are interested in combining larger structures, i.e. in having a kernel over regions rather than over single points. One very simple way to achieve this was suggested in (Ronneberger et al., 2002): by applying a Gaussian smoothing of the input data which directly depends on the selected size of the local support, we can define a "**multi-scale**" kernel which has different sizes of local support in each point.

This class of **local sparse kernel** functions provides a more structured but still very flexible framework for the design of local invariant features. However, even with a support reduced to n discrete points, naive kernel computation is still very expensive since the local support has to be integrated over the entire transformation group. (Schulz-Mirbach, 1995b)(Schael and Siggelkow, 2000)(Burkhardt and Siggelkow, 2001) suggested to overcome this problem by the use of Monte Carlo methods, but this approach is only effective when features are computed via integration over the entire dataset (i.e. integration over the translation group). For the computation of local features, i.e. a Monte Carlo integration over the rotation group is not suitable.

To make group-integral features applicable to large data sets, (Ronneberger et al., 2002) introduced a sub-class of sparse kernel-functions. For these so called **separable kernels**, the kernel can be split into a linear combination of non-linear sub-kernels such that:

$$\kappa\left(X(s_g(\mathbf{x}_1)),\ X(s_g(\mathbf{x}_2)),\dots\right) = \kappa_1\left(X(s_g(\mathbf{x}_1))\right) \cdot \kappa_2\left(X(s_g(\mathbf{x}_2))\right) \cdot \dots \tag{7.5}$$

This separability constraint is not a strong limitation of the original class of sparse kernel-functions since in many cases it is possible to find approximative decompositions of non-separable kernels via Taylor series expansion.

Besides the non-linearity, the choice of the sub-kernels κ_i is theoretically not further constrained, but in most cases very simple non-linear mappings such as $\kappa(x) = x^2, \kappa(x) = x^3, \dots$ or $\kappa(x) = \sqrt{x}$ are powerful enough (see experiments in part III).

Based on these separable kernels, (Ronneberger et al., 2002) derived a fast convolution method for the evaluation of kernels with a support of only two sparse points on continuous 2D images - so called "2-point" kernels (see section 7.1).

7.1 2-Point Haar-Features ($2p$)

Our first feature which makes use of the general group integration framework (7.2) is the so-called 2-Point or $2p$-Haar feature. It was first introduced as a global feature for 2D images in (Ronneberger et al., 2002). We later extended this approach to local features on scalar 3D volume data in (Ronneberger and Fehr, 2005) and (Ronneberger et al., 2005) with an application to biomedical 3D image analysis in (Fehr et al., 2005) (see part III).

$2p$-Features use a sub-class of the previously introduced separable kernel functions (7.5). The name 2-Point derives from the constraint that we restrict kernels to have just two separable kernel points x_1, x_2. This restriction allows a reformulation of the initial parameterization λ of the rotation group $\mathcal{SO}(3)$, which is drastically reducing the computational complexity necessary to obtain rotation invariance. However, this comes at the price of reduced discrimination power as we discuss at the end of this section.

7.1.1 Feature Design

The selection of the kernel points x_1 and x_2 is bound by the following design principle for the 2-Point features: For the extraction of a local $2p$-Feature at a given point x in X of the scalar (or possibly multi-channel) 3D input volume X, x_1 is fixed at the center of the neighborhood, i.e. $x_1 := X(x)$. The second kernel point is chosen from the local neighborhood: $x_2 \in S[r](x)$ (see 2.12 for the neighborhood definition).

Since x_1 is fixed, we only have to choose the parameters for x_2: the local neighborhood r and the spherical coordinates Φ, Θ which can be neglected later on.

We are using the scheme for separable kernels (7.5), we can write the $2p$-Kernels as:

$$\kappa\Big(X(x_1), X(x_2)\Big) = \kappa_1\Big(X(x_1)\Big) \cdot \kappa_2\Big(X(x_2)\Big). \tag{7.6}$$

Figure 7.2 shows a schematic example of a local 3D $2p$ kernel on volume data.

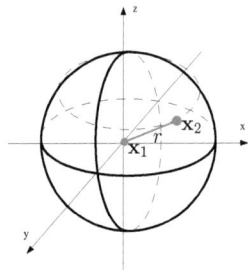

Figure 7.2: Schematic example of a $2p$-Haar Feature: the first kernel point is set to the center of the local features extraction $x_1 := X(x)$, while the second kernel point lies on the spherical neighborhood with radius r: $x_2 \in S[r](x)$

Rotation Invariance

As for all other local features, we want to obtain rotation invariance. If we plug the $2p$ kernel (7.6) into the general Haar framework (7.2), we can achieve invariance regarding rotations $\mathcal{R}(\phi, \theta, \psi) \in \mathcal{SO}(3)$

parameterized in Euler angles (see section 3.2) with local transformations (7.5) $s_{\mathcal{R}}(\phi, \theta, \psi) \in \mathcal{SO}(3)$. Since $\mathbf{x}_1$ is by definition always in the rotation center, it is not affected by any rotation. Hence we can simplify the Haar-Integration for the multiplicative and separable $2p$-Kernel functions:

$$T[r, \mathbf{x}_2](\mathbf{x}) := \kappa_1\Big(X(\mathbf{x})\Big) \cdot \int_{\mathcal{SO}(3)} \kappa_2\Big(X(s_{\mathcal{R}(\phi,\theta,\psi)}(\mathbf{x}_2))\Big) \sin\theta d\phi d\theta d\psi. \tag{7.7}$$

Fast Computation

In order to compute (7.7) we have to evaluate the integral over all possible rotations at each point $X(\mathbf{x})$, which turns out to be quite expensive in terms of computational complexity. At this point, the restriction of (7.5) to two points provides us with a fast solution: due to the fact that we have to integrate only over the position of a single point $\mathbf{x}_2 \in S[r]\left(X(\mathbf{x})\right)$, the integral over ψ becomes a constant factor and we can rewrite (7.7) as:

$$T[r, \mathbf{x}_2](\mathbf{x}) = \kappa_1\Big(X(\mathbf{x})\Big) \cdot \int_{\phi,\theta} \kappa_2\Big(X(s_{\mathcal{R}(\phi,\theta,\psi)}(\mathbf{x}_2))\Big) \sin\theta d\phi d\theta. \tag{7.8}$$

Since $\mathbf{x}_2 \in S[r](\mathbf{x})$ is also parameterized in ϕ, θ, we can further reformulate the integral and simply solve:

$$T[r, \mathbf{x}_2](\mathbf{x}) = \kappa_1\Big(X(\mathbf{x})\Big) \cdot \int_{\mathbf{x}_i \in \mathcal{S}[r](\mathbf{x})} \kappa_2\Big(X\big|_{\mathcal{S}[r](\mathbf{x})}(\mathbf{x}_i)\Big). \tag{7.9}$$

Finally, the integration over a spherical neighborhood $S[r](\mathbf{x})$ can easily be formulated as convolution of $X\big|_{\mathcal{S}[r](\mathbf{x})}$ with a spherical template $S_t[r]$ with $S_t[r](\Phi, \Theta) = 1, \quad \forall \Phi \in [0, \dots, 2\pi], \Theta \in [0, \dots, \pi]$:

$$T[r](\mathbf{x}) = \kappa_1\Big(X(\mathbf{x})\Big) \cdot \Big(\kappa_2(X\big|_{\mathcal{S}[r](\mathbf{x})}) * S_t[r](\mathbf{x})\Big). \tag{7.10}$$

In the same way, we can evaluate the $2p$-Feature at all positions in X at once, using fast convolution in the Fourier domain:

$$T[r](X) = \kappa_1(X) \cdot \Big(\kappa_2(X) * S_t[r]\Big). \tag{7.11}$$

7.1.2 Implementation

The implementation is straightforward: given discrete input data, we apply the convolution theorem to compute the convolution via FFT:

$$T[r](X) = \kappa_1(X) \cdot FFT^{-1}\Big(FFT(\kappa_2(X)) \cdot FFT(S_t[r])\Big). \tag{7.12}$$

The only thing we have to handle with some care is the implementation of the spherical template $S_t[r]$. To avoid sampling issues, we apply the same implementation strategies as in the case of the Spherical Harmonic base functions (see section 4.1 for details).

Multi-Channel Data: Naturally, the application of $2p$-Features to multi-channel data is limited to two channels per feature, but this is straightforward: we can simply set the kernel points to be on different data channels c_i:

$$T[r](X) = \kappa_1\Big(X[c_1]\Big) \cdot \Big(\kappa_2(X[c_2]\big|_{\mathcal{S}[r](\mathbf{x})}) * S_t[r]\Big). \tag{7.13}$$

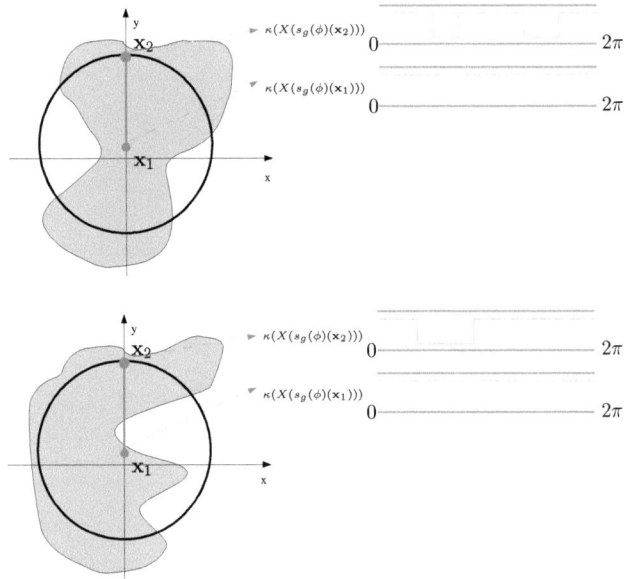

Figure 7.3: Ambiguities of $2p$-Features: This binary toy example illustrates the rather weak separability performance of $2p$-Features. The integral $\int_{\phi=0}^{2\pi} \kappa(X(s_g(\phi)(\mathbf{x}_2)))d\phi$ returns equal values for different local neighborhoods.

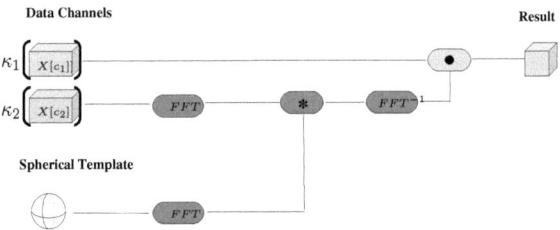

Figure 7.4: Schematic overview of the implementation of $2p$-Features.

Complexity: By reducing the feature computation to a fast convolution, we end up with a complexity of $O(m \log m)$ for an input volume with m voxels.

Parallelization: Since there is no easy way to parallelize the Fourier Transformation, we do not further parallelize the computation of $2p$-Features. However, because $2p$-Features can be computed so fast anyway, this is not a real drawback.

7.1.3 Discussion

The best property of $2p$-Features is their computational speed: no other spherical local 3D feature, neither in the context of this thesis nor in the literature can be computed this fast. However, the speed comes at the price of a rather low discrimination power and the lack of gray-scale robustness. While one might try to compensate the missing gray-scale robustness by pre-normalization of the input data, the discrimination power hardly can be improved.

The problem is caused by the fact that $2p$-Features are not only invariant under rotations, but also under arbitrary permutations of signals on the sphere. This causes problematic ambiguities, as illustrated in figure 7.3.

7.2 3-Point Haar-Features ($3p$)

3-Point Haar-Features (or $3p$-Features) are a direct extension of separable kernels (7.5) from two (7.6) to three kernel points. The main motivation for this extension derives from the discussion of the $2p$-Features (see section 7.1.3), where we pointed out that even though 2-point kernels (7.6) provide computationally very efficient features, the resulting discrimination power is flawed by the fact that these kernels are also invariant to arbitrary permutations.

To overcome this major drawback, we introduced the $3p$-Features in (Ronneberger and Fehr, 2005) and (Fehr et al., 2008). The basic idea is to add a third kernel point $\mathbf{x}_3$ to the separable kernel function κ (7.5) (see figure 7.5), which cancels out the permutation ambiguities:

$$\kappa\Big(X(\mathbf{x}_1), X(\mathbf{x}_2), X(\mathbf{x}_3)\Big) = \kappa_1\Big(X(\mathbf{x}_1)\Big) \cdot \kappa_2\Big(X(\mathbf{x}_2)\Big) \cdot \kappa_3\Big(X(\mathbf{x}_3)\Big). \qquad (7.14)$$

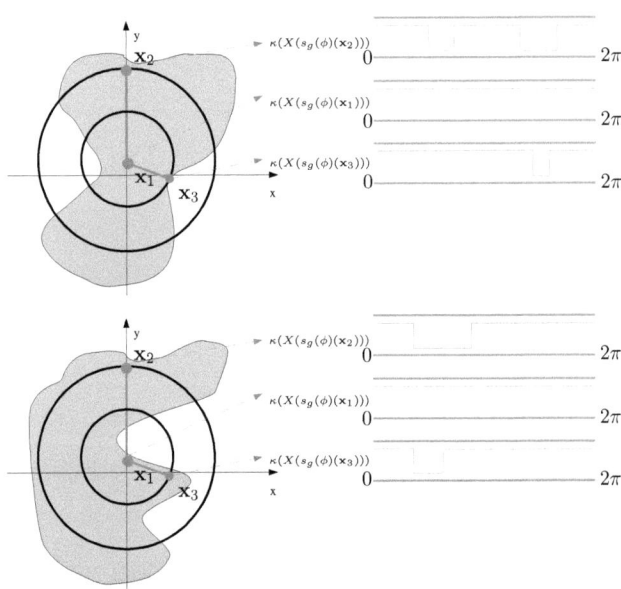

Figure 7.5: Reducing ambiguities of $2p$-Haar features: for the same binary toy example as in figure 7.3, the addition of a third kernel point leads to different results of the integral $\int\limits_{\phi=0}^{2\pi} \kappa(X(s_g(\phi)(\mathbf{x}_2)))\kappa(X(s_g(\phi)(\mathbf{x}_3)))d\phi$ for different local neighborhoods.

7.2.1 Feature Design

As in the $2p$ case, we fix the first kernel point $\mathbf{x}_1 := X(\mathbf{x})$ at the point of the local feature extraction, while the other two points are placed at the concentric spherical neighborhoods surrounding the first point: $\mathbf{x}_2 \in S[r_2](\mathbf{x}), \mathbf{x}_3 \in S[r_3](\mathbf{x})$.

Of course, both kernel points $\mathbf{x}_2, \mathbf{x}_3$ can be on the same sphere, resulting in $r_2 = r_3$, and are parameterized in spherical coordinates Φ_2, Φ_3 and Θ_2, Θ_3. Figure 7.6 shows examples of such 3p-Kernels.

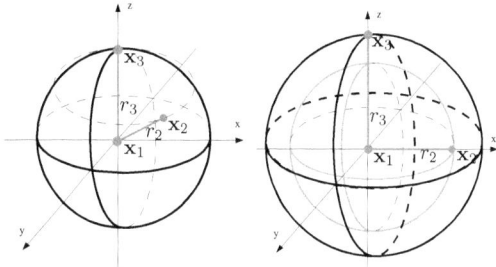

Figure 7.6: Schematic examples of 3p-Kernels. **Left:** both kernel points $\mathbf{x}_2, \mathbf{x}_3$ are located on the same concentric sphere ($r_2 = r_3$). **Right:** ($r_2 \neq r_3$). The first kernel point is set to the center of the local features extraction $\mathbf{x}_1 := X(\mathbf{x})$, while the other kernel points lie on the spherical neighborhoods with radii r_2, r_3: $\mathbf{x}_i \in S[r_i](\mathbf{x})$

Rotation Invariance

If we plug the 3p kernel (7.14) into the general Haar framework (7.2), we can achieve invariance regarding rotations $\mathcal{R}(\phi, \theta, \psi) \in \mathcal{SO}(3)$ parameterized in Euler angles (see section 3.2) with local transformations (7.5) $s_\mathcal{R}(\phi, \theta, \psi) \in \mathcal{SO}(3)$. As in the 2p case, $\mathbf{x}_1$ is by definition always in the rotation center, hence it is not affected by any rotation. This way, we end up with the Haar-Integration approach for the separable 3p-kernel functions:

$$T[r_1, r_2, \mathbf{x}_2, \mathbf{x}_3](\mathbf{x}) := \kappa_1\Big(X(\mathbf{x})\Big) \cdot \tag{7.15}$$

$$\int\limits_{\mathcal{SO}(3)} \kappa_2\Big(X(s_{\mathcal{R}(\phi,\theta,\psi)}(\mathbf{x}_2))\Big) \cdot \kappa_2\Big(X(s_{\mathcal{R}(\phi,\theta,\psi)}(\mathbf{x}_3))\Big) \cdot \sin\theta \, d\phi \, d\theta \, d\psi$$

We can further simplify this integral by the same considerations we made in (7.8): since the kernel points $\mathbf{x}_2, \mathbf{x}_3$ are not rotated independently, we express (without loss of generality) $\mathbf{x}_3$ in dependency of $\mathbf{x}_2$ (see Figure 7.7). The integral over ψ is a constant factor in $\mathbf{x}_2$ (as shown in (7.8)), but for each position of $\mathbf{x}_2$ the dependency of $\mathbf{x}_3$ is expressed in terms of the angle ψ. Hence we have to integrate over all ψ in $\mathbf{x}_3$:

$$T[r_1, r_2, \mathbf{x}_2, \mathbf{x}_3](\mathbf{x}) := \kappa_1\Big(X(\mathbf{x})\Big) \cdot \tag{7.16}$$

$$\int\limits_{\phi,\theta} \kappa_2\Big(X(s_{\mathcal{R}(\phi,\theta)}(\mathbf{x}_2))\Big) \int\limits_{\psi} \kappa_2\Big(X(s_{\mathcal{R}(\phi,\theta)}(\mathbf{x}_3))\Big) \sin\theta \, d\phi \, d\theta \, d\psi.$$

Fast Computation

It is obvious that the introduction of the 3rd kernel point makes it impossible to solve (7.16) by the same convolution approach as in (7.11). But the formulation of (7.16) leads us to an intuitive re-parameterization of the original problem. Without loss of generality, we consider the case where both

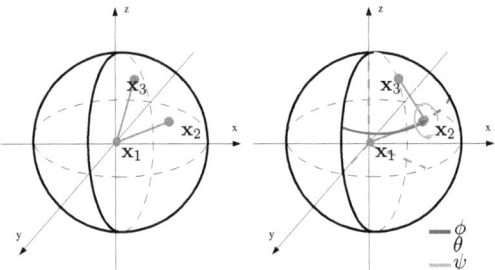

Figure 7.7: **Left:** Arbitrary $3p$ kernel with an independent formulation of the points x_2, x_3. **Right:** formulation x_3 in dependency of x_2.

kernel points x_2, x_3 are located on the same sphere, i.e. $r_2 = r_3$. Further we can fix x_2 at the "north pole" x_N and reduce its parameterization to the radius r_2.

Since x_3 is bound to x_2 by the angle ψ, we can express the possible positions of x_3 in terms of the points on the circle which lies on the same sphere as x_2 and is centered in x_2. As figure 7.8 shows, this way we can reduce the parameterization of x_3 to the radius r_c of this circle (Note: if we assume $r_2 \neq r_3$, the circle simply lies on a sphere with radius r_3).

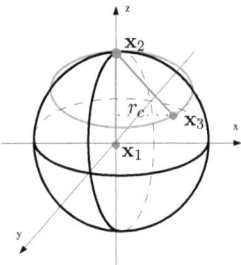

Figure 7.8: Re-parameterization of the kernel points. Given rotations in $\mathcal{SO}(3)$, x_3 is parameterized by the radius r_c of a circle centered in x_2

Given this re-parameterization, we can give a fast algorithm for the evaluation of (7.16): the integral over ψ can be expressed as a convolution of a circular template on a sphere (analogous to (7.11)) in spherical coordinates (we denote this operation by $*$):

$$T[r, r_c](\mathbf{x}) = \kappa_1 \left(X(\mathbf{x}) \right) \cdot \int_{S^2} \left(\kappa_2 \left(X(s_{\mathcal{R}(\phi, \theta)}(\mathbf{x}_2)) \right) \right) \cdot \qquad (7.17)$$

$$\left(\kappa_3 \left(X \Big|_{S[r](\mathbf{x})} \right) * C_t[r_c] \right) \sin\theta \, d\phi \, d\theta.$$

The key step towards a fast algorithm is to transfer the evaluation of (7.17) to the Spherical Harmonic domain: we expand the kernelized spherical neighborhoods

$$\widehat{\mathbf{x}}_2 := \mathcal{SH}[r]\left(\kappa_2\left(X\Big|_{S[r](\mathbf{x})}\right)\right), \quad \widehat{\mathbf{x}}_3 := \mathcal{SH}[r]\left(\kappa_3\left(X\Big|_{S[r](\mathbf{x})}\right)\right)$$

and the circle template $\widehat{C_t} := \mathcal{SH}[r]\left(C_t[r_c]\right)$ into the harmonic domain. Hence, we can apply the methods for fast convolution (see section 3.5), or "left-convolution" (see section 3.5.1) in case of the convolution with the circle template, in order to evaluate (7.17).

Using these the techniques and exploiting the orthonormal dependencies of the harmonic base functions, we can directly derive a fast algorithm for the computation of the $3p$ integral (Ronneberger and Fehr, 2005):

$$T[r, r_c](\mathbf{x}) \quad = \quad \kappa_1\left(X(\mathbf{x})\right) \cdot \sum_{l=0}^{\infty} \sum_{m=-l}^{l} \left(\widehat{\mathbf{x}_2}\right)_m^l \cdot \left(\widehat{\mathbf{x}_3} * \widehat{C_t}\right)_m^l. \tag{7.18}$$

7.2.2 Implementation

The transformation into the harmonic domain is implemented as described in section 4.1. Hence, we can also obtain the expansions at all points in X at once using the convolution approach (4.3).

The implementation of the circular template $C_t[r_c]$ has to be handled with some care: to avoid sampling issues, we apply the same implementation strategies as in the case of the Spherical Harmonic base functions (see section 4.1 for details).

Finally, we can even further simplify the computation of the "left convolution" (3.59),

$$\left(\widehat{\mathbf{x}_3} * \widehat{C_t}\right)_m^l = 2\pi\sqrt{\frac{4\pi}{2l+1}}(\widehat{\mathbf{x}_3})_m^l \widehat{C}_{t0}^l. \tag{7.19}$$

Since the 0th order of the harmonic base functions Y_0^l always has constant values for a fixed latitude Θ (3.2), given by the Legendre Polynomials $P_0^l(\sin \Theta)$ (3.7), and C_t only holds ones on a fixed latitude, we can compute (7.19) by a simple multiplication with a scalar value.

Figure 7.9 gives a schematic overview of the implementation of $3p$-Features:

Multi-Channel Data: Naturally, the application of $3p$-Features to multi-channel data is limited to three channels per feature but straightforward: we can simply set the kernel points to be on different data channels as shown in the $2p$ case.

Complexity: Given input data X with m voxels, we need to compute the Spherical Harmonic transformation three times, to obtain $\widehat{\mathbf{x}}_2$, $\widehat{\mathbf{x}}_3$ and $\widehat{C_t}$. Depending on the maximum expansion band $b_{\max}$, this lies in $O(b_{\max} \cdot m \log m)$ (see section 4.1). The convolution with the circular template and the dot-product take another $O(m \cdot b_{\max}^2)$, followed by the voxel-wise multiplication with $\kappa_1(X)$ in $O(m)$.

Parallelization: As stated in section 4.1, we can gain linear speed-up in the number of cores for the parallelization of the harmonic transformation. Further, we could also split the computation of the convolution and the dot-product into several threads, but in practice this speed-up hardly falls into account.

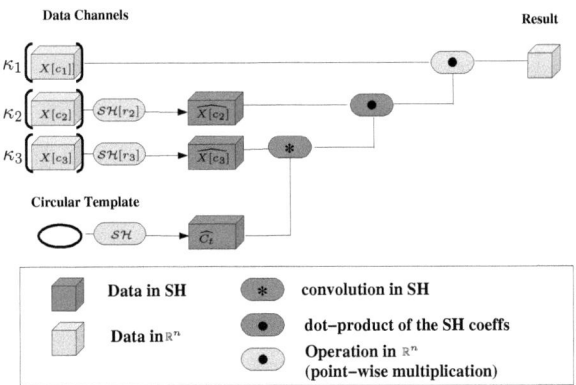

Figure 7.9: Schematic overview of the implementation of $3p$-Features.

7.2.3 Discussion

The 3-Point Haar-Features solve the permutation invariance problem of the 2-Point Features. However, this comes at the price of increased computational complexity, where the transformation to the harmonic domain makes up most of the additional cost.

Another issue is the growing parameter set: for $3p$ kernels we have to set $\kappa_1, \kappa_2, \kappa_3, r$ and r_c. which rises the question of an appropriate feature selection. We tackle this problem in depth in section 10, but it is evident that such a selection will become more difficult with a growing number of parameters.

7.3 n-Point Haar-Features (np)

In this section, we introduce a generic algorithm for the implementation of the general scheme for separable kernels (7.5) which can handle an arbitrary number of kernel points $\mathbf{x}_1, \ldots, x_n$. Just as we obtain an increase in discrimination power by going from two to three kernel points (see section 7.2), we motivate the strategy to add further points to the kernel by the goal of deriving even more selective features.

The actual number of needed kernel points depends on the application: i.e. for a single feature, the use of four points might deliver more discriminative texture features than $3p$ kernels, while one might use kernels with eight or more points to locate very specific structures in an object detection task (see part III).

As in (7.6) and (7.14), we formalize the n-Point kernels as given by (7.5):

$$\kappa := \kappa_1 \left(X(s_g(\mathbf{x}_1)) \right) \cdot \kappa_2 \left(X(s_g(\mathbf{x}_2)) \right) \cdot \cdots \cdot \kappa_n \left(X(s_g(\mathbf{x}_n)) \right). \tag{7.20}$$

7.3.1 Feature Design

As in the case of local 2- and 3-Point features, the primary goal is to achieve rotation invariance. Hence, the transformation group $\mathcal{G}$ is given by the group of 3D rotations $\mathcal{SO}(3)$. If we parameterize these global rotations $\mathcal{R} \in \mathcal{SO}(3)$ as local rotations of the kernel points in Euler angles $s_g(\phi, \theta, \psi)$ (see Fig. 3.4), we can rewrite (7.20) as:

$$T[\Lambda](X) := \int\limits_{\mathcal{SO}(3)} \kappa_1 \left(s_{g_{(\phi,\theta,\psi)}} X(\mathbf{x}_1) \right) \cdot \kappa_2 \left(s_{g_{(\phi,\theta,\psi)}} X(\mathbf{x}_2) \right) \cdot \ldots$$

$$\cdot \kappa_n \left(s_{g_{(\phi,\theta,\psi)}} X(\mathbf{x}_n) \right) \sin\theta d\phi d\theta d\psi. \tag{7.21}$$

where Λ is the set of parameters, i.e. including $\kappa_1, \ldots, \kappa_n$ - we define Λ in detail when we present the parameterization of the kernel in the next section (7.3.1).

It is obvious that a direct and naive computation of these n-Point features is hardly tractable in terms of computational costs. For the computation of every single (voxel-wise) feature, we would have to evaluate the kernel at all possible combinations of ϕ, θ, ψ while transforming the n kernel points respectively.

To cope with this massive computational complexity, we generalize the methods for the fast computation of 3D 2- and 3-Point features (Ronneberger and Fehr, 2005) via fast convolution in the harmonic domain. The main challenge for this generalization is that we need to be able to couple the n sparse kernel points during the rotation in order to meet the separability criteria (7.5) in (7.21).

Previously, we were able to avoid the coupling problem: in the case of "2-point" kernels no coupling is needed, and the 3-Point kernels take advantage of the exception that the third point always lies on a circle centered in the second point (see section 7.2.1).

For the general np case, we need to derive a new approach which actually solves the coupling problem.

As in the previous sections, we will first derive the theory in a continuous setting before we deal with the implementation issues for actual applications in a discrete world (see section 7.3.2).

Parameterization

As in the $2p$ and $3p$ case, we fix the first kernel point $\mathbf{x}_1 := X(\mathbf{x})$ at the point of the local feature extraction, while the other points $\mathbf{x}_i, i \in \{2, \ldots, n\}$ are placed at concentric spherical neighborhoods with radii r_i: $x_i \in S[r_i](x)$. Hence, each x_i is parameterized by the spherical angles $\Phi_i \in [0,\ldots,2\pi], \Theta_i \in [0,\ldots,\pi]$, the input data channel c_i and the radius $r_i \in \mathbb{R}$ (also see figure 7.10).

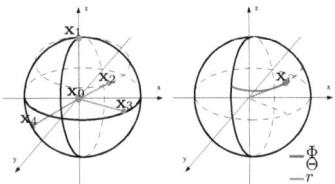

Figure 7.10: Parameterization of n-Point kernels. **Left**: The n kernel points are parameterized as points on a sphere with exception of $x_1 = x$ which is by definition placed in the origin of the local kernel support x. Note: the points must not necessarily lie on the same sphere as indicated in this scheme. **Right**: Each kernel point $x_i \in S[r_i](x)$ is parameterized by it's spherical coordinates in Φ_i, Θ_i and distance to the origin (= radius of the sphere) r_i.

Overall, we end up with set of kernel parameters:

$$\Lambda := \left\{ \kappa_1, \{\kappa_2, r_2, c_2, \Phi_2, \Theta_2\}, \ldots, \{\kappa_n, r_n, c_n, \Phi_n, \Theta_n\} \right\}. \tag{7.22}$$

Given this spherical parameterization, we first treat each x_i independently and perform the angular coupling of all points later on. We represent the x_i by a spherical delta-function $T_i[r_i] \in S^2$ with radius r_i:

$$T_i[r_i](\Phi, \Theta) := \delta(\Phi - \Phi_i)\delta(\Theta - \Theta_i). \tag{7.23}$$

In its harmonic representation, $T_i[r_i]$ is given by the according Spherical Harmonic base functions:

$$T_i[r_i](\Phi, \Theta) = \sum_{l=0}^{\infty} \sum_{m=-l}^{l} \overline{Y_m^l}(\Phi, \Theta) Y_m^l(\Phi_i, \Theta_i). \tag{7.24}$$

Hence, we can obtain the Spherical Harmonic transformation of $T_i[r_i]$ directly from the harmonic base functions:

$$\left(\widehat{T_i}[r_i, \Phi_i, \Theta_i] \right)_m^l = Y_m^l(\Phi_i, \Theta_i). \tag{7.25}$$

In the next step, we evaluate the contribution of the kernel points at the constellation of the $T_i[r_i]$ given the local support of each feature extraction point x.

Due to the separability of our kernels (7.5), each kernel point is associated with a potentially different non-linear sub-kernel κ_i and might operate on a different data channel c_i. For each feature evaluation, we perform Spherical Harmonic expansions around the center voxel at the radii r_i (associated with the respective kernel points) of the non-linearly transformed input data $\kappa_i(X[c_i])$:

$$\widehat{X[r_i, c_i]}(x) = \mathcal{SH}[r_i]\left(\kappa_i(X[c_i]\big|_{S[r_i](x)}) \right). \tag{7.26}$$

With the data and the kernel points represented in the harmonic domain, we can now apply a fast correlation to evaluate the contribution of each kernel point on the local data and perform this evaluation over all rotations. Given a point at position x, we compute the result $C_i^{\#}$ of this fast correlation over all spherical angles for the i-th kernel point as shown in (3.45):

$$C_i^{\#} = \widehat{X[r_i, c_i]}(x) \# \widehat{T_i}. \tag{7.27}$$

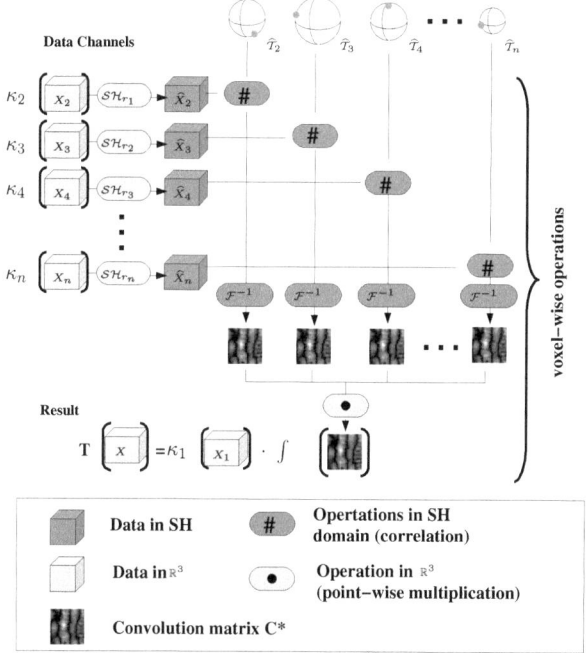

Figure 7.11: Schematic overview of the fast computation of np-Features.

Rotation Invariance

The key issue regarding the construction of n-Point" kernels is that we need to couple the contributions of the individual kernel points in such a way that only the chosen kernel constellation (given by the Φ_i, Θ_i, r_i) has a contribution when we rotate over all possible angles, i.e. the kernel points must not rotate independently.

Since the correlation matrices $C_i^\#$ hold the contribution at each possible angle in a 3D Euclidean space with a (ϕ, θ, ψ) coordinate-system (see section 3.4), we can perform the multiplicative coupling of the separate sub-kernels (7.5) by an angle-wise multiplication of the point-wise correlation results: $\prod_{i=2}^n C_i^\#$.

Finally, by integrating over the resulting Euclidean space of this coupling, we easily obtain rotation invariance as in (7.21):

$$\int_{\mathcal{SO}(3)} \left(\prod_{i=2}^n C_i^\# \right) \sin\theta \, d\phi \, d\theta \, d\psi. \tag{7.28}$$

With the additional coupling of x_1, we are now able to compute the n-Point Haar-Feature as shown in figure (7.11):

$$T[\Lambda](\mathbf{x}) \quad := \quad \kappa_1\Big(X(\mathbf{x})\Big) \cdot \int\limits_{\mathcal{SO}(3)} \left(\prod_{i=2}^{n} \mathcal{C}_i^{\#}\right) \sin\theta d\phi d\theta d\psi. \tag{7.29}$$

Gray-Scale Invariance

A nice side effect of the kernel point coupling via fast correlation (7.29) is the fact that we can obtain real invariance towards additive and multiplicative gray-value changes: we simply use the normalized cross-correlation (3.57) to compute the

$$\mathcal{C}_i^{\#} = \widehat{X[r_i, c_i]}(\mathbf{x}) \# \widehat{\mathcal{T}_i}$$

where the individually normalized correlations are independent of gray-scale changes.

7.3.2 Implementation

The transformation into the harmonic domain is implemented as described in section 4.1. Hence, we can also obtain the expansions at all points in X at once using the convolution approach (4.3).

The implementation of the template $\mathcal{T}_t$ has to be handled with some care: to avoid sampling issues, we apply the same implementation strategies as in the case of the Spherical Harmonic base functions (see section 4.1 for details).

The computation of the correlation matrices $\mathcal{C}^{\#}$ follows the algorithm given in section 3.4.5. The size of the padding p we need to apply strongly depends on the angular resolution necessary to resolve the given configuration of the kernel points.

Finally, the evaluation of the Haar-Integration over all possible rotations is approximated by the sum over the combined (ϕ, θ, ψ)-space:

$$T[\Lambda](\mathbf{x}) \quad \approx \quad \kappa_1\Big(X(\mathbf{x})\Big) \cdot \sum \left(\prod_{i=2}^{n} \mathcal{C}_i^{\#}\right). \tag{7.30}$$

Multi-Channel Data: As in the other cases of scalar Haar-Features, the application of np-Features to multi-channel data is limited to n channels per feature, but straightforward: we can simply set the kernel points to be on different data channels as shown in the $2p$ case.

Complexity The computational complexity of the np-Feature is dominated by the n Spherical Harmonic expansions needed to transform the kernelized input data into the harmonic domain which takes $O(n \cdot b_{\max} \cdot m \log m)$ for input data of size m. The costs for the correlation and multiplication of the correlation matrices are negligible.

Parallelization As stated in section 4.1, we can gain linear speed-up in the number of cores for the parallelization of the harmonic transformation. Further, we could also split the computation of the correlation matrices into several threads, but as mentioned before, this speed-up hardly falls into account.

7.3.3 Further Speed-up

Concerning computational complexity, the main bottleneck of the *np*-Feature is actually the transformation to the Spherical Harmonic domain. Due to the non-linear mappings κ_i of the separable kernel, we have to compute the harmonic expansion at all points **x** in X for each kernel point independently (7.27). Without the κ_i, we would only need a single transformation for all kernel points which lie on the same radius and the same data channel (a setting which is very common in practice). However, we cannot simply neglect the non-linear kernel mappings.

On the other hand, we are not bound to the class of separable kernels, which were only introduced to

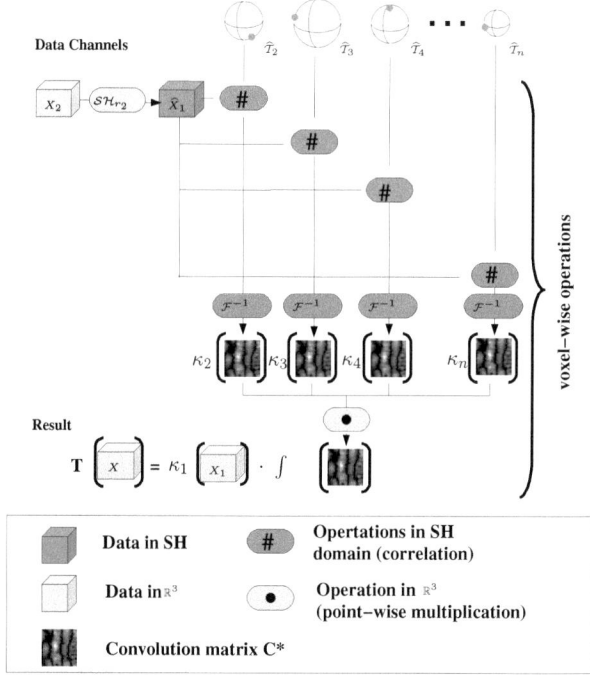

Figure 7.12: Schematic overview of the optimized computation of "np"-features.

support the development of fast algorithms. Hence, we construct a new kernel, which is separating the kernel point $\mathbf{x}_1 = X(\mathbf{x})$ in the center from the points $\mathbf{x}_i \in S[r_i](\mathbf{x})$ in the local spherical neighborhood of **x**:

$$\kappa := \kappa_1 \left(X(s_g(\mathbf{x}_1)) \right) \cdot \kappa_s \left(X(s_g(\mathbf{x}_2)), \dots, X(s_g(\mathbf{x}_n)) \right), \tag{7.31}$$

where κ_s is some non-linear mapping of $(n-1)$ arguments (just like in (7.1)).

Instead of a non-linear weighting of the underlying data sensed by the kernel points (as before), we choose κ_s to provide a non-linear weighting of the combination of the kernel points. Technically this is only a small change, but it enables us to move the κ_i into the harmonic domain, weighting the contribution of the kernel points to the Integral:

$$T[\Lambda](\mathbf{x}) \quad := \quad \kappa_1\Big(X(\mathbf{x})\Big) \cdot \int\limits_{\mathcal{SO}(3)} \left(\prod_{i=2}^{n} \kappa_i\Big(c_i^{\#}\Big)\right) \sin\theta\, d\phi\, d\theta\, d\psi. \tag{7.32}$$

Figure 7.12 shows the changes in the overall computation scheme. It should be noted that this optimized approach is similar but not equivalent to the original np formulation.

7.3.4 Discussion

The np-Features provide a powerful framework for the implementation of local features which are able obtain invariance towards rotations and multiplicative gray-scale changes via Haar-Integration.

In practice, np-Features are especially suitable for the design of highly specific features with a strong discriminative power used in challenging image analysis tasks justifying the higher computational costs. For less complex problems, we are better off using some of the less complex feature methods.

A major problem concerning the application of np-Features is the huge set of kernel parameters Λ (7.22) we have to choose. In practice, it is infeasible to try all possible parameter combinations in a feature selection process, like we suggest for other features. Neither is it practically possible to select the best parameter settings by hand. To overcome this problem, we introduce an automatic, data driven algorithm which learns the kernel parameters on given training samples (see section 10.3).

8 $\mathcal{VH}$-Features

In this chapter, we derive a set of local, rotation invariant features which are directly motivated by the mathematical formulation of the Vectorial Harmonics (see section 3.6). Analogous to the $\mathcal{SH}$-Features, we take advantage of the nice properties of the harmonic representation which allow us to perform fast feature computations in the frequency domain.

Given 3D vector fields $\mathbf{X}$, the transformation $\mathcal{VH}[r](\mathbf{x})$ (3.65) of local vectors on a sphere with radius r around the center $\mathbf{x}$ in $\mathbf{X}$ in Vectorial Harmonics is nothing more than a change of the base-functions representing the initial data. So the new base might provide us with a nice framework to operate on spheres, but we still have to perform the actual feature construction. Primarily, we want to obtain rotation invariance.

First we introduce a method to obtain rotational invariance which is the simple extension of $\mathcal{SH}_{abs}$-Features (see section 5.1) to vector fields: In section 8.1 we introduce $\mathcal{VH}_{abs}$-Features, which use the fact that the band-wise energies of a $\mathcal{VH}$ representation do not change under rotation.

The second member of the $\mathcal{VH}$-Feature class is also derived from its $\mathcal{SH}$ counter part: the fast and also rotation invariant auto-correlation feature $\mathcal{VH}_{autocorr}$ (section 8.2) is based on the fast correlation in Vectorial Harmonics introduced in section 3.8.

Finally, since we transfer all $\mathcal{VH}$-Features directly from the class of $\mathcal{SH}$-Features, one might ask if the other two $\mathcal{SH}$-Features, $\mathcal{SH}_{phase}$ and $\mathcal{SH}_{bispectrum}$ could also be extended to the $\mathcal{VH}$ domain. And in fact, theoretically both extension could be done without much effort, but practically, none of them make much sense: the bispectrum features (see section 5.4) simply become exceptionally expensive when we have to add additional couplings over the sub-bands k. For the vectorial phase, we could simply somehow define a phase in $\mathcal{VH}$, however, it is actually not evident how such a phase should be chosen and what it actually represents with respect to the mapping of the input data.

8.1 $\mathcal{VH}_{abs}$

$\mathcal{VH}_{abs}$-Features are the direct extension of $\mathcal{SH}_{abs}$-Features (see section 5.1) to vector fields. Again, we use the fact that the band-wise energies of a $\mathcal{VH}$ representation does not change under rotation.

8.1.1 Feature Design

Rotations $\mathcal{R}(\phi, \theta, \psi) \in i\mathcal{SO}(3)$ on 3D vector fields $\mathbb{R}^3 \times \mathbb{R}^3$ (see section 3.7) are represented in the Vectorial Harmonic domain in terms of band-wise multiplications of the expansions $\widehat{f^l}$ with Wigner D-Matrices D^l (3.73). Hence, we can directly follow the very same power spectrum approach as for the $\mathcal{SH}_{abs}$-Features. This way we easily obtain a rotation invariant scalar entry for the l-th frequency in the power spectrum:

$$\left(\mathcal{VH}_{abs}[r](\mathbf{x})\right)^l := \sqrt{\sum_{k=-1}^{1} \sum_{m=-(l+k)}^{(l+k)} \left(\left(\mathcal{VH}[r](\mathbf{x})\right)_{k,m}^l\right)^2}. \tag{8.1}$$

Since the rotation invariance is achieved band wise, the approximation of the original data via harmonic expansion can be cut off at an arbitrary band, encoding just the level of detail needed for the application.

8.1.2 Implementation

The implementation of the $\mathcal{VH}_{abs}$ is straightforward. We follow the implementation of the Vectorial Harmonic transformation as described in section 4.2.

Multi-Channel Data: $\mathcal{VH}_{abs}$-Feature cannot directly combine data from several channels into a single feature. In case of multi-channel data, we would have to compute features for each channel separately.

Complexity

Following the implementation given in section 4.2, we obtain the harmonic expansion to band b_{max} at each point of a volume with m voxels in $O(m(b_{max})^2 + (m \log m))$. The computation of the absolute values takes another $O((b_{max})^3)$.
The additional loop over k does not effect the O-Complexity, but in practice, $\mathcal{VH}_{abs}$ takes about factor three longer to compute than $\mathcal{SH}_{abs}$.

Parallelization Further speed-up can be achieved by parallelization (see section 4): the data can be transformed into the harmonic domain by parallel computation of the coefficients and the computation of the absolute values can also be split into several threads. For $\mathcal{C}$ CPU cores with $\mathcal{C} \leq (b_{max})^2$ and $\mathcal{C} \leq m$ we obtain:

$$O(\frac{m(b_{max})^3}{\mathcal{C}}) + O(\frac{m(b_{max})^2 + (m \log m)}{\mathcal{C}}).$$

8.1.3 Discussion

The $\mathcal{VH}$-Features are a simple and straightforward extension of $\mathcal{SH}_{abs}$ to 3D vector fields. They are computationally efficient and easy to implement. However, the discriminative properties are even more limited than the $\mathcal{SH}_{abs}$-Features. The band-wise absolute values capture only the energy of the respective frequencies in the overall spectrum. Hence, we loose all the phase information which leads to strong ambiguities within the feature mappings. The additional sub-bands k further increase this problem compared to $\mathcal{SH}_{abs}$. In many applications it is possible to reduce these ambiguities by combining $\mathcal{VH}$-Features extracted at different radii.

8.2 $\mathcal{VH}_{autocorr}$

The second member of the $\mathcal{VH}$-Feature class is also derived from its $\mathcal{SH}$ counter part: based on the auto-correlation feature $\mathcal{SH}_{autocorr}$ (section 5.3) we compute invariant features directly from the Vectorial Harmonic representation. Again, this is motivated by the introduction of the fast normalized cross-correlation in the Vectorial Harmonic domain (see introduction of chapter 3.8). The cross-correlation $\mathcal{VH}_{corr}(f, g)$ of two vectorial signals $\mathbf{f}, \mathbf{g} \in S^2$ is a binary operation $\mathcal{VH}_{corr} : S^2 \times S^2 \rightarrow \mathbb{R}$. Hence, it cannot be used directly as a feature, where we require a mapping of individual local signals $\mathbf{f} \in S^2 \rightarrow \mathcal{H}$ into some feature space $\mathcal{H} \subseteq \mathbb{R}^n$ (see section 2).

A general and widely known method for obtaining features from correlations is to compute the auto-correlation, e.g. (Kangl et al., 2005). In our case, we propose the local $\mathcal{VH}_{autocorr}$-Feature, which performs a fast auto-correlation of $\mathbf{f} \in (S^2 \times \mathbb{R}^3)$ with itself.

We use local dot-products of vectors to define the auto-correlation under a given rotation $\mathcal{R}$ in Euler angles ϕ, θ, ψ as:

$$(\mathbf{f} \# \mathbf{f})(\mathcal{R}) := \int_{\Phi, \Theta} \langle \mathbf{f}(\Phi, \Theta), \mathcal{R}\mathbf{f}(\Phi, \Theta) \rangle \quad \sin \Theta d\Phi d\Theta. \tag{8.2}$$

8.2.1 Feature Design

We first expand the local neighborhood f at radius r around the point $\mathbf{x} \in X$ in Vectorial Harmonics, $\hat{\mathbf{f}} := \mathcal{VH}[r](\mathbf{X}(\mathbf{x}))$.
Then we follow the fast correlation method which we introduced in section 3.8 to obtain the full correlation $C^{\#}$ from equation (3.80).

Invariance: In order to obtain rotation invariant features, we follow the Haar-Integration approach (see section 7.0.4) and integrate over the auto-correlations at all possible rotations $\mathcal{R}$. $C^{\#}$ holds the necessary auto-correlation results in a 3D (ϕ, θ, ψ)-space (3.44), hence we simply integrate over $C^{\#}$,

$$\mathcal{VH}_{autocorr} := \int_{\phi, \theta \psi} \kappa \left(C^{\#}(\phi, \theta, \psi) \right) \sin \theta d\phi d\theta d\psi \tag{8.3}$$

and obtain a scalar feature. Additionally, we insert a non-linear kernel function κ to increase the separability. Usually, very simple non-linear functions, such as $\kappa(x) := x^2, \kappa(x) := x^3$ or $\kappa(x) := \sqrt{x}$, are sufficient.

8.2.2 Implementation

We follow the implementation of the Vectorial Harmonic transformation as described in section 4.2 and the implementation of the fast correlation from (3.53).
In practice, where the harmonic expansion is bound by a maximal expansion band $b_{\max}$, the integral (8.3) is reduce to the sum over the then discrete angular space $C^{\#}$:

$$\mathcal{VH}_{autocorr} = \sum_{\phi, \theta \psi} \kappa \left(C^{\#}(\phi, \theta, \psi) \right). \tag{8.4}$$

Multi-Channel Data: $\mathcal{VH}_{autocorr}$ cannot directly combine data from several channels into a single feature. In case of multi-channel data, we would have to compute features for each channel separately.

Complexity

Following the implementation given in section 4.2, we obtain the harmonic expansion to band b_{max} at each point of a volume with m voxels in $O(m(b_{\mathrm{max}})^2 + (m \log m))$. The complexity of the auto-correlation depends on b_{max} and the padding parameter p (3.53) and can be computed in $O(m(b_{\mathrm{max}} + p)^3 \log(b_{\mathrm{max}} + p)^3))$. The summ over $C^{\#}$ takes another $O((b_{\mathrm{max}} + p)^3)$ at each point.

Parallelization: Further speed-up can be achieved by parallelization (see section 4): the data can be transformed into the harmonic domain by parallel computation of the coefficients and the computation of the absolute values can also be split into several threads. For $\mathcal{C}$ CPU cores with $\mathcal{C} \leq (b_{\mathrm{max}})^2$ and $\mathcal{C} \leq m$ we obtain:

$$O(\frac{m\left((b_{\mathrm{max}} + p)^3 + (b_{\mathrm{max}} + p)^3 \log(b_{\mathrm{max}} + p)^3\right)}{\mathcal{C}}) + O(\frac{m(b_{\mathrm{max}})^2 + (m \log m)}{\mathcal{C}})$$

8.2.3 Discussion

Auto-correlation can be a very effective feature to encode texture properties. The discriminative power of $\mathcal{VH}_{autocorr}$ can be further increased by combining the correlation at several different radii into a correlation result $C^{\#}$ as described in section 3.4.6.

9 Vectorial Haar-Features

In this chapter we derive several features operating on vectorial data which obtain invariance via Haar-Integration. All of the methods are strongly related to the features presented in the chapter 7 and are based on the Haar-Integration framework 7.2. In the case of vectorial data, we take advantage of the Vectorial Harmonic (see section 3.6) representation of local spherical neighborhoods $\mathcal{S}[r](\mathbf{x})$ of radii r at position $\mathbf{x} \in \mathbb{R}^3$ of the 3D vector fields $\mathbf{X} : \mathbb{R}^3 \rightarrow \mathbb{R}^3$ with vectorial elements $\mathbf{X}(\mathbf{x}) \in \mathbb{R}^3$.

Please refer to the sections 7.0.4 and 7.0.5 for an in-depth introduction of the Haar approach. It also might be useful to take a look at the scalar kernels in 7.1, 7.2 and 7.3 first.

Analogical to the $2p$, $3p$ and np kernels, where the name indicated the number of scalar kernel points in a local, sparse and separable kernel (7.5), we also denote the local, sparse and separable vectorial kernels by $1v, 2v$ and nv:

The $1v$-Feature (section 9.1) uses a kernel with a single vector component and acts as vectorial extension of the $2p$-Feature. Basically, it integrates the local similarities of the data vectors with the normal vectors of a spherical neighborhood template. The $1v$ kernel is especially suitable for the detection of sphere like convex structures and is primarily a shape feature, not a texture feature.

The $2v$-Feature (section 9.2) applies a variation of the $1v$ kernel: instead of using the normal vectors of a spherical neighborhood template, the $2v$ kernel integrates over the similarities of the data vectors with the centering vector $\mathbf{X}(\mathbf{x})$. $2v$ kernels return more texture based and less shape based features.

Finally, we introduce the nv-Feature (section 9.3) where we apply the direct extension of the np kernel (section 7.3) to 3D vector fields in order to derive highly specific local features.

Related Work: In general, there have not been many publications on local invariant features for 3D vector fields. One exception is the work of (Schulz et al., 2006), which uses a voting scheme in a 3D gradient vector field to detect spherical structures. The results of this feature are practically identical to those of our $1v$-Features - both just follow different approaches to implement a detector which could be considered as Hough-Transform for spheres.

9.1 1-Vector Features ($1v$)

The $1v$-Feature uses a kernel with a single vector component and acts as vectorial extension of the $2p$-Feature. Basically, it integrates the local similarities of the data vectors with the normal vectors of a spherical neighborhood template.

9.1.1 Feature Design

Given a 3D vector field $\mathbf{X} : \mathbb{R}^3 \to \mathbb{R}^3$, we extract local features from the spherical neighborhoods $\mathcal{S}[r](\mathbf{x})$ at positions $\mathbf{x}$. We integrate over the dot-products between the vectorial data $\mathbf{X}(\mathbf{x}_i)$ and the normal vectors $\mathbf{x}_i^\perp$ at all positions $\mathbf{x}_i \in \mathcal{S}[r](\mathbf{x})$ on the sphere around $\mathbf{x}$. The normal vectors are defined as:

$$\mathbf{x}_i^\perp := \alpha\left(\mathbf{x} - \mathbf{x}_i\right), \tag{9.1}$$

where the $\alpha \in \{-1, 1\}$ factor determines whether the normal vector points towards or away from the feature extraction point. Figure 9.1 illustrates the basic kernel design

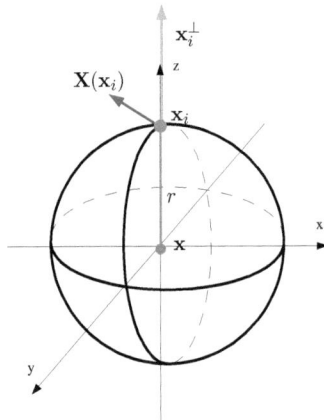

Figure 9.1: Example for the basic design of the $1v$ kernel with $\alpha = 1$.

Rotation Invariance

If we plug the dot-product into the general Haar framework (7.2), we can achieve invariance regarding rotations $\mathcal{R}(\phi, \theta, \psi) \in \mathcal{SO}(3)$ parameterized in Euler angles (see section 3.2).
It is obvious that all possible positions $\mathbf{x}_i$ lie on the spherical neighborhood $\mathcal{S}[r](\mathbf{x})$ with the radius

$$r = \left|\mathbf{x} - \mathbf{x}_i\right|, \tag{9.2}$$

whereas the normal vector $\mathbf{x}_i^\perp$ changes with the position according to (9.1). Because we are considering a singe kernel vector, we can reduce the integral over all rotations to an integral over all points of the spherical neighborhood parameterized by the angles ϕ and θ (see 7.9 for a detailed justification). The final formulation of the $1v$-Feature is then:

$$T[r, \alpha](\mathbf{x}) := \int_{x_i \in \mathcal{S}[r](\mathbf{x})} \left\langle \mathbf{x}_i^\perp, \mathbf{X}(\mathbf{x}_i) \right\rangle \sin\theta \, d\phi \, d\theta. \tag{9.3}$$

9.1.2 Implementation

The evaluation of (9.3) could be implemented straightforward. However, usually we want to compute features at all voxels $\mathbf{x}$ simultaneously. Therefore, we propose an optimized algorithm: we pre-compute a vectorial template $T[r, \alpha]$, which simply holds the normal vectors of the spherical neighborhood $\mathcal{S}[r](\mathbf{x})$ weighted by α. Figure 9.2 shows such a template. We then reformulate the dot-product

Figure 9.2: Sample $T[r, \alpha]$, with $\alpha = -1$.

in (9.3) as component-wise convolution of $T[r, \alpha]$ with $\mathcal{S}[r](\mathbf{x})$:

$$T[r, \alpha](\mathbf{x}) := \sum_{c=0}^{2} \mathbf{X}[c]\Big|_{\mathcal{S}[r](\mathbf{x})} * T[r, \alpha][c], \tag{9.4}$$

where $\mathbf{X}(\mathbf{x})[c]$ returns the cth directional component of $\mathbf{X}(\mathbf{x})$. Hence, we can apply a fast convolution to simultaneously evaluate (9.4) at all voxels $\mathbf{x}$:

$$T[r, \alpha](\mathbf{X}) := \sum_{c=0}^{2} FFT^{-1}\Big(FFT(\mathbf{X}[c]) \cdot FFT(T[r, \alpha][c])\Big). \tag{9.5}$$

For discrete input data we have to handle the implementation of the spherical template $T[r, \alpha]$ with some care. To avoid sampling issues, we apply the same implementation strategies as in the case of the Spherical Harmonic base functions (see section 4.1 for details).

Multi-Channel Data: $1v$-Features cannot directly combine data from several channels into a single feature. In case of multi-channel data, we would have to compute features for each channel separately.

Complexity

Using the convolution approach, we end up with a complexity of $O(m \cdot m \log m)$ for an input volume of size m.

Parallelization: Since there is no easy way to parallelize the Fourier Transform, we do not further parallelize the computation of $1v$-Features. But since $1v$-Features can be computed so fast anyway, this is not a real drawback.

9.1.3 Discussion

The $1v$-Feature provides a very fast and rotation invariant method for the extraction of local features from 3D vector fields. The nature of the kernel vectors given as normals of the spherical neighborhood makes the $1v$ kernel an optimal detector for spherical structures which relies mostly on shape and hardly on texture properties of the underlying data. The α factor then indicates if we detect the inner or the outer surface of a spherical shape.

In an alternative interpretation, the $1v$ approach could be seen as Hough-Transform (Hough, 1962) for spheres. This could be reinforced by an additional integration over several radii.

9.2 2-Vector Features ($2v$)

The $2v$-Feature uses a variation of the $1v$ kernel: instead of using the normal vectors of a spherical neighborhood template, the $2v$ kernel integrates over the similarities of the data vectors of the centering vector $\mathbf{X}(\mathbf{x})$.

9.2.1 Feature Design

Given a 3D vector field $\mathbf{X} : \mathbb{R}^3 \rightarrow \mathbb{R}^3$, we extract local features from the spherical neighborhoods $\mathcal{S}[r](\mathbf{x})$ at positions $\mathbf{x}$.

The basic idea of the $2v$ kernel is to compute the similarity (in terms of the dot-product) of the direction of the data vectors $\mathbf{X}(\mathbf{x}_i), \forall \mathbf{x}_i \in \mathcal{S}[r](\mathbf{x})$ with the direction of the center vector $\mathbf{X}(\mathbf{x})$.

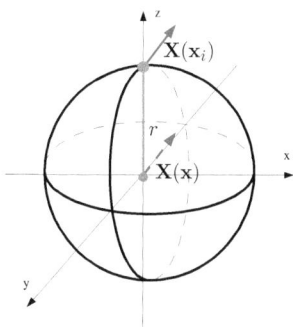

Figure 9.3: Basic design of the $2v$ kernel.

Rotation Invariance: If we plug the $2v$ kernel into the general Haar framework (7.2), we can achieve invariance regarding rotations $\mathcal{R}(\phi, \theta, \psi) \in \mathcal{SO}(3)$ which are parameterized in Euler angles (see section 3.2).

Just as in the $1v$ case, we use the fact that all possible positions of the $\mathbf{x}_i$ lie on the spherical neighborhood $\mathcal{S}[r](\mathbf{x})$ with the radius:

$$r = \left| \mathbf{x} - \mathbf{x}_i \right|, \tag{9.6}$$

And again, since we are considering only a singe kernel vector, we can reduce the integral over all rotations to an integral over all points of the spherical neighborhood parameterized by the angles ϕ and θ (see 7.9 for a detailed justification). The final formulation of the $2v$-Feature is then:

$$T[r](\mathbf{x}) := \int\limits_{x_i \in \mathcal{S}[r](\mathbf{x})} \left\langle \mathbf{X}(\mathbf{x}), \mathbf{X}(\mathbf{x}_i) \right\rangle \sin\theta d\phi d\theta. \tag{9.7}$$

9.2.2 Implementation

The implementation strictly follows the convolution based algorithm introduced for the $1v$ case (see section 9.1.2). The only difference is that the vectors in the template $\mathcal{T}$ are oriented in the same direction as $\mathbf{X}(\mathbf{x})$.

Multi-Channel Data: $v2$-Features can combine data from two channels into a single feature: we can simply extract the kernel direction $\mathbf{X}[c_1](\mathbf{x})$ and the neighborhood data $\mathbf{X}[c_2](\mathbf{x}_i)$ from different channels.

Complexity

Using the convolution approach, we end up with a complexity of $O(m \cdot m \log m)$ for an input volume of size m.

Parallelization: Since there is no easy way to parallelize the Fourier Transformation, we do not further parallelize the computation of $2v$-Features. But as $2v$-Features can be computed so fast anyway, this is not a real drawback.

9.2.3 Discussion

The fast $2v$ kernels return more texture based and less shape based features. Intuitively, $2v$-Features are an indicator for the local homogeneity of the vector field. The name $2v$-Feature might miss leading to some degree, since we only consider a single kernel vector. But in contrast to the $1v$-Feature approach, we actually combine two vectors from the input data $\mathbf{X}(\mathbf{x})$ and $\mathbf{X}(\mathbf{x}_i)$.

9.3 n-Vector Features (nv)

The nv-Features are the direct extension of the np-Features (see section 7.3) to 3D vector fields. Analogous to the properties of np kernels on scalar (multi-channel) data, the goal is to derive highly specific local features for the detection of local structures (objects) in 3D vector fields.

To obtain a strong discrimination power, we introduce a vectorial kernel which is able to handle an arbitrary number of kernel vectors $\mathbf{v}_1, \ldots, \mathbf{v}_n$ instead of only one or two (as for $1v, 2v$-Features).

Since the entire derivation of the nv kernel strongly relies on the very same methods and algorithms that were introduced for the derivation of the np kernel, the reader may to refer to section 7.3 for some technical details.

Given a 3D vector field $\mathbf{X} : \{\mathbb{R}^3 \to \mathbb{R}^3\}$, we extract local features from the spherical neighborhoods $\mathcal{S}[r](\mathbf{x})$ at positions $\mathbf{x}$. For the kernel vectors $\mathbf{v}_i \in \{\mathbb{R}^3 \times \mathbb{R}^3\}$, we write $\dot{\mathbf{v}}_i \in \mathbb{R}^3$ and $\vec{\mathbf{v}}_i \in \mathbb{R}^3$ to address their position and direction.

There are two major differences in the basic formulation between general sparse and local scalar (np) and vectorial (nv) kernels: first, we do not explicitly consider a center vector for nv kernels (even though the framework would allow such a constellation). The main reason to do so is given by the second difference: since non-linear mappings (like the κ_i in the np kernel) are not well defined on vectorial data, we do not use a separable kernel approach (7.5) for the construction of the nv kernel. Instead, we are following the alternative (fast) approach (7.31), which allows us to formalize the n-Vector kernels in a more abstract way: (7.5):

$$\kappa \left(s_g(\mathbf{v}_1), \ldots, s_g(\mathbf{v}_n) \right). \tag{9.8}$$

Figure 9.4 shows an example nv kernel. Later on, we give the actual kernel mapping κ, which is still non-linear, but does not operate directly on vectorial data.

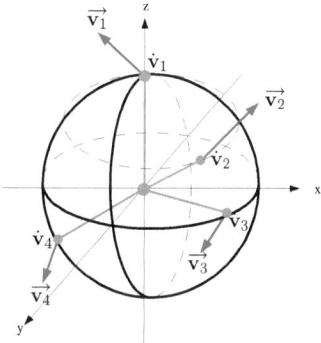

Figure 9.4: Example for the basic design of the nv kernel with four kernel vectors. Note that the kernel vectors are not necessarily bound to the same radius as illustrated in this example.

9.3.1 Feature Design

The primary goal is to achieve rotation invariance. Hence, the transformation group $\mathcal{G}$ is given by the group of 3D rotations $\mathcal{SO}(3)$. If we parameterize these global rotations $\mathcal{R} \in \mathcal{SO}(3)$ as local rotations of the kernel vectors in Euler angles $s_g(\phi, \theta, \psi)$ (see Fig. 3.4), we can rewrite (9.8) as:

$$T[\Lambda](\mathbf{x}) := \int_{SO(3)} \kappa \left(s_{g(\phi,\theta,\psi)}(\mathbf{v}_1), \dots, s_{g(\phi,\theta,\psi)}(\mathbf{v}_n) \right) \sin\theta \, d\phi \, d\theta \, d\psi, \tag{9.9}$$

where Λ is the set of parameters, i.e. including κ - we define Λ in detail when we present the parameterization of the kernel in the next sub-section(9.3.1).

Parameterization

The key for a fast computational evaluation of (9.9) is the smart parameterization of the kernel. Following the approach for the np kernels, we parameterize the position of the kernel vectors as points $\dot{\mathbf{v}}_i$ with $i \in \{1, \dots, n\}$ located at concentric spherical neighborhoods $S[r_i](\mathbf{x})$ with radii r_i surrounding the point of the feature extraction $\mathbf{x}$. Hence, each $\dot{\mathbf{v}}_i$ is parameterized by the spherical angles $\Phi_i \in [0, \dots, 2\pi], \Theta_i \in [0, \dots, \pi]$ and $r_i \in \mathbb{R}$ (also see figure 7.10).
The overall parameter set Λ thus includes the parameterized position $\dot{\mathbf{v}}_i$, the direction $\overrightarrow{\mathbf{v}_i}$ (which is normalized to $|\overrightarrow{\mathbf{v}_i}| = 1$) and the non-linear mapping κ which will be split into $\kappa_1, \dots, \kappa_n$ later on:

$$\Lambda := \left\{ \{\kappa_1, r_1, \Phi_1, \Theta_1, \overrightarrow{\mathbf{v}_1}\}, \dots, \{\kappa_n, r_n, \Phi_n, \Theta_n, \overrightarrow{\mathbf{v}_n}\} \right\}. \tag{9.10}$$

Given this parameterization, we further follow the approach from the np derivation and introduce "delta like" vectorial template functions T_i which represent the kernel vectors $T_i[r_i]$ in the harmonic domain:

$$\left(\widehat{T}_i[r_i, \Phi_i, \Theta_i, \overrightarrow{\mathbf{v}_i}] \right)^l_{km} = \overrightarrow{\mathbf{v}_i}^T \mathbf{Z}^l_{km}(\Phi, \Theta). \tag{9.11}$$

Now we have a frequency representation of the individual kernel vectors. In the next step, we evaluate the contribution of the input data at these kernels. For each feature evaluation, we perform Vectorial Harmonic expansions around $\mathbf{x}$ at the radii r_i (associated with the position of the respective kernel vectors) of the input vector field X:

$$\widehat{S[r_i]}(\mathbf{x}) = \mathcal{VH}[r_i](\mathbf{x}). \tag{9.12}$$

With the data and the kernel vectors represented in the harmonic domain, we can apply a fast correlation to evaluate the contribution of each kernel point on the local data and perform this evaluation over all rotations. Given a vector at position $\mathbf{x}$, we compute the result $C_i^{\#}$ of this fast correlation over all spherical angles for the i-th kernel vector as shown in (3.80):

$$C_i^{\#} = \widehat{S[r_i]}(\mathbf{x}) \# \widehat{T}_i. \tag{9.13}$$

Rotation Invariance

As in the case of n-Point kernels, we need to couple the contributions of the individual kernel vectors in such a way that only the chosen kernel constellation (given by the Φ_i, Θ_i, r_i) has a contribution to the feature while rotating over all possible angles, i.e. the positions of the kernel vectors must not rotate independently. Note that the correct orientation of the kernel vectors under the rotation is guaranteed by the Vectorial Harmonic formulation.
Since the $C_i^{\#}$ hold the contribution at each possible angle in a 3D Euclidean space with a (ϕ, θ, ψ) coordinate-system (see section 3.8), we can perform the multiplicative coupling of the separate sub-kernels (7.5) by a angle-wise multiplication of the point-wise correlation results: $\prod_{i=2}^n C_i^{\#}$.

By integrating over the resulting Euclidean space of this coupling, we easily obtain rotation invariance as in (9.9):

$$\int_{\mathcal{SO}(3)} \left(\prod_{i=2}^{n} \mathcal{C}_i^{\#} \right) \sin\theta d\phi d\theta d\psi. \tag{9.14}$$

Finally, we still have to introduce the non-linear mapping into (9.14) to satisfy (9.8). We follow the fast approach from (7.31), where we split κ into n non-linear mappings $\kappa_1, \ldots, \kappa_2$ which act directly on the correlation matrices. This leads to the final formulation of the nv-Feature:

$$T[\Lambda](\mathbf{x}) \quad := \quad \int_{\mathcal{SO}(3)} \left(\prod_{i=1}^{n} \kappa_i \left(\mathcal{C}_i^{\#} \right) \right) \sin\theta d\phi d\theta d\psi. \tag{9.15}$$

Figure 9.5 shows a schematic overview of the computation of nv-Features.

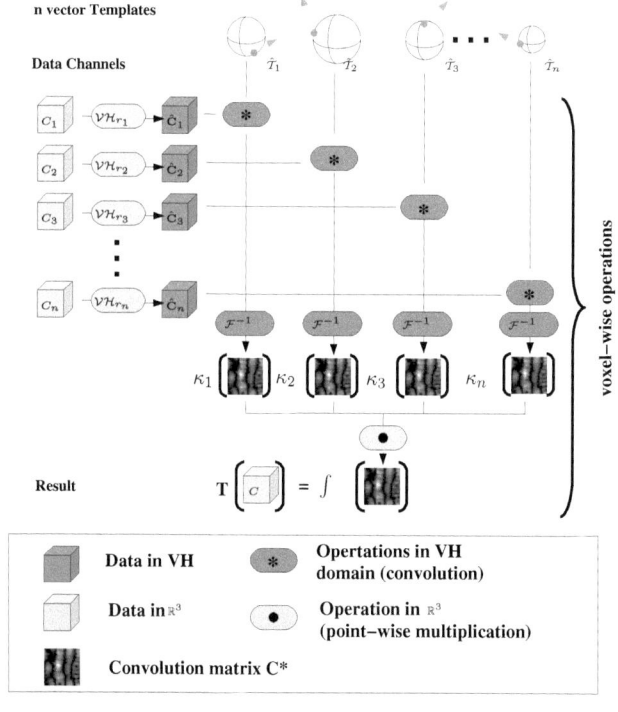

Figure 9.5: Schematic overview of the computation of nv-Features.

113

9.3.2 Implementation

The transformation into the harmonic domain is implemented as described in section 4.2. Hence, we can also obtain the expansions at all points in X at once using the convolution approach analogous to (4.3).

The implementation of the template $\mathcal{T}_t$ has to be handled with some care: to avoid sampling issues, we apply the same implementation strategies as in the case of the Spherical Harmonic base functions (see section 4.2 for details).

The computation of the correlation matrices $\mathcal{C}^{\#}$ follows the algorithm given in section 3.8. The size of the padding p we need to apply strongly depends on the angular resolution necessary to resolve the given configuration of the kernel points.

Finally, the evaluation of the Haar-Integration over all possible rotations is approximated by the sum over the combined (ϕ, θ, ψ)-space:

$$T[\Lambda](\mathbf{x}) \approx \sum \left(\prod_{i=2}^{n} \mathcal{C}_i^{\#} \right). \tag{9.16}$$

Multi-Channel Data: nv-Features cannot directly combine data from several channels into a single feature. In case of multi-channel data, we have to compute features for each channel separately.

Complexity

The computational complexity of the nv-Feature is dominated by the Vectorial Harmonic expansions needed to transform the input data and the kernel vector templates into the harmonic domain. This takes $O(b_{\max} \cdot m \log m)$ for input data of size m and $O(n \cdot b_{\max} \cdot m' \log m')$ for a template size of m'. The costs for the correlation and multiplication of the correlation matrices are negligible.

Parallelization: As stated in section 4.1, we can gain linear speed-up in the number of cores for the parallelization of the harmonic transformation. Further, we could also split the computation of the correlation matrices into several threads, but as mentioned before, this speed-up hardly falls into account.

9.3.3 Discussion

The nv-Features provide a powerful framework for the implementation of local features which are able obtain invariance towards rotation via Haar-Integration.

In practice, nv-Features are especially suitable for the design of highly specific features with a strong discriminative power used in challenging image analysis tasks justifying the higher computational costs. For less complex problems, we are better off using some of the less complex feature methods.

A major problem concerning the application of nv-Features is the huge set of kernel parameters Λ (9.10) we have to choose. In practice, it is infeasible to try all possible parameter combinations in a feature selection process, as we suggest for other features. Neither is it practically possible to select the best parameter settings by hand. To overcome this problem, we use the same automatic, data driven algorithm which learns the kernel parameters on given training samples as for the selection of the np-Features (see section 10.3).

10 Feature Selection

Basically all the features we have introduced in the previous chapters take some parameters like radius, maximum expansion band or non-linear mappings κ_i. The correct selection of these parameters is absolutely vital to the feature performance.

While it is possible to use some a-priori knowledge and expert experience to set some of the parameters, i.e. the radius, it is in most cases not possible to determine the other parameters directly. Therefore, we apply automatic feature selection methods that use labeled training samples to determine the most discriminative features.

We distinguish between two different types of feature selection methods: first, the class of **combinatorial** algorithms. These generic selection algorithms are most common in literature. Basically, they perform an "intelligent" combinatoric search over all possible feature combinations. This is more or less a "brute force" approach, where we have to compute all features and search the best combination. For this purpose, we use two different methods, MMD (Vasconecelos, 2003) and SIMBA (Gilad-Bachrach et al., 2004) which are well known from literature.

For some features, like np- and nv-Features, the parameter space is simply to large for even the smartest combinatoric search: it is simply not feasible to compute all possible features. For these cases, we introduce the second class of specialized (feature dependent) **constructive** data driven feature selection methods which use labeled training samples to actually learn the best feature parameters.

Structure: The remainder of this chapter is structured as follows: first, before we review the two combinatoric feature selection methods MMD (section 10.1) and SIMBA (section 10.2), we state basic mathematical definitions which found the basis for both methods.

Then, we introduce and derive our constructive feature selection algorithm for np- and vp-Features in section 10.3.

10.0.4 Mathematical Background

Given two random variables X and Y with marginal probabilities $p_1(x), p_2(x)$ and the joint probability distribution $p(x, y)$, we define the following terms:

Mutual Information: of two random variables is a quantity that measures the mutual dependence of the two variables:

$$I(X;Y) := \sum_{y \in Y} \sum_{x \in X} p(x, y) \log \frac{p(x, y)}{p_1(x) p_2(y)}. \tag{10.1}$$

Kullback-Leibler Divergence: is a non-commutative measure of the difference between two probability distributions P and Q:

$$KL(P\|Q) := \sum_i P(i) \log \frac{P(i)}{Q(i)}. \tag{10.2}$$

10.1 Maximum Marginal Diversity (MMD)

The first of the two combinatoric feature selection algorithms we choose to apply for several of our problems (see part III) is the Maximum Marginal Diversity (MMD) approach by (Vasconecelos, 2003). MMD is fast, easy to implement and under certain constraints, MMD is able to compute the best n features in a minimum Bayesian error sense by applying the **Infomax Principle** (Linsker, 1988).

Infomax Principle: For classification problems, Infomax (Linsker, 1988) endorses the selection of features that maximize the mutual information between features and class labels:

Lemma: *Given a classification problem (see section 12) with m classes and features $\mathbf{X} := T(\mathbf{Z})$ which are drawn from the random variables (input data) $\mathbf{Z}$, then the best feature space is the one that maximizes the mutual information $I(Y; \mathbf{X})$* (Linsker, 1988).

It has been shown in (Vasconecelos, 2003), that the Infomax solution of a problem is in fact a very close approximation of the Bayesian Error estimate of this classification problem. However, it is very hard to actually compute an Infomax solution without searching the all possible feature combinations or using numerical approximations.

One way to overcome this problem was also introduced in (Vasconecelos, 2003), where it has been observed that Infomax emphasizes solutions with large marginal diversities.

Marginal Diversity (MD):   Given a classification problem (see section 12) with features $\mathbf{X} = (X_1, \ldots, X_n)$, the Marginal Diversity (MD) for a single feature X_k is given by the divergence of the probability densities for single classes $P_{X_k|Y}(x|i)$ with all classes:

$$md(X_k) := \langle KL(P_{X_k|Y}(x|i) \| P_{X_k}(x) \rangle_Y. \tag{10.3}$$

10.1.1 Feature Selection with the Maximum Marginal Diversity (MMD)

Using the Marginal Diversity formulation (10.3), (Vasconecelos, 2003) was able to show that in cases where the knowledge of the class label does not change the mutual information between the features, selecting features of maximal marginal diversity results in the same solution as the Infomax algorithm.

Following these results, (Vasconecelos, 2003) also introduced a very simple and easy to implement algorithm for computation of the MMD, which uses histogram approximations of the probability densities:

Algorithm 1 MMD feature selection

---
    for all features X_k with $k \in \{1, \ldots, n\}$ **do**
      for all labels $i \in \{1, \ldots, m\}$ **do**
        compute the histogram $h_{k,i}$ of $P_{X_k|Y}(x|i)$
      end for
      compute $h_k = 1/m \sum_i h_{k,i}$
    end for
    compute $md(X_k) = \sum_i p_i \mathbf{h}_{k,i}^T \log \mathbf{h}_{k,i}/h_k$
    sort X_k by $md(X_k)$
    RETURN top N X_k

The main advantage of the MMD algorithm is that it is able to perform the Infomax approximation of n features in $O(n)$.

10.1.2 Discussion

The Maximum Marginal Diversity algorithm is easy to implement and provides an accurate and fast approximation of the Infomax principle. However, the fact that MMD treats all features independently can cause some unexpected drawbacks in the quality of the selected features: in cases (and the nature of our features endorses theses cases) where two or more features are redundant, MMD will rank all features the same - even though just one of these features would provide the same separability properties as all of them together.

This behavior makes it very hard to decide how many features are actually needed and causes the risk to neglect generally weaker features which actually would provide additional information. Hence, MMD only provides the best individual features, but not the best feature combination.

10.2 SIMBA

We try to overcome the shortcomings of the MMD algorithm (see 10.1.2) with a second feature selection method: the so-called SIMBA approach (Gilad-Bachrach et al., 2004).

SIMBA uses an iterative search over the possible feature combinations in order to find the best feature combination. Hence, SIMBA does not have the same problems as MMD, but we have to expect a higher computational complexity.

While there are numerous other feature selection methods which apply smart combinatoric search strategies, we have chosen SIMBA because it utilizes a maximum margin measure to evaluate the quality of feature combinations. This is a natural choice, since we are applying maximum margin classifiers, i.e. support vector machines (SVM), later on (see chapter 13).

While SVMs optimize the **sample-margin**, i.e. the distance between the instances and the decision boundary (see chapter 13 for details), (Gilad-Bachrach et al., 2004) showed that a lower bound to the sample-margin is given by the much easier to compute **hypothesis-margin** $\Theta_P(\mathbf{x})$ (10.4). Given a set of points P and the feature vector $\mathbf{x}$,

$$\Theta_P(\mathbf{x}) := \frac{1}{2}\Big(\|\mathbf{x} - nearmiss(\mathbf{x})\| - \|\mathbf{x} - nearhit(\mathbf{x})\|\Big), \tag{10.4}$$

where $nearmiss(\mathbf{x})$ and $nearhit(\mathbf{x})$ denote the nearest points in P with a different/same class label.

Using this definition of the margin, (Gilad-Bachrach et al., 2004) introduce a weighting $\mathbf{w}$ of the individual features, such that:

$$\Theta_P^{\mathbf{w}}(\mathbf{x}) := \frac{1}{2}\Big(\|\mathbf{x} - nearmiss(\mathbf{x})\|_{\mathbf{w}} - \|\mathbf{x} - nearhit(\mathbf{x})\|_{\mathbf{w}}\Big) \tag{10.5}$$

$$\text{with } \|z\|_{\mathbf{w}} := \sqrt{\sum_i \mathbf{w}_i^2 z_i^2}.$$

Given such a weighting, (Gilad-Bachrach et al., 2004) use a leave one out (LOO) (see section 12.1) strategy to compute the quality of the margin induced by a set S of features with weights $\mathbf{w}$:

$$e(\mathbf{w}) := \sum_{\mathbf{x} \in S} \Theta_{S\backslash\mathbf{x}}^{\mathbf{w}}(\mathbf{x}). \tag{10.6}$$

In order to apply a gradient decent algorithm for the iterative search of the best feature weighting, one differentiates (10.6):

$$
\begin{aligned}
(\bigtriangledown e(\mathbf{w}))_i \quad &:= \quad \frac{\partial e(\mathbf{w})}{\partial \mathbf{w}_i} \\
&= \quad \sum_{\mathbf{x} \in S} \frac{\partial \Theta(\mathbf{x})}{\partial \mathbf{w}_i} \\
&= \quad \frac{1}{2} \sum_{\mathbf{x} \in S} \left(\frac{(\mathbf{x}_i - nearmiss(\mathbf{x})_i)^2}{\|\mathbf{x} - nearmiss(\mathbf{x})\|_{\mathbf{w}}} - \frac{(\mathbf{x}_i - nearhit(\mathbf{x})_i)^2}{\|\mathbf{x} - nearhit(\mathbf{x})\|_{\mathbf{w}}} \right) \mathbf{w}_i .
\end{aligned}
\tag{10.7}
$$

Based on this gradient formulation, (Gilad-Bachrach et al., 2004) derived an easy to implement and reasonably fast algorithm for maximum margin feature selection called SIMBA (see algorithm 2).

Algorithm 2 SIMBA feature selection

initialize $\mathbf{w} = (1, 1, \ldots, 1)$
for $t = 1, \ldots, T$ **do**
    pick random $\mathbf{x} \in S$
    compute $nearmiss(\mathbf{x})$ with respect to $S \setminus \mathbf{x}$
    compute $nearhit(\mathbf{x})$ with respect to $S \setminus \mathbf{x}$
    for $i = 1, \ldots, N$ **do**
        compute $(\bigtriangledown e(\mathbf{w}))_i$
    end for
    $\mathbf{w} = \mathbf{w} + \bigtriangledown e(\mathbf{w})$
end for
$\mathbf{w} \leftarrow \mathbf{w}^2 / \|\mathbf{w}^2\|_\infty$ where $(\mathbf{w}^2)_i := (\mathbf{w}_i)^2$

10.2.1 Discussion

The SIMBA algorithm computes a maximum margin guided feature selection which runs in $\Omega(TNm)$ for m training samples with N features. The number of needed iterations T depends on the individual problem, but we empirically experienced quite good convergence behavior and usually set $T < 100$.

10.3 Data Driven Feature Selection

All of the combinatoric methods are actually performing a "smart" search for the optimal features (or feature combinations). No matter how "smart" this search may be, it always requires that large quantities of the features in the search space are actually computed. For features like $2p$-Haar (7.1) or $\mathcal{SH}_{phase}$ (5.2) that have only few parameters where the parameter space can be limited by a-priori knowledge, these combinatoric methods are quite suitable.

However, for features like np (7.3) or vp-Haar (9.3) which have a huge set of parameters, e.g. the infinitely many possible combinations of the kernel points, the combinatoric method are completely infeasible. Thus, especially for those features where a automatic feature selection really is needed, the previous methods cannot be applied.

We tackle this problem by introducing a novel, feature specific (non-generic) selection algorithm, where we learn the optimal feature parameters from labeled training data. Hence, this approach is constructive and tries to avoid searching large parameter spaces at all.

Throughout the rest of this section we use the np-Feature (see chapter 7.3) to derive the selection algorithm. However, the same method can also be directly applied to nv-Features (see chapter 9.3). Let us recall the parameterization of the np-Features from (7.22). Regardless of whether we use the original separable formulation (7.29) or the fast kernel (7.31), we need to choose the following parameters for each feature:

$$\Lambda := \Big\{ \kappa_1, \{\kappa_2, r_2, c_2, \Phi_2, \Theta_2\}, \dots, \{\kappa_n, r_n, c_n, \Phi_n, \Theta_n\} \Big\}. \tag{10.8}$$

While the selection of the input channels c_i and a limitation of the radii r_i to reasonable values can be done according to a-priori knowledge of the problem, we derive two data driven methods for the learning of suitable kernel point positions (Φ_i, Θ_i) and the non-linear mappings κ_i.

10.3.1 Learning the Position of the Kernel Points

Let us start with the more difficult problem, the positioning of the kernel points. Given the parameterization recalled from figure 7.10, we need to determine the number of kernel points and their position parameterized in Φ_i, Θ_i:

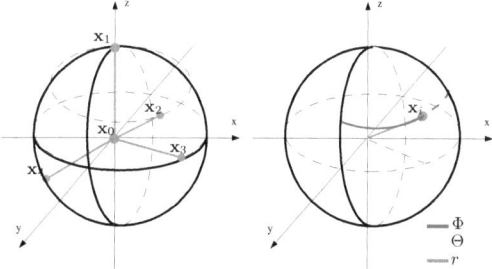

Figure 10.1: Parameterization of n-point kernels. **Left**: The n kernel points are parameterized as points on a sphere with exception of x_0, which is by definition placed in the origin of the local kernel support **x**. **Right**: Each kernel point $x_i \in S[r_i]$ (**x**) is parameterized by its spherical coordinate (Φ_i, Θ_i) and distance to the origin (= radius of the sphere) r_i.

Recall that np-Features (see chapter 7.3) are designed to be quite specific features which should detect certain structures. Hence, the kernel points have to be selected such that the structure of the target objects is reflected in the kernel constellation. We derive the final algorithm in a constructive manner:

Step 1: Clustering: We begin by applying an unsupervised clustering (see 12.1), by applying the k-Means algorithm on the labeled training data. We utilize the maximum of the simultaneous fast correlation (see section 3.4.5) over several radii of the local harmonic expansions of the training data as distance measure for the clustering.

After clustering, we use the labels of the training data to select homogeneous clusters, i.e. clusters which are mostly containing members of the target classes. The number of the selected clusters reflects the number of proposed features. Hence, we tune the clustering such that it returns the number of desired clusters. We then construct a feature for each of these selected clusters. Figure 10.2 shows an example for the clustering step.

Figure 10.2: Step 1: sample result of the clustering for the np-Feature selection on neuronal spine data
(see section 20). The voxel-wise clustering was performed with $k = 30$ k-Means using
the fast correlation over several concentric radii at once.

Step 2: Registration of the Cluster Members: For each of the selected clusters from step 1,
we take the centroid of this cluster as reference and un-rotate all other cluster members according to the
results form the correlation (see section 3.4.4. This way we obtain a registration of all cluster members.
Figure 10.3 illustrates[1] this step for a toy example.

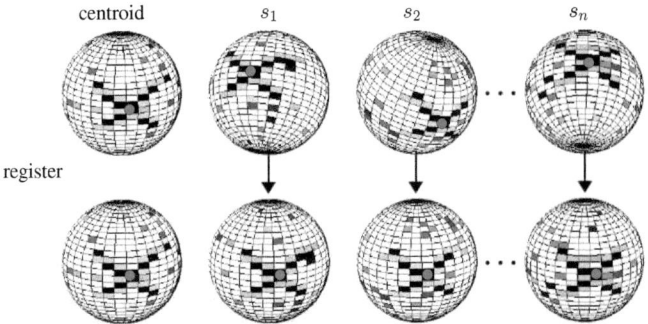

Figure 10.3: Step 2 (toy example): for each cluster, we register all cluster members $s_1, \ldots, s_n$ to the
cluster centroid. The red dot marks the position of the maximum correlation with the
centroid which is obtained from the correlation matrices from step 1.

Step 3: Construction of the Cluster Representative: Next, we transform all aligned cluster
members back to the spatial domain. Hence, we obtain a discrete 3D volume grid representation of
spherical surfaces for each considered radius. Then, we compute the voxel-wise variance $\sigma(r, \Phi_i, \Theta_i)$
at fixed voxel positions r, Φ_i, Θ_i over all cluster members (see figure 10.4). Finally, we locate regions
on the surfaces which have a locally stable low variance and the same number of regions with a high
variance.

Step 4: Placing the Kernel Points: In the last step, we place the kernel points at the regions of
low variance (see figure 10.5). Hence, we obtain the number of needed kernel points, as well as the

---

[1]Thanks to A. Streicher for the Matlab visualization tool.

cluster members

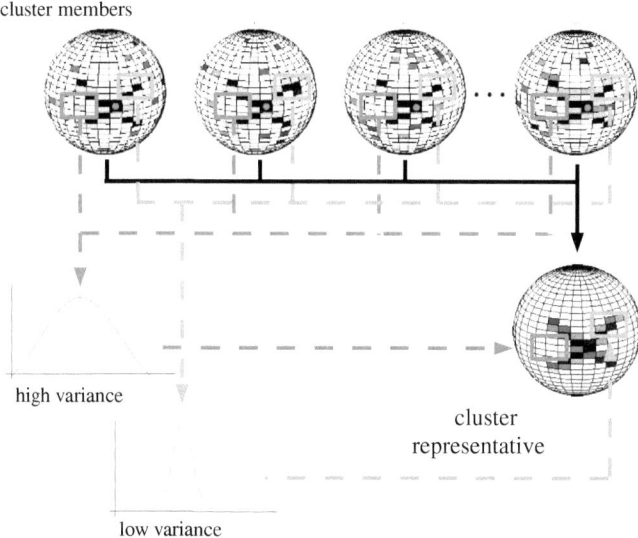

high variance

cluster
representative

low variance

Figure 10.4: Step 3 (toy example): generation of the cluster representative. We compute the variance for each discrete position r, Φ_i, Θ_i over all registered cluster members. Voxels with a low variance (an example for such a voxel is marked in green) are mapped to the representative while voxels with a high variance (an example for such a voxel is marked in red) are set to zero.

corresponding parameters r_i, Φ_i and Θ_i. The regions with high variance are needed later on for the learning of the non-linear mappings.

An overview of the entire procedure is given in algorithm 3. Placing the kernel points in positions of low variance guaranties that the points are actually sensing information which is stable and representative for the cluster while neglecting noise. Since we required that the cluster member have to belong to the same class, the correlation based clustering ensures that the selected points are discriminative. The usage of the unsupervised clustering enables us to uncover the different types of appearance within the variation of a class.

Algorithm 3 Feature selection: np kernel point positions
---
   cluster the labeled input data
   select clusters mostly containing the target or background class
   for all clusters **do**
      register the cluster members
      transform cluster members to spatial domain
      compute voxel-wise variance
      place kernel points in regions of low variance
      obtain r_i, Φ_i and Θ_i
   end for

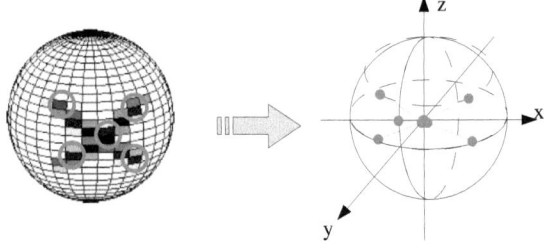

Figure 10.5: Step 4 (toy example): placing of the kernel points at regions of low variance.

10.3.2 Learning the Non-Linear Kernel Mappings

After selecting the positions for the kernel points, we still need the associated non-linear mappings κ_i. This problem appears to be non-trivial, because searching for suitable functions is a variational problem which tend be very difficult to solve. To overcome these difficulties, we turn to well known regression algorithms which describe the variational problem in terms of easier to handle parameter optimization problems.

For our case, we recall that it is feasible enough to draw the mappings κ_i from a rather small set of very simple but essentially non-linear functions, i.e. functions like $\kappa_1(x_1) = x_1^2, \kappa_2(x_2) = x_2^3, \kappa_3(x_3) = x_3^4, \ldots, \kappa_n(x_4) = \sqrt{(x_4)}, \ldots$. Hence, the parameters are the weights of the given mappings. They can be found by a combinatoric search using MMD or SIMBA.

For each feature, we return to the corresponding registered cluster, where we collect the data from the n kernel points as positive labeled training samples (x_i, y_i) for the i-th cluster member and assign $y_i = 1$. The entries of x_i are given by the gray-values at the kernel points.

Additionally, we generate the same number of negative training samples from the cluster members by rotating the kernel such that random kernel points are positioned in also randomly selected regions with high variance. We label these samples by $y_i = -1$. All x_i training samples are combined row-wise in the matrix X and the labels are stored in the vector Y.

Using X, we then construct the matrix K containing all possible combinations of the non-linear mappings κ_i: Given n points and m possible non-linear mappings, each row K_i holds a possible assignment of the κ_i. Without loss of generality, we assume $m = n$. Hence, K contains all possible permutations of the κ_i assignments to the kernel points x_i:

$$\mathbf{K}_i := \left(\kappa_1\left(\mathbf{x}_1\right) \cdot \kappa_2\left(\mathbf{x}_2\right) \cdot \cdots \cdot \kappa_n\left(\mathbf{x}_n\right), \right. \tag{10.9}$$
$$\cdots,$$
$$\left. \kappa_n\left(\mathbf{x}_1\right) \cdot \kappa_{n-1}\left(\mathbf{x}_2\right) \cdot \cdots \cdot \kappa_1\left(\mathbf{x}_n\right) \right). \tag{10.10}$$

Then we apply the fast MMD algorithm (see section 10.1) on K to find the best combination of the mapping given Y. The ranking that is returned by MMD then indicates which feature combination is most suitable. At this point we can then decide to select one or more features with the same kernel constellation but different non-linear mappings from each cluster.

11 Experiments

In the final chapter of the first part, we evaluate the feature methods which were introduced in the previous chapters. We start with the evaluation of the speed and accuracy of our fast correlation in Spherical Harmonics in section 11.1 and the correlation in Vectorial Harmonics in section 11.3.
Section 11.2 evaluates the computational complexity of our features on real world data. Then we use a database of semi-artificial 3D textures (see Appendix A) to perform a series of 3D texture classification (see section 11.4).

11.1 Evaluating $\mathcal{SH}$-Correlation

Unlike previous publications (Makadia and Daniilidis, 2006)(Makadia et al., 2004)(Makadia and Daniilidis, 2003), which only performed a small set of experiments with a fixed number of predefined example rotations, we evaluate our methods with a series of large scale experiments on real word data.
We use the "Princeton Shape Benchmark" (PSB) (see Appendix B) (Shilane et al., 2004) dataset (which contains about 1800 3D objects) for our experiments. If not mentioned otherwise, all experiments have the same basic setup: for each parameter set, we evaluate the error statistics of 100 random rotations of random objects. We generate the rotations over all possible angles $\phi, \psi \in [0, 2\pi[$ and $\theta \in [0, \pi[$ with a resolution of $0.001 \approx 0.1°$. Note that an error of $1° \approx 0.017$. All given error rates are the sums over the errors of all three angles.

Rotating Objects in the Harmonic Domain

In this first series of experiments, we extract a harmonic expansion with a fixed radius around the object center and then rotate this expansion using (3.19).

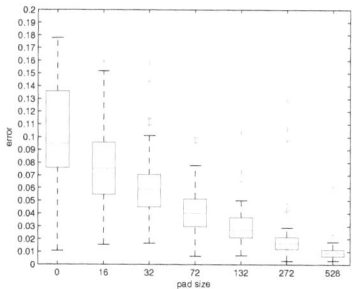

Figure 11.1: Estimation errors with $b = 24$ and increasing pad size p.

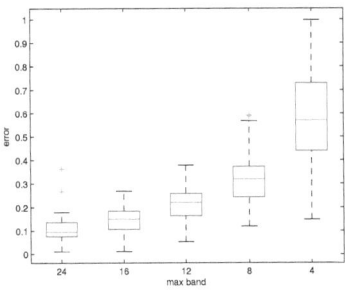 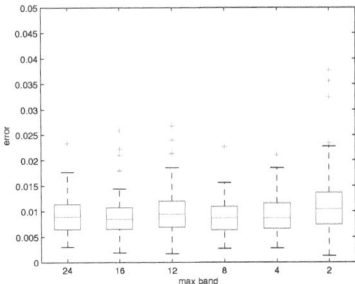

Figure 11.2: Estimation errors with increasing maximum expansions. Left: $p = 0$. Right: $p > 512$ (p is not fix due to the padding to optimal FFT sizes). Note that the experiment with $p = 0, b = 2$ is left out because the result was so poor that it did not fit into the the chosen error scale.

Pad Size: In a first experiment, we are able to show the effect of our padding method on the estimation accuracy. Figure (11.1) clearly shows the correlation of the pad size and the expected error. It is also evident that we are able to achieve a high precision with errors below 1 degree. Hence, the experimental errors are found to be well within the theoretical bounds given in (3.52).

Maximum Band: The next two experiments investigate the practical influence of the maximum expansion band on the estimation errors. Figure (11.2) strongly supports our initial assumption that the original formulation is not able to achieve accurate estimates for low expansions. Our method on the other hand achieves very low error rates even for extremely low expansions with $b = 2$.

Rotational Invariance and Computational Costs: Rotational Invariance and Computational Costs are investigated in the last two experiments (figure (11.3)) of the first series. We rotate the object in $\pi/8$ steps in every angle to show that the correlation maximum is stable and indeed independent of the rotation. The computational complexity is largely dominated by the costs for the inverse FFT, hence growing with the pad size. So accuracy comes at some cost but reasonable accuracy can still be achieved well within 1 second.

Rotating Objects in $\mathbb{R}^3$

The results of figure (11.2) suggest that the maximum expansion band has no influence on the quality of the rotation estimation - of course, this is only true if we are considering input signals that are limited to the very same maximum band. This is very unlikely for very low bands in the case of real data. In order to evaluate the actual influence of the maximum expansion band, we need to rotate the objects in $\mathbb{R}^3$ and extract a second harmonic expansion after the rotation. As mentioned before, the usability of our sinc interpolation approach is limited to correctly sampled (concerning the Sampling Theorem) input signals (also see section 4 for more details on sampling issues). Hence, one must not expect to obtain precise rotation estimates for low band expansions, which act as a low pass filter, of high frequent input signals. Luckily, for most input data, we are not depending on the high frequent components in order to find the maximum correlation. Hence, we can apply a low pass filter (Gaussian) on the input data prior to the harmonic expansion. Figure (11.4) shows the impact of the maximum band and

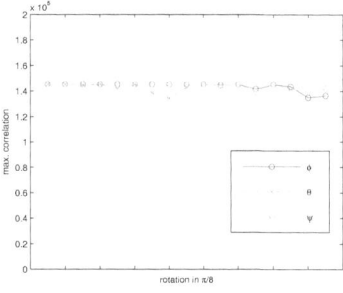 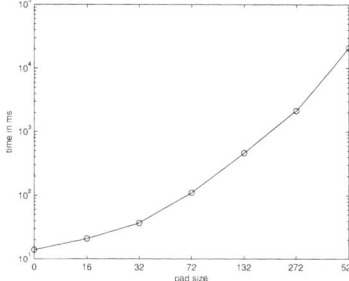

Figure 11.3: Left: Maximum correlation for separate rotations in each angle. Right: Computational costs in ms on a standard 2GHz PC.

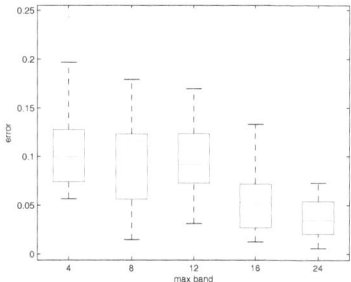 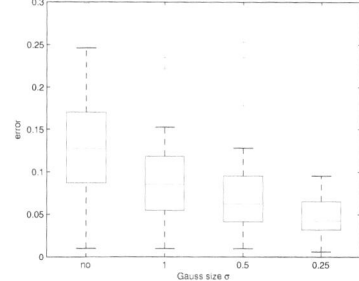

Figure 11.4: Accuracy for rotations in $\mathbb{R}^3$. Left: Influence of the maximum band b, $p > 512$, $\sigma = 0.25$. Right: Correct sampling does matter! Without Gaussian smoothing and with different values for σ, $p > 512$, $b = 24$

smoothing for rotations in $\mathbb{R}^3$. Overall, the estimation results are slightly worse than before, but are still quite reasonable.

11.2 Evaluating the Feature Complexity

We evaluated the computational complexity on dummy volume data. All experiments were conducted on a 3GHz machine with 16 CPU cores and 128GB Ram. However, only a single CPU was used if not noted otherwise.

11.2.1 Complexity of the Spherical Harmonic Transformation

We conducted two experiments to show the complexity of the voxel-wise Spherical Harmonic trans-formation of 3D volume data. The complexity is independent of the actual data and is only influenced by the maximum expansion band (b_{max}) and the data size as shown in figure 11.5.

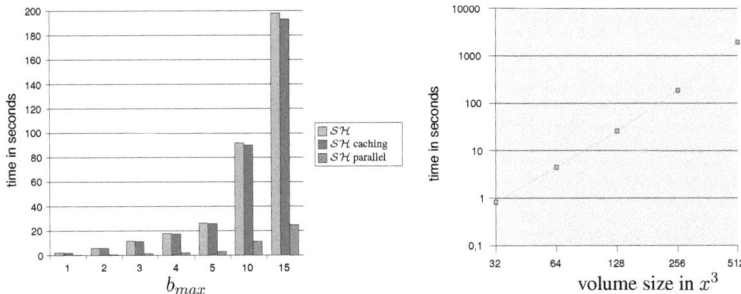

Figure 11.5: **Left:** Computational complexity of the $\mathcal{SH}$ transformation: voxel-wise computation at
radius $r = 10$ on a $(128 \times 128 \times 128)$ test volume. The parallel computation was performed
with 8 cores and shows an almost linear speed-up, while the caching of the $\mathcal{SH}$ coefficients
has only a small effect.

Right: Computational complexity in dependency of the volume size (single core results
with $b_{max} = 5$). The logarithmic increase in the complexity clearly indicates that the
underlying Fourier Transform, which is used for the convolution of the base functions
with the data, is dominating the overall complexity of the harmonic transformation.

11.3 Evaluating $\mathcal{VH}$-Correlation

We use a sample 3D vector field (see figure 11.6) which is rotated around the center of one spherical
patch parameterized by a single radius of $r = 10$.

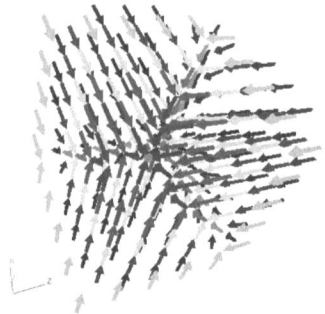

Figure 11.6: Artificial 3D vector field used for the rotation estimation experiments. The red dot indicates the position **x** of the rotation center, at which the spherical test patches have been
extracted.

For each experiment, we evaluate the error statistics of 100 random rotations of this vector field.
We generate the rotations over all possible angles $\varphi, \psi \in [0, 2\pi[$ and $\theta \in [0, \pi[$ with a resolution of
$0.001 \approx 0.1°$. Note that an error of $1° \approx 0.017$. All given error rates are the accumulated errors of all
three angles. Figure 11.7 shows the direct effect of the maximum expansion band b_{max} on the rotation
estimate. But even for expensive "higher band" expansions, we encounter strong outliers and a rather

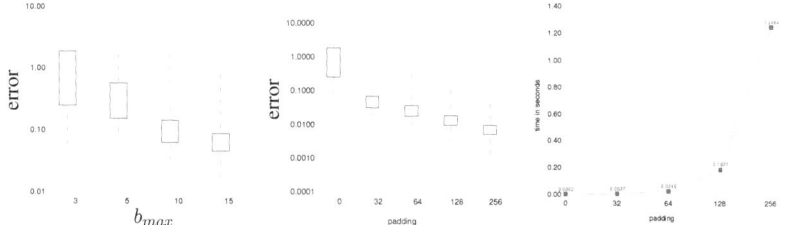

Figure 11.7: **Left:** Accumulated rotation estimation error for increasing b_{max} and without using the Sinc interpolation method ($p = 0$). **Center:** Accumulated rotation estimation error for increasing pad size p of the Sinc interpolation with $b_{max} = 5$. **Right:** Computational complexity for increasing pad size p of the Sinc interpolation with $b_{max} = 5$. The experiments were performed on a standard 2GHz PC, using the FFTW (Frigo and Johnson, 2005) implementation of the inverse FFT.

poor average accuracy.

This can be compensated by our Sinc interpolation approach (3.49): Figure 11.7 shows how we can reduce the rotation estimation error well below $1°$, just by increasing the pad size p. The additional computational costs caused by the padding are also given in figure 11.7.

Summarizing these first experiments, we are able to show that our proposed method is able to provide a fast and accurate rotation estimation even for rather low band expansions, e.g. if we choose $p = 64$ and $b_{max} = 5$, we can expect an average estimation error below $1°$ at a computation time of less than 25ms.

Key Point Detection. In a second series of experiments, we evaluate the performance of our methods in a key point (or object) detection problem on artificial data. Figure 11.8 shows the 3D vector fields of two of our target structures. Our goal is to detect the center of such X- and Y-like shaped bifurcations under arbitrary rotations in larger vector fields. For each target structure, we extract a single patch, parameterized in four different radii with $b_{max} = 3$, at the center of the bifurcations.

Using (4.6), we extract patches with the same parameterization at each point of the test samples and apply our fast, combined (see section 3.4.6) and normalized (3.57) cross-correlation to detect the target structures in the test vector fields. Figures 11.9 and 11.10 show some example test data together with the correlation results.

Figure 11.8: Sample target structures for the detection problem: 3D vector fields of X- and Y-like shaped bifurcations.

It should be noted that the test bifurcations are only similar in terms of a X or Y shape, but not

127

identical to the given target structures. We also rotate the test data in a randomized procedure over all angles.

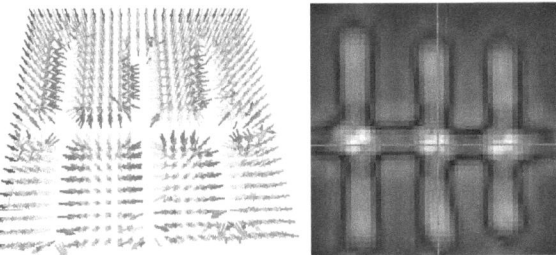

Figure 11.9: **Left:** Sample test data. **Right:** xy-slice of a sample correlation result for the X-bifurcation target. The red cross indicates the position of the maximum correlation value.

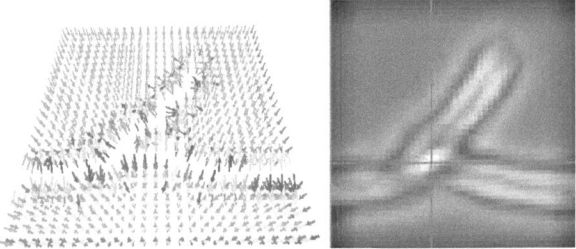

Figure 11.10: **Left:** Sample test data. **Right:** xy-slice of the correlation result for the Y-bifurcation target. The red cross indicates the position of the maximum correlation value.

Applying a threshold of 0.9 to the correlation results, we were able to detect the correct target structures in all of our test samples without false positives.

11.3.1 Complexity of the Vectorial Harmonic Transformation

We also performed the experiment measuring the complexity in dependency of the maximum expansion band (b_{max}) for the voxel-wise Vectorial Harmonic transformation of 3D volume data. Figure 11.11 clearly shows that the complexity of the transformation in the vectorial case is much higher than in the scalar case. This can only be compensated by the parallelization of the transformation.

11.3.2 Complexity of a voxel-wise Feature Extraction

In the final experiment regarding the computational complexity, we evaluated all features on a ($250 \times 250 \times 250$) volume texture sample. We extracted voxel-wise features simultaneously at all voxels. We used a fixed radius of $r = 10$ and evaluated the computation time on a single core with $b_{max} = \{3, 5, 8\}$.

Figure 11.12 illustrates the computation time for all features which is also given in table 11.1. The complexity of the individual features has a wide range: from about 3 seconds for the computation of

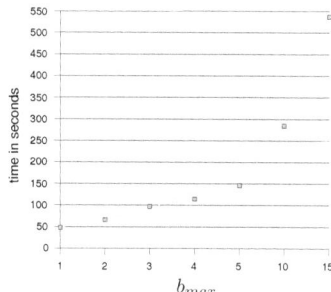

Figure 11.11: Computational complexity of the $\mathcal{VH}$ transformation: voxel-wise computation at radius $r = 10$ on a $(128 \times 128 \times 128)$ test vector field. The computation was performed using 8 cores in parallel.

the simple $2p$-Feature (which is not based on a Spherical Harmonic transformation), to almost 4 hours needed to compute a $4v$-Feature with $b_{max} = 8$ at every voxel of the $(250 \times 250 \times 250)$ volume.

It is obvious that some of the features are too complex to be of practical use in such a setting as presented here. Especially, a computation of the highly specialized np and vp-Features at all voxels and at a high expansion band b_{max} appears to be practically intractable.

However, it turns out that this is not a major drawback in practice: First of all, as figure 11.13 shows, the features are well suited for parallelization, and second, it is usually not necessary to compute such specific features at all 256^3 voxels. Typically, it is very easy to reduce the number of candidate voxels drastically, if one uses the response of "cheap" features to perform a rough pre-segmentation.

Multicore Speed-up: We examined the potential speed-up of a parallelization of the feature computation at the example of the $5p$ (5) feature (see table 11.1). Using 8 instead of a single CPU core, the complexity drops from 6350s (almost 2 hours) to 1700s ($\approx$ 30min). Figure 11.13 shows how the parallelization affects the different computation steps like the $\mathcal{SH}$ transformation, the correlation step or the non-linear transformations and multiplications.

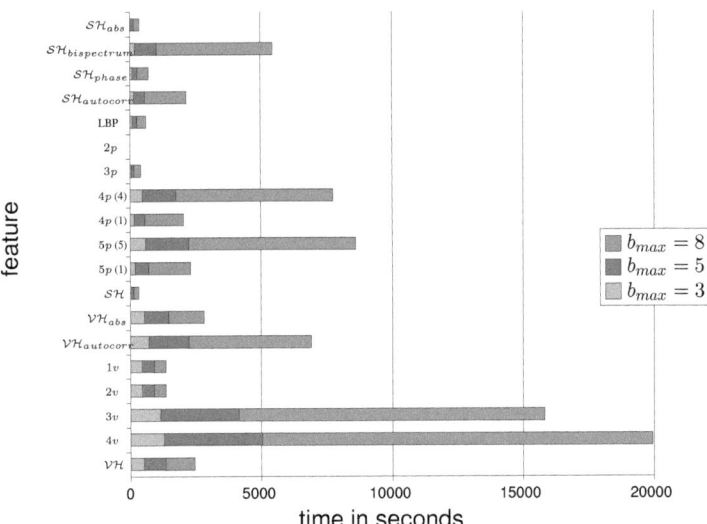

Figure 11.12: Illustrates the computational complexity of the individual features as given in table 11.1. The complexity was measured on a $(250 \times 250 \times 250)$ volume texture sample with $r = 10$ and $b_{max} = \{3, 5, 8\}$ using only a single CPU core. We also give the complexity for the $\mathcal{SH}$ and $\mathcal{VH}$ transformations as reference values. $4p$ (4) indicates that the $4p$-Feature was computed with kernel points in 4 different channels (7.29), whereas $4p$ (1) indicates the fast np-Feature version (7.31), where all kernel points are located in the same channel.

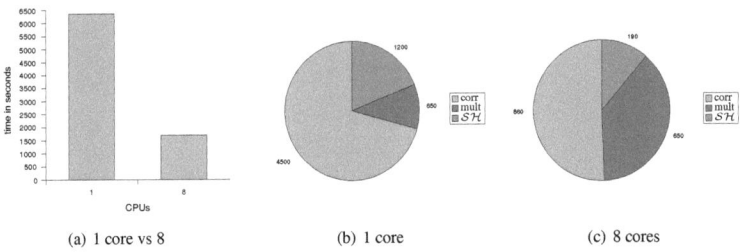

(a) 1 core vs 8   (b) 1 core   (c) 8 cores

Figure 11.13: Comparing the computational complexity of a $5p$-Feature on a single and a 8 core system. (a) Parallelization speed-up. (b) Distribution of the computation time with a single core. (c) Distribution of the computation time at the parallelization to 8 cores.

feature	$b_{max} = 3$	$b_{max} = 5$	$b_{max} = 8$
$\mathcal{SH}_{abs}$	46	102	229
$\mathcal{SH}_{phase}$	190	848	4431
$\mathcal{SH}_{autocorr}$	90	201	441
$\mathcal{SH}_{bispectrum}$	157	422	1596
LBP	87	175	365
$2p$	3	3	3
$3p$	50	114	257
$4p$ (4)	470	1290	5965
$4p$ (1)	156	416	1468
$5p$ (5)	604	1624	6358
$5p$ (1)	201	506	1589
$\mathcal{SH}$	40	93	198
$\mathcal{VH}_{abs}$	558	896	1359
$\mathcal{VH}_{autocorr}$	719	1515	4655
$1v$	455	455	455
$2v$	455	455	455
$3v$	1146	3003	11671
$4v$	1283	3751	14905
$\mathcal{VH}$	513	823	1105

Table 11.1: Computational complexity of the individual features as illustrated in figure 11.12. The complexity was measured on a $(250 \times 250 \times 250)$ volume texture sample with $r = 10$ and $b_{max} = \{3, 5, 8\}$ using only a single CPU core.

11.4 Evaluating 3D Texture Discrimination

In a final experiment, we evaluated the texture discrimination performance of our proposed features. The experiments were conducted on our artificial 3D volume texture database (see appendix A for details on this database).

Using the SIMBA feature selection algorithm (see section 10.2), we extracted the top 10 parameter

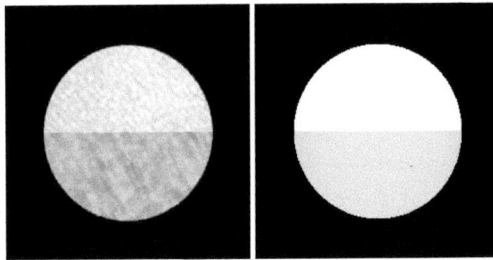

Figure 11.14: Example 3D texture database entry. **Left:** the xy-slice shows how two randomly selected textures are combined in one test sample. **Right:** ground-truth labeling.

combinations for each of our features. Scalar features were expanded to the 5th band, vectorial features were computed on the gradient field of the scalar input data and expanded to the 3rd band.
Given these feature vectors, we used a voxel-wise SVM classification (see chapter 13) to evaluate the 3D texture segmentation performance of the individual features.

feature	rotations	rotations and gray-scale changes
$S\mathcal{H}_{abs}$	91%	82%
$S\mathcal{H}_{phase}$	90%	90%
$S\mathcal{H}_{autocorr}$	93%	94%
$S\mathcal{H}_{bispectrum}$	94%	89%
LBP	91%	91%
$2p$	85%	78%
$3p$	86%	79%
$4p$ (4)	93%	93%
$4p$ (1)	92%	92%
$5p$ (5)	91%	91%
$5p$ (1)	91%	91%
$\mathcal{VH}_{abs}$	94%	94%
$\mathcal{VH}_{autocorr}$	**95%**	**95%**
$3v$	91%	91%
$4v$	93%	93%

Table 11.2: 3D texture segmentation benchmark. Voxel-vise error rate in percent. $4p$ (4) indicates that the $4p$-Feature was computed with kernel points in 4 different channels(7.29), whereas $4p$ (1) indicates the fast np-Feature version (7.31), where all kernel points are located in the same channel.

Our evaluation clearly shows that those features that are not invariant towards gray-scale changes strongly suffer in the case of such changes. The vectorial features appear to be very stable, however this comes at the cost of higher computational complexity (see table 11.1).

The highly specific np and vp-Features are not able to outperform the other approaches. These features are probably too selective to be able to describe the large variations in the textures by just 10 parameter settings. However, these features anyway have been designed for key point and object detections (see section 11.3) rather than texture description.

Part II

Learning

12 Introduction

Following the design of our general *framework* (see section 1.2), we combine the local invariant features from part I with learning techniques. Hence, in the second part of this thesis we focus on learning methods.

Most of our learning problems can be solved sufficiently by using standard, "off the shelf" algorithms like Support Vector Machines (SVM) (see chapter 13) or Markov Random Fields (MRF) (see chapter 15). However, the classification speed of these methods is in most cases far to low to meet the requirements of our applications. Therefore, we introduced several speed-up techniques for SVMs in (Zapién et al., 2006), (Fehr et al., 2007) and (Fehr and Zapién, 2007) as well as for MRFs (Petersen et al., 2008).

Structure of Part II   The second part is structured as follows: first, we give a general introduction to learning techniques in section 12.1 and briefly review some notable related work in section 12.2. Next, we take a closer look at Support Vector Machines in chapter 13 before we introduce our SVM speed-up algorithms in chapter 14.

Chapter 15 then introduces Markov Random Fields and discusses the most common inference methods, including "Generalized Belief Propagation" which we speed-up in chapter 16.

Finally, we present some benchmarking experiments for all of our speed-up algorithms in chapter 17.

12.1 Learning Decision Functions

We follow the initial definition of general classification problems from section 2.1: given an arbitrary set of patterns $\{X_i | X_i \in \mathcal{X}, i = 1, \ldots, n\}$, we are looking for some function $\Gamma : X_i \to y_i$ which denotes each pattern with a semantic label $y_i \in Y$ from the category space $Y \subset \mathbb{Z}$. Y holds the semantic meaning (categorization) from the real world. Each category y_i defines an equivalence class.

The actual task of assigning the label y is called classification and Γ is often referred to as decision function or classifier.

The objective is to learn Γ from a set $\mathcal{X}_{train} \subset \mathcal{X}$ of training examples. The two most important properties of a Γ, which are derived from (2.1), are **separability** and **generalization** ability.

Separability is the obvious requirement that the decision function Γ should classify all samples correctly. Given a training set $\mathcal{X}_{train}$, this results in (2.1):

$$X_1, X_2 \in \mathcal{X}_{train} : \quad X_1 \sim_y X_2 \Leftrightarrow \Gamma(X_1) = \Gamma(X_2)$$

The separability is usually measured by the so-called training error, where all m training samples are classified:

$$\textbf{Training Error:} \quad Err_{train} \quad := \quad \frac{m}{\sum_{i=0}^{m} \delta\left(\Gamma(X_i) - y_i\right)}, \tag{12.1}$$

$$\text{with} \quad \delta(x) \quad := \quad \begin{cases} 1 & x \neq 0 \\ 0 & \text{otherwise} \end{cases} \tag{12.2}$$

However, a low training error does not guarantee a good overall classification performance. The main problem is that the number of training examples is usually much lower than the number of possible samples. Hence, a good classifier has to correctly classify not only the known samples correctly, but also the unknown. This is called **generalization ability**.

If the training causes Γ to be dominated by the training samples in such a way that the training error is very low but the generalization is poor, Γ is a so-called **overfitting** solution which we try to avoid in any case.

In order to estimate the generalization ability of Γ, one usually splits the available data into fixed and strictly separated training and evaluation (test) sets. Another statistically valid option is the so-called cross validation (Kohavi, 1995).

Cross Validation: The advantage of cross validation is that this algorithm takes all available training vectors into account when estimating the quality of Γ. The basic idea is to iteratively and randomly split the set of n available samples $\mathcal{X}_{train}$ into $m = \frac{n}{k}$ pairs of sets randomly. Each pair consists of a training set $\mathcal{X}_{train}$ of size $l = n - k$ and a test set $\mathcal{X}_{test}$ of size k:

$$\forall \delta = 1, ..., m : \quad \mathcal{X}_{train}^{l_\delta} \bigcup \mathcal{X}_{test}^{k_\delta} = \mathcal{X} \quad \text{with } \mathcal{X}_{train}^{l_\delta} \bigcap \mathcal{X}_{test}^{k_\delta} = \varnothing$$

For all pairs, a model is trained and the samples from $\mathcal{X}_{test}$ are classified. This leads to the test error of each pair

$$\text{Err}_{test}^{k_\delta}(\Gamma_\delta) = \frac{1}{k} \sum_{(\mathbf{x}_1, y_i) \in \mathcal{X}_{test}^{k_\delta}} \frac{k}{\sum_{i=0}^{k} \delta\Big(\Gamma(X_i) - y_i\Big)} \tag{12.3}$$

Averaging over all test errors gives an approximation of the model error rate

$$\text{Err}_{cross_m} := \frac{1}{m} \sum_{\delta=1}^{m} \text{Err}_{test}^{k_\delta}(\Gamma_\delta) \tag{12.4}$$

The quality of the approximation by Err_{cross_m} depends on the choice of k. A small k reduces the negative bias on the estimate but increases computation time. The best results can be expected for the most expensive case, called Leave One Out (LOO) (Kohavi, 1995), where k is set to 1.

Supervised vs. Unsupervised Learning: So far, we implicitly assumed that we have a labeled training set, where each data sample $(X_i, y_i) \in \{\mathcal{X} \times Y\}$ comes with its label. Theses cases are called supervised learning. The "correct" label is usually provided by a human expert, which makes the generation of suitable training sets expensive. Both, SVM and MRF are supervised learning techniques.

We also face situations where no labeling of the data is available or where we apply learning techniques to discover regularity in the structure of the training data. Theses cases are called unsupervised or clustering learning algorithms. These methods are not covered in this part, please refer to chapter 10, where we apply clustering methods for the data driven (unsupervised) selection of features.

12.2 Related Work

The selection of a suitable learning algorithm from the almost countless number of available methods is not an easy task. While we choose to use two of the most popular algorithms, SVMs and MRFs, we neglect other powerful methods. In this section, we briefly motivate our choice. Please refer to sections 14 and 16 for reviews of related work on SVM and MRF speed-up.

The main requirement for the application of learning algorithms within our *framework* (see section 1.2), besides accuracy and speed, is flexibility. We need learning techniques that can easily be adapted to new problem settings without expert user interference.

The choice to use Markov Random Fields for contextual learning tasks does not need much motivation - there are simply not many alternatives available. The only notable methods are from (Lampert and Blaschko, 2008), who tried to embed the contextual learning directly into the SVM. But this approach is by far less flexible than MRFs.

The choice for the Support Vector Machines is not that obvious: even though SVMs are one of the most popular methods and meet the flexibility criteria much better than e.g. traditionally used Neuronal Networks (Bishop, 2006) (because SVMs guarantee the global optimum solution), there are at least two prominent alternatives: Boosting (Schapire, 2002) and Random Forests (Breiman, 2001).
For many applications, both algorithms outperform SVMs in terms of classification speed at equal accuracy. So why do we use SVMs? We actually implemented Boosting and Random Forest algorithms and performed a series of experiments within our *framework*. Both are not able to meet the accuracy of the SVM. The main reason for the weaker performance is specific to our problem: both methods use an ensemble of "weak decision functions". This makes them fast but also causes problems within our *framework*: the features we extract prior to the classification step are usually highly correlated. This makes it very hard to split the overall decision function into an ensemble of "weak" subproblems which are limited to only a few features at a time. The SVM on the other hand, generates a global solution which is able to separate these problems.
A possible solution would be to uncorrelate the data via (kernelized) PCA or LDA (Schölkopf and Smola, 2002) prior to the classification, but this would annihilate the speed advantage.

13 Support Vector Machines (SVM)

In this chapter, we briefly review the basic concepts of Support Vector Machines and introduce some important ideas, methods and formulations we are utilizing in chapter 14 to derive a fast SVM classification algorithm.

The reader may refer to (Schölkopf and Smola, 2002) for a comprehensive background on SVMs.

13.1 Introduction

Support Vector Machines (SVM) were introduced in the mid nineties by (Cortes and Vapnik, 1995) and turned out to be a very efficient and easy to handle classifier which has become the method of choice in many areas of classification and machine learning.

SVMs are based on the principles from statistical learning theory (Vapnik, 1995) which lead to the formulation of a supervised two class maximum margin learning algorithm. In the trivial case, the set of labeled training vectors given as

$$(\mathbf{x}_1, y_1), ..., (\mathbf{x}_n, y_n) \in \mathbb{R}^d \times \{-1, +1\}$$

is **linear separable**. The SVM computes a decision function in form of a hyperplane in the feature space $\mathbb{R}^d$, which separates the feature-vectors $\mathbf{x}_i$ of different classes with the largest possible margin. Figure 13.2 shows on a SVM solution for a typical toy problem.

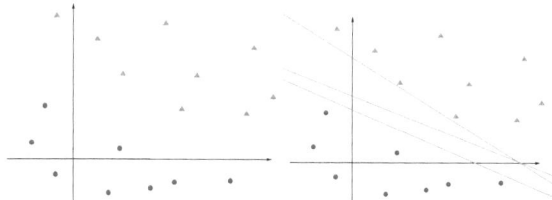

Figure 13.1: 2D two-class toy problem (**left**) and possible solutions for the separating hyperplane (**right**).

The separating hyperplane is specified by a normal vector $\mathbf{w} \in \mathbb{R}^d$, an offset $b \in \mathbb{R}$ (see figure 13.2) and the set of vectors $\mathbf{x}$ which hold:

$$\mathbf{w} \cdot \mathbf{x} + b = 0. \tag{13.1}$$

Given such a hyperplane as decision function Γ, the classification of a feature vector $\mathbf{x}_i$ with label

$y_i \in \{-1, +1\}$ is obtained via:

$$\Gamma_{svm}(\mathbf{x}_i) \quad = \quad \sigma(\langle \mathbf{w}, \mathbf{x} + b \rangle) = y_i \tag{13.2}$$

$$\text{with} \tag{13.3}$$

$$\sigma(x) \quad := \quad \begin{cases} 1 & \text{for } x \geq 0 \\ -1 & \text{otherwise} \end{cases}. \tag{13.4}$$

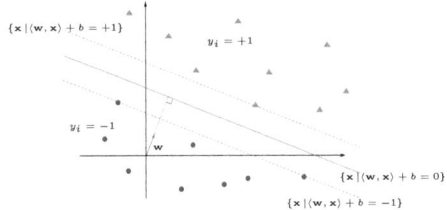

Figure 13.2: The Hyperplane with largest margin separates the two classes.

13.2 Primal Optimization Problem

The classification of unknown samples using (13.2) is fairly simple - but the question remains how we can actually learn the hyperplane (in form of $\mathbf{w}$ and b) from a set of labeled training samples. Given such a set of m training samples with $(\mathbf{x}_i, y_i) \in \mathbb{R}^d \times \{-1, +1\}, i \in \{1, \ldots, m\}$, the hyperplane is retrieved via a convex optimization process.

Considering two samples $\mathbf{x}_1, \mathbf{x}_2$, one of each class

$$\langle \mathbf{w}, \mathbf{x}_1 \rangle + b \quad = \quad 1 \tag{13.5}$$

$$\langle \mathbf{w}, \mathbf{x}_2 \rangle + b \quad = \quad -1, \tag{13.6}$$

which are located at the margin boarders, the margin width is normalized to

$$\langle \mathbf{w}, \mathbf{x}_1 - \mathbf{x}_2 \rangle + b = 2. \tag{13.7}$$

This normalization is then used to re-formulate the maximization of the margin in terms of a minimization of $\|w\|$ considering:

$$\langle \frac{\mathbf{w}}{\|w\|}, \mathbf{x}_1 - \mathbf{x}_2 \rangle + b = \frac{2}{\|w\|}. \tag{13.8}$$

This leads to the following convex optimization problem for the computation of the optimal hyperplane, which is only constrained by the obvious condition that all training samples have to be classified correctly:

$$\underset{\mathbf{w} \in \mathcal{H}, b \in \mathbb{R}}{\text{minimize}} \quad \tau(\mathbf{w}) = \tfrac{1}{2} \|\mathbf{w}\|^2, \tag{13.9}$$

$$\text{subject to} \quad y_i(\langle \mathbf{x}_i, \mathbf{w} \rangle + b) \geq 1, \ i = 1, .., m,. \tag{13.10}$$

Following (Nocedal and Wright, 1999) and (Schölkopf and Smola, 2002), the constrained optimization problem in 13.10 can be transfered to a *Lagrangian* optimization process with *Lagrange* multipliers α:

$$L(\mathbf{w}, b, \boldsymbol{\alpha}) = \frac{1}{2}\|\mathbf{w}\|^2 - \sum_{i=1}^{m} \alpha_i(y_i(\langle \mathbf{x}_i, \mathbf{w} \rangle + b) - 1). \tag{13.11}$$

The KKT conditions for $Lagrangian$ processes state that the gradient of the original optimization variables must be equal to zero:

$$\frac{\partial}{\partial b}\mathcal{L}(\mathbf{w}, b, \boldsymbol{\alpha}) = 0 \quad \text{and} \tag{13.12}$$

$$\frac{\partial}{\partial \mathbf{w}}\mathcal{L}(\mathbf{w}, b, \boldsymbol{\alpha}) = 0. \tag{13.13}$$

which leads to the following constraints in (13.11):

$$\sum_{i=1}^{m} \alpha_i y_i = 0 \quad \text{and} \tag{13.14}$$

$$\mathbf{w} = \sum_{i=1}^{m} \alpha_i y_i \mathbf{x}_i. \tag{13.15}$$

Equation 13.11 also nicely illustrates the concept of Support Vectors: the solution to $\mathbf{w}$ is found in the span of the training samples (13.15), where only the samples $\mathbf{x}_i$ with $\alpha_i \neq 0$ contribute to the modeling of the decision function. These $\mathbf{x}_i$ are called **Support Vectors (SV)**.

The offset b is then computed as:

$$b = \frac{1}{2}\left(min\left\{ \langle \mathbf{x}_i, \mathbf{w} \rangle \right\} + max\left\{ \langle \mathbf{x}_i, \mathbf{w} \rangle \right\} \right). \tag{13.16}$$

13.3 Dual Optimization Problem

By substituting (13.14) and (13.15) into the primal Lagrangian formulation (13.11), one can eliminate the primal variables $\mathbf{w}$ and b, obtaining a dual problem which is usually solved in practice since it only depends on the sample vectors:

$$\underset{\boldsymbol{\alpha} \in \mathbb{R}^m}{\text{maximize}} \quad W(\boldsymbol{\alpha}) = \sum_{i=1}^{m} \alpha_i - \frac{1}{2}\sum_{i,j=1}^{m} \alpha_i \alpha_j y_i y_j \langle \mathbf{x}_i, \mathbf{x}_j \rangle, \tag{13.17}$$

$$\text{subject to} \quad \alpha_i \geq 0, \ i = 1, ..., m, \tag{13.18}$$

$$\sum_{i=1}^{m} \alpha_i y_i = 0. \tag{13.19}$$

Using (13.17), the hyperplane decision function (13.2) is re-formulated as:

$$\Gamma(\mathbf{x}) = sign\left(\sum_{i=1}^{m} y_i \alpha_i \langle \mathbf{x}_i, \mathbf{x} \rangle + b \right). \tag{13.20}$$

Figure 13.2 shows a solution for the toy example in Figure 13.1. The visualization also illustrates one of the key properties of SVMs: the final decision function only depends the few initial training samples which directly lie on the margin boundary.

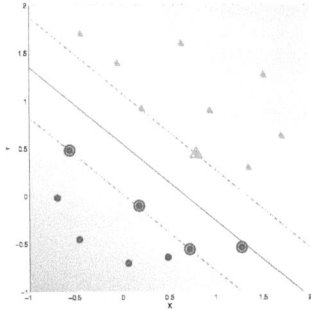

Figure 13.3: Visialization of a two-class classification problem with a linear soft margin solution where the Support Vectors $\mathbf{x}_i$ with $\alpha_i \neq 0$ have been marked.

13.4 Soft Margin SVM

In practice, cases where the classification problem is so simple that the classes can be separated by a linear decision function are very rare. Hence, the SVM formulation given in (13.17 and 13.20) is not powerful enough to solve most of the classification problems occurring in real world applications. Basically, there are two strategies to extend the original formulation in order to cope with this problem: the introduction of non-linear SVMs (see section 13.5) and the introduction of a so-called soft margin SVM.

One property of the original formulation is making it difficult to obtain solutions for the linear decision function: this constraint $\sum_{i=1}^{m} \alpha_i y_i = 0$ in (13.17), which requires that all training samples have to be classified correctly. The obvious consequence is that a single outlier can dominate the entire solution.

The solution to this problem is the formulation of a soft margin SVM, which weakens the original hard constraint and allows solutions where not all training samples are classified correctly. This can be achieved via the introduction of a penalty term in form of a slack variable ξ.

For a two-class problem, the primal optimization problem with slack variables is then defined as:

$$\underset{\mathbf{w} \in \mathcal{H}, b \in \mathbb{R}, \boldsymbol{\xi} \in \mathbb{R}^m}{\text{minimize}} \quad \tau(\mathbf{w}, \boldsymbol{\xi}) = \tfrac{1}{2} \|\mathbf{w}\|^2 + \sum_{i=1}^{m} C_i \xi_i, \qquad (13.21)$$

$$\text{subject to} \quad y_i(\langle \mathbf{x}_i, \mathbf{w} \rangle + b) \geq 1 - \xi_i, \ i = 1, .., m, \qquad (13.22)$$

$$\xi_i \geq 0, \ i = 1, .., m. \qquad (13.23)$$

Again, using (13.14) and (13.15) leads to the dual formulation:

$$\underset{\boldsymbol{\alpha} \in \mathbb{R}^m}{\text{maximize}} \quad W(\boldsymbol{\alpha}) = \sum_{i=1}^{m} \alpha_i - \tfrac{1}{2} \sum_{i,j=1}^{m} \alpha_i \alpha_j y_i y_j \langle \mathbf{x}_i, \mathbf{x}_j \rangle, \qquad (13.24)$$

$$\text{subject to} \quad 0 \leq \alpha_i \leq C_i, \ i = 1, ..., m, \qquad (13.25)$$

$$\sum_{i=1}^{m} \alpha_i y_i = 0. \qquad (13.26)$$

The decision function remains as in (13.20), but the computation of the threshold b has to be adapted

(Keerthi et al., 1999):

$$b = \frac{1}{2}\left(\min_{i \in I_0 \cup I_1 \cup I_2} \left\{ \langle \mathbf{x}_i, \mathbf{w} \rangle \right\} + \max_{i \in I_0 \cup I_3 \cup I_3} \left\{ \langle \mathbf{x}_i, \mathbf{w} \rangle \right\} \right),$$ (13.27)

where,

$$
\begin{align}
I_0 &= \{i | 0 < \alpha_i < C_i\}; & (13.28)\\
I_1 &= \{i | y_i = 1, \alpha_i = 0\}; & (13.29)\\
I_2 &= \{i | y_i = -1, \alpha_i = C_i\}; & (13.30)\\
I_3 &= \{i | y_i = 1, \alpha_i = C_i\}; & (13.31)\\
I_4 &= \{i | y_i = -1, \alpha_i = 0\}. & (13.32)
\end{align}
$$

13.5 Non-Linear SVM

The introduction of the soft margin SVM (13.24) solves only a small portion of the separability problem by allowing the negligence of outliers. This has a very positive effect on the generalization capabilities (see 12.1) of the model, but does not solve the general problem that SVMs are bound to linear decision functions.

This can be solved by the introduction of non-linear SVMs. However, the non-linearity of the decision function cannot be embedded directly to the strictly linear formulation of the SVM. Instead, the feature vectors are mapped into some higher dimensional Hilbert space $\mathcal{H}$, using some non-linear function

$$\Psi(\mathbf{x}) : \mathbb{R}^n \rightarrow \mathcal{H}.$$ (13.33)

Ψ is chosen such that the classes can be separated in $\mathcal{H}$ by the original linear SVM decision function. Hence, one can apply the original linear decision function in $\mathcal{H}$:

$$\Gamma(\mathbf{x}) = sign\left(\sum_{i=1}^{m} y_i \alpha_i \langle \Psi(\mathbf{x}), \Psi(\mathbf{x}_i) \rangle + b \right).$$ (13.34)

Neither the determination of an appropriate function Ψ nor computations in the space $\mathcal{H}$ via $\Psi(\mathbf{x}_i)$ are usually simple tasks. To avoid these difficulties, one uses techniques often referred to as "kernel-methods":

Taking a close look at (13.34) reveals that the only computation that has to be performed in $\mathcal{H}$ is the evaluation of the **inner products** $\langle \Psi(\mathbf{x}), \Psi(\mathbf{x}_i) \rangle$. These products measure the distances, or more generally spoken the similarities, between the test samples $\mathbf{x}$ and the Support Vectors $\mathbf{x}_i$. So, rather than looking for some mapping Ψ, it is adequate to find an analogous equivalence measure

$$k(\mathbf{x}, \mathbf{x}') = \langle x, x' \rangle = \langle \Psi(\mathbf{x}), \Psi(\mathbf{x}') \rangle.$$ (13.35)

in $\mathcal{H}$. $k(\mathbf{x}, \mathbf{x}_i)$ is referred to as **kernel function** or simply as **kernel**. In the linear case, this is exactly the inner product.

One can simply plug a kernel (13.35) into the original formulation (13.34) and obtain a potentially non-linear decision function:

$$\Gamma(\mathbf{x}) = sign\left(\sum_{i=1}^{m} y_i \alpha_i k(\mathbf{x}, \mathbf{x}_i) + b \right),$$ (13.36)

with the threshold b defined as:

$$b = \frac{1}{2} \left(\min_{i \in I_0 \cup I_1 \cup I_2} \left\{ k(\mathbf{x}_i, \mathbf{w}) \right\} + \max_{i \in I_0 \cup I_3 \cup I_3} \left\{ k(\mathbf{x}_i, \mathbf{w}) \right\} \right), \tag{13.37}$$

where the indices I_k are defined as in (13.28).

The embedding of the non-linear mapping by substitution of the initial dot-product with a kernel function is usually referred to as the "**Kernel Trick**", which is also directly applied to the SVM training process:

$$\underset{\boldsymbol{\alpha} \in \mathbb{R}^m}{\text{maximize}} \quad W(\boldsymbol{\alpha}) = \sum_{i=1}^{m} \alpha_i - \frac{1}{2} \sum_{i,j=1}^{m} \alpha_i \alpha_j y_i y_j k(\mathbf{x}_i, \mathbf{x}_j), \tag{13.38}$$

$$\text{subject to} \quad 0 \leq \alpha_i \leq C_i, \; i = 1, ..., m, \tag{13.39}$$

$$\sum_{i=1}^{m} \alpha_i y_i = 0. \tag{13.40}$$

The remaining question is, how the actual kernel functions should be constructed.

13.5.1 Kernel Functions

Theoretically, the only restriction on kernels is that the eigenvalues have to satisfy $\lambda \geq 0$. Thus, k has to be *semi positive definite*. In general, k is a kernel if and only if k holds $\sum_{i,j=1}^{m} \alpha_i \alpha_j k(\mathbf{x}_i, \mathbf{x}_j) \geq 0$. This is stated by the Mercer theorem (Schölkopf and Smola, 2002):

Mercer Theorem :
$k(\mathbf{x}_i, \mathbf{x}_j) = \langle \Phi(\mathbf{x}_i), \Phi(\mathbf{x}_j) \rangle$ iff for arbitrary $g(\mathbf{x})$ with $\int g(\mathbf{x})^2 d\mathbf{x} < \infty$ holds:

$$\int k(\mathbf{x}_i, \mathbf{x}_j) g(\mathbf{x}_i) g(\mathbf{x}_j) d\mathbf{x}_i d\mathbf{x}_j \geq 0. \tag{13.41}$$

The Mercer theorem guarantees the convexity of the resulting optimization problem and that the kernels fulfill the triangle inequality. For $\mathbf{x} \in \mathbb{R}^n$ there are several standard kernels (Schölkopf and Smola, 2002):

Linear

$$k(\mathbf{x}, \mathbf{x}') = \langle \mathbf{x}, \mathbf{x}' \rangle \tag{13.42}$$

Polynomial

$$k(\mathbf{x}, \mathbf{x}') = \langle \mathbf{x}, \mathbf{x}' \rangle^d \tag{13.43}$$

Gaussian or Radial Basis Function (RBF)

$$k(\mathbf{x}, \mathbf{x}') = exp \left(-\frac{\|\mathbf{x} - \mathbf{x}'\|^2}{2\sigma^2} \right) \tag{13.44}$$

Sigmoid

$$k(\mathbf{x}, \mathbf{x}') = tanh(\kappa \langle \mathbf{x}, \mathbf{x}' \rangle + \vartheta) \tag{13.45}$$

Histogram Intersection

$$k(\mathbf{x}, \mathbf{x}') = |\mathbf{x} - \mathbf{x}'|$$
(13.46)

The Gaussian kernel, also known as Radial Basis Function (RBF), proposed by (Boser et al., 1992), (Guyon et al., 1993) and (Vapnik, 1995) is usually the first choice because it combines good performance with a strong theoretical foundation. Additionally, we also use the Histogram Intersection kernel.

(Schölkopf and Smola, 2002) showed that the RBF-kernel is equivalent to the dot product of elements in an infinite dimensional space, while the Histogram Intersection kernel implements a $\mathbb{L}^1$-norm.

13.5.2 Example

To show the capacity of the kernel trick, we illustrate a toy example in Figure 13.4. It is easy to see that there is no hyperplane in the original space that can separate all training samples. If we try to adjust a

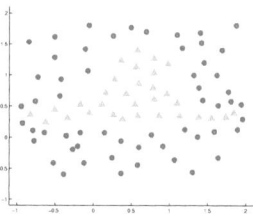

Figure 13.4: Example of a two-class problem without linear solution.

soft margin solution to this problem, a result like the one shown in Figure 13.5 would be obtained.

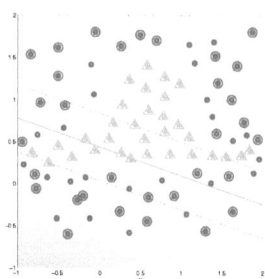

Figure 13.5: Two-class problem with the best adjusted hyperplane

Finally, a non-linear solution to the problem is shown in Figure 13.6, where a Gaussian kernel is able to properly separate the training samples.

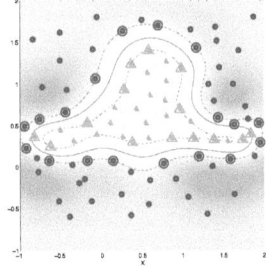

Figure 13.6: Solution for a two-class problem with Gaussian Kernel.

13.6 Multi-Class SVM

Originally, the SVM is only capable of solving two-class problems, but there are different strategies to extend SVMs to muti-class problems (Hsu and Lin, 2001).

One vs. One If there are n classes, $\binom{n}{2}$ binary classifiers are trained pairwise. For classification, vectors are tested in all models giving a probability of belonging to a class. The following is an example of a one vs. one classifier.

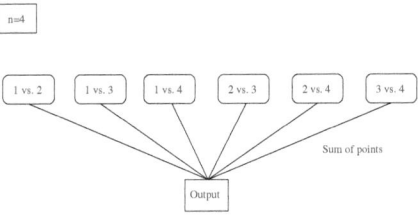

Figure 13.7: One-vs.-one classifier for 4 classes

One vs. Rest If there are n classes, n two-class classifiers are trained, where one class is differentiated from all the others. New samples are tested in all models and the results are compared. The following is an example of a one vs. rest classifier.

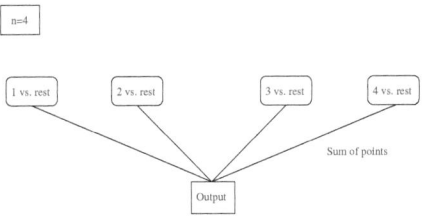

Figure 13.8: One-vs.-rest classifier for 4 classes

14 Speeding Up SVM Classification

In this chapter, we derive a very fast algorithm for the SVM classification of huge datasets. Our original approach of this method was published in (Zapién et al., 2006) and later extended in (Fehr et al., 2007). Here, we only present the theoretical background of the entire approach and show its application within the context of this thesis - please refer to (Fehr and Zapién, 2007) for an in-depth coverage of the quite "tricky" technical details of the actual implementation.

In terms of classification-speed, SVMs are still outperformed by many standard classifiers when it comes to the classification of large problems. For a non-linear kernel function k, the classification function can be written as in Eq. (14.1). Thus, the classification complexity lies in $\Omega(n)$ for a problem with n SVs. However, for linear problems, the classification function has the form of Eq. (14.2), allowing classification in $\Omega(1)$ by computing the dot product with the normal vector $\mathbf{w}$ of the hyperplane. In addition, the SVM has the problem that the complexity of a SVM model always scales with the most difficult samples, forcing an increase in the number of Support Vectors.

However, we observed that many large scale problems can easily be divided in a large set of rather simple subproblems and only a few difficult ones. Following this assumption, we propose a classification method based on a tree whose nodes mostly consist of linear SVMs.

$$\Gamma_{non-linear}(\mathbf{x}) = \text{sign} \left(\sum_{i=1}^{m} y_i \alpha_i k \left(\mathbf{x}_i, \mathbf{x} \right) + b \right) \tag{14.1}$$

$$\Gamma_{linear}(\mathbf{x}) = \text{sign} \left(\langle \mathbf{w}, \mathbf{x} \rangle + b \right) \tag{14.2}$$

This way, each node in the decision tree will contain a decision hyperplane, and the classification complexity only depends on the number of nodes. The classification is then computed with the dot product of a test sample with the orthogonal vector to the corresponding hyperplane of each node.

The remainder of this chapter is structured as follows: first, we review some related speed-up algorithms in section 14.1. Then, in Section 14.2 we introduce the proposed algorithm and give an extensive example. Finally, we take an in-depth look at the theoretical pitfalls of the algorithm and their solutions in section 14.3.

14.1 Related Work

There have been various approaches to speed-up the SVM classification time. We review the most prominent approaches known from literature:

Direct reduction of number of SVs. (Burges and Schölkopf, 1997) proposed a method to approximate $\mathbf{w}$ by a $\mathbf{w}'$ which can also be expressed by a list of vectors associated with corresponding coefficients α_i. However, the method for determining the reduced set is computationally very expensive. Later, (Downs et al., 2001) developed a method to identify and discard unnecessary SVs - especially those SVs that linearly depend on other SVs - while leaving the SVM decision unchanged. A reduction in SVs as high as 40.96% has been reported.

Indirect reduction of the number of SVs by reducing the size of the quadratic problem (QP). This method called *RSVM* (Reduced Support Vector Machines) was proposed by (Lin and Lin, 2003). It preselects a subset of training samples as support vectors and solves a smaller QP. The authors reported that RSVM needs much less computation time and memory usage than standard SVMs. A comparative study on RSVM and SVM by (Lin and Lin, 2003) showed that standard SVM possesses higher generalization ability, while RSVM may be suitable in very large training problems or those provlems that have a large portion of training samples becoming SVs.

Reduction of the number of vector components. (Lin H. and L., 2005) proposed a reduction of the feature space using principal component analysis (PCA) and Recursive Feature Elimination (RFE).

Enlarging margins in Perceptron Decision Trees. (Bennett et al., 2000) experimentally proved that inducing large margins into decision trees with linear decision functions improved the generalization ability. Their method relies on several parameters that have to be tuned in order to achieve satisfactory results.

Wavelet approximation of the SVM. (Kropatsch W., 2005) developed an approximation of a SVM decision function for face classification. This can be achieved by an over-complete Haar wavelet transformation of the raw data using a set of rectangles with constant gray-level values, allowing a very significant speed-up. However, this method is only suitable for direct image classification like face classification and does not work for arbitrary feature vectors.

Overall, our typical applications (see part III for more details) require the classification of millions of samples in seconds. To realize this would require more drastic speed-ups of large constant factors. Hence, we can conclude that none of the previously known approaches is fast enough for our purposes.

14.2 Description of the Algorithm

Let us motivate our approach by an example toy problem: Figure 14.1 shows a typical two-class classification problem in $\mathbb{R}^2$.

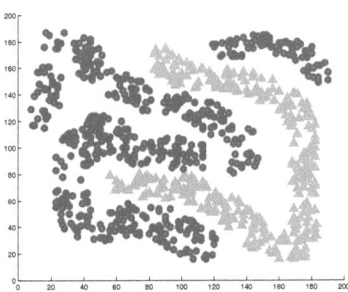

Figure 14.1: Example toy problem *Fourclass* from (Chang and Lin, 2005)

Without loss of generality, we define that the class C_1 shall be represented by green triangles and class C_2 by blue circles. Further, we use the following extended class definitions for C_1 and C_2:

Let m_1 and m_2 be two natural numbers that fulfill $m = m_1 + m_2$, $m_1 > 0$, $m_2 > 0$ and $\mathbb{C} = \{1, ..., m\}$. Without loss of generality, we can define:

Class 1 (Positive Class) of size m_1, with index $\mathbb{C}_1 = \{1, ..., m_1\}$, is conformed by the set $\{\mathbf{x}_i\}, i \in \mathbb{C}_1$, has a gravity center $\mathbf{s}_1 = \frac{1}{m_1} \sum_{i \in \mathbb{C}_1} \mathbf{x}_i$, a label $y_i = 1$ for all $i \in \mathbb{C}_1$, and for some later applications, a global penalty value D_1 is defined such that $C_i = D_1 \; \forall i \in \mathbb{C}_1$; C_i represent individual penalty values.

Class 2 (Negative Class) of size m_2, with index $\mathbb{C}_2 = \{m_1 + 1, ..., m_1 + m_2\}$, is conformed by the set $\{\mathbf{x}_i\}, i \in \mathbb{C}_2$, has a gravity center $\mathbf{s}_2 = \frac{1}{m_2} \sum_{i \in \mathbb{C}_2} \mathbf{x}_i$, $y_i = -1$ for all $i \in \mathbb{C}_2$, and for some later applications, a global penalty value D_2 is assigned to this class such that $C_i = D_2 \; \forall i \in \mathbb{C}_2$; C_i represent the individual penalty values.

Throughout this chapter we only consider two-class problems - an extension to multi-class problems can easily be obtained by following the methods given in section 13.6.

Returning to our example in figure 14.1: It clearly has a non-linear solution, so a SVM with Gaussian Kernel can be used to obtain a suitable decision function. The graphical representation of such a possible solution is given in Figure 14.2,

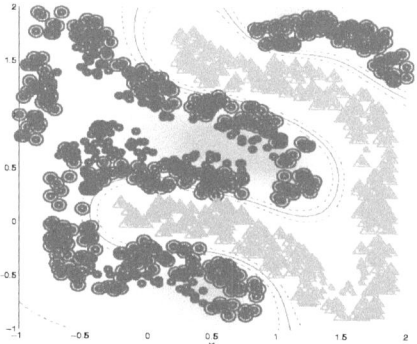

Figure 14.2: The solution for the *fourclass* problem with a Gaussian kernel needs 135 SV out of 287 training samples.

where the decision function is marked with a solid red line and the margin between the two classes by spotted red lines. The marked points are the resulting support vectors.

Since there appear to be hardly any un-marked training samples, we can conclude that the classification problem in figure 14.2 is not trivial, and that the high number of SVs results in a high computational complexity for the classification. In fact, the Gaussian solution in this case needs 135 SVs out of 287 training samples.

14.2.1 Decision Tree with Linear SVM Nodes

We propose to combine the speed of linear kernels with the separation power of non-linear kernels to achieve a fast and powerful SVM classification. The basic idea to realize this combination is to approximate a virtual non-linear decision function by a combination of several linear kernels.

For this purpose, we consecutively build a binary decision tree which holds a linear SVM in each node (see figure 14.6). The tree is built up during the training and each classification sample is simply run down the tree like in an ordinary decision tree. The building process is consecutive, performing the same steps in each node until the algorithm converges.

In each node, we train a linear SVM where we select one class to be the so-called *hard class* $\mathbf{C}_k$ and the other class to be the *soft class* $\mathbf{C}_{\bar{k}}$. The term *hard* indicates the margin property for this class should not allow any miss-classifications of the training samples in $\mathbf{C}_k$ and as little miss-classifications as possible in $\mathbf{C}_{\bar{k}}$.

In the first training step of our example, the class 1 (green triangles) is chosen to be the hard class $\mathbf{C}_k = 1$. Figure 14.3 illustrates the resulting linear decision function for the first SVM node: The

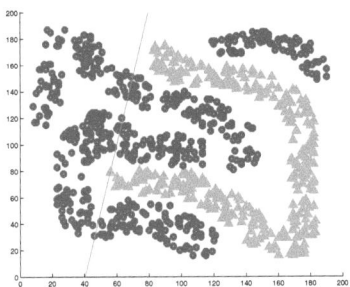

Figure 14.3: First hyperplane solution for the *fourclass* problem (hard class = triangles).

training of the linear SVM leaves the training samples of $\mathbf{C}_{\bar{k}}$ exclusively on one side of the decision function, while samples of $\mathbf{C}_k$ may appear on both sides. Hence, it is "safe" to give all samples which fall on the $\mathbf{C}_{\bar{k}}$ side (blue area in figure 14.4) of the decision function the label of $\mathbf{C}_{\bar{k}}$.

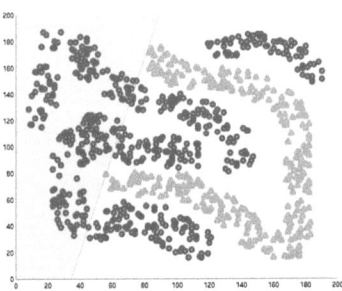

Figure 14.4: Labeling after the first hyperplane solution for the *fourclass* problem.

In a final step, we reduce the problem by leaving out the samples that lie in the previously marked region and hand the remaining training samples as new problem to the next node (figure 14.5).

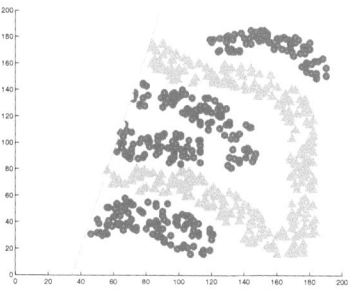

Figure 14.5: Reduced problem after the first hyperplane solution for the *fourclass* problem.

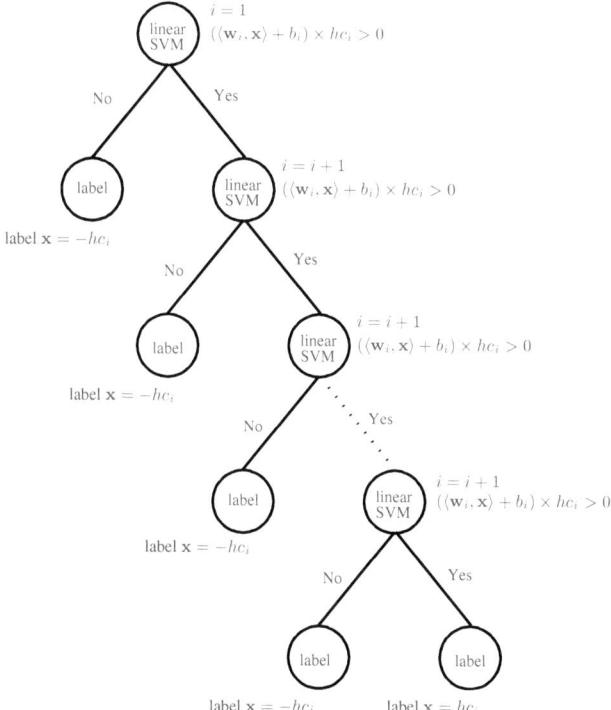

Figure 14.6: Decision tree with linear SVM in each node.

This procedure is repeated node by node with altering ***hard classes*** until it converges to the point where all remaining samples belong to the same class. Figures 14.7 to 14.9 show all of the remaining consecutive linear nodes for our toy problem:

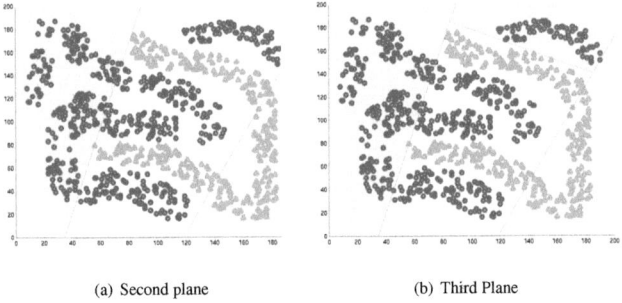

(a) Second plane (b) Third Plane

Figure 14.7: Second and third plane for the *fourclass* problem

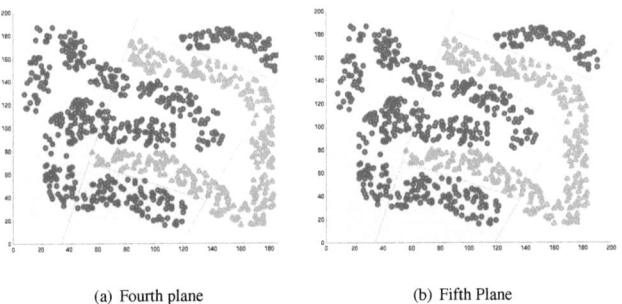

(a) Fourth plane (b) Fifth Plane

Figure 14.8: Fourth and fifth plane for the *fourclass* problem

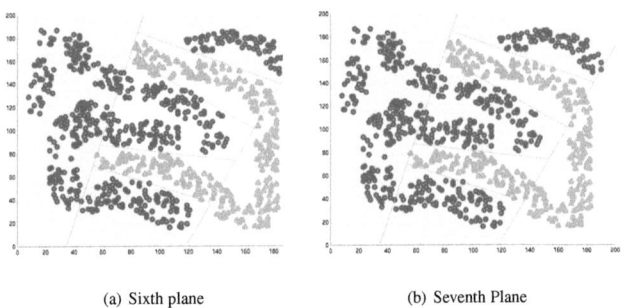

(a) Sixth plane (b) Seventh Plane

Figure 14.9: Sixth and seventh plane for the *fourclass* problem

The final solution of the SVM-Tree is shown in figure 14.10. Compared to the the non-linear solution (see figure 14.2), the linear approximation of the Gaussian decision function works quite well and need only 7 nodes. Hence, the complexity is reduced from 135 SV in the non-linear case to 7. This is a speed-up of roughly factor 20.

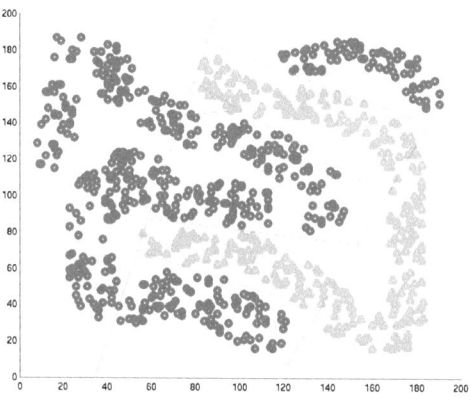

Figure 14.10: Final solution for the fourclass problem

14.3 Theoretical Details

The proposed algorithm appears to be quite simple, yet there are two major questions we still have to answer: first, how should the **hard class** be selected in each step? And second, how can we construct linear SVMs which have the desired margin property that the **hard class** is always classified correctly with minimum possible error penalties for the other class.
We first tackle the second problem and engage the **hard class** selection in section 14.3.3.

Trying to construct a linear SVM which fulfills the properties for our SVM-Tree, one runs into an unexpected but major problem: The SVM training (13.40) often converges to a trivial (zero vector) solution in cases where the training data is not linearly separable. This phenomenon is independent of the underlying optimization method. Hence, in order to construct our linear SVM-nodes we first have to investigate the zero solution problem.

14.3.1 Zero Solutions in the SVM Optimization Process

Given two classes C_1, C_2 (defined as in 14.2), a standard soft margin SVM is usually trained such that it makes as little mistakes as possible while the errors are treated equally for both classes $D_1 = D_2$ (14.2)(13.40). However, for the purpose of our linear SVM nodes, we have to use different class weights D_1, D_2, which turns out to make zero solutions even more likely.

We showed the connection of the class weights and the occurrence of zero solutions together with the derivation of a general theorem for trivial convergence in linear SVMs in (Zapién et al., 2006):

Theorem 1 (Zero Solution) *Let class* $\mathbf{C}_k$ *and class* $\mathbf{C}_{\bar{k}}$ *be defined as in (14.2). If the convex hull of class* $\mathbf{C}_k$ *intersects the convex hull of the other class* $\mathbf{C}_{\bar{k}}$, *then* $\mathbf{w} = \mathbf{0}$ *is a feasible solution for the primal Problem 13.23 if* $D_{\bar{k}} \geq \max_{i \in \mathbf{C}_k}\{\lambda_i\} \cdot D_k$, *where the* λ_i *are such that*

$$\mathbf{p} = \sum_{i \in \mathbf{C}_k} \lambda_i \mathbf{x}_i, \tag{14.3}$$

for a point $\mathbf{p}$ *that belongs to both convex hulls.*

Proof: Note that if $i \in \mathbb{C}_k$ and $j \in \mathbb{C}_{\bar{k}}$ then $y_i \cdot y_j = -1$; similarly, if $i \in \mathbb{C}_k$ and $j \in \mathbb{C}_k$ then $y_i \cdot y_j = 1$. Without loss of generality, let class $\mathbf{C}_k = \mathbf{C}_1$ and class $\mathbf{C}_{\bar{k}} = \mathbf{C}_2$, then the dual problem (13.40) can be written as follows

$$\text{maximize} \quad \sum_{i \in \mathbb{C}_1} \alpha_i + \sum_{i \in \mathbb{C}_2} \alpha_i + \sum_{i \in \mathbb{C}_1, j \in \mathbb{C}_2} \alpha_i \alpha_j \langle \mathbf{x}_i, \mathbf{x}_j \rangle \tag{14.4}$$

$$-\frac{1}{2} \sum_{i,j \in \mathbb{C}_1} \alpha_i \alpha_j \langle \mathbf{x}_i, \mathbf{x}_j \rangle - \frac{1}{2} \sum_{i,j \in \mathbb{C}_2} \alpha_i \alpha_j \langle \mathbf{x}_i, \mathbf{x}_j \rangle \tag{14.5}$$

$$\text{subject to} \quad \sum_{i \in \mathbb{C}_1} \alpha_i y_i + \sum_{i \in \mathbb{C}_2} \alpha_i y_i = 0 \tag{14.6}$$

$$0 \leq \alpha_i \leq D_1 \text{ for all } i \in \mathbb{C}_1 \tag{14.7}$$

$$0 \leq \alpha_j \leq D_2 \text{ for all } j \in \mathbb{C}_2. \tag{14.8}$$

If $\mathbf{p}$ belongs to the convex hull of both classes, then, it can be written as follows

$$\mathbf{p} = \sum_{i \in \mathbb{C}_1} \lambda_i \mathbf{x}_i \quad \text{and} \quad \mathbf{p} = \sum_{j \in \mathbb{C}_2} \lambda_j \mathbf{x}_j, \tag{14.9}$$

with $\lambda_i \geq 0$ for all $i \in \mathbb{C}_1$, $\sum_{i \in \mathbb{C}_1} \lambda_i = 1$ and $\lambda_j \geq 0$ for all $j \in \mathbb{C}_2$, $\sum_{j \in \mathbb{C}_2} \lambda_j = 1$.

Let $\alpha_i = \lambda_i D_1 \leq D_1$ for all $i \in \mathbb{C}_1$ and $\alpha_j = \lambda_j D_1 \leq \max_{j \in \mathbb{C}_2}\{\lambda_j\} D_1 \leq D_2$ for all $j \in \mathbb{C}_2$, then

$$\sum_{i \in \mathbb{C}_1} \alpha_i y_i + \sum_{j \in \mathbb{C}_2} \alpha_j y_j \;=\; \sum_{i \in \mathbb{C}_1} \lambda_i D_1 - \sum_{j \in \mathbb{C}_2} \lambda_j D_1 \tag{14.10}$$

$$=\; D_1 \sum_{i \in \mathbb{C}_1} \lambda_i - D_1 \sum_{j \in \mathbb{C}_2} \lambda_j \tag{14.11}$$

$$=\; D_1 - D_1 \tag{14.12}$$

$$=\; 0. \tag{14.13}$$

Therefore $\alpha_i = \lambda_i D_1$ for all $i \in \mathbb{C}_1$ and $\alpha_j = \lambda_j D_1$ for all $j \in \mathbb{C}_2$ is a feasible solution for the dual problem. If we calculate the vector $\mathbf{w}$ with these values, we obtain:

$$\mathbf{w} \;=\; \sum_{i \in \mathbb{C}_1} \alpha_i \mathbf{x}_i y_i + \sum_{j \in \mathbb{C}_2} \alpha_j \mathbf{x}_j y_j \tag{14.14}$$

$$=\; \sum_{i \in \mathbb{C}_1} \lambda_i D_1 \mathbf{x}_i - \sum_{j \in \mathbb{C}_2} \lambda_j D_1 \mathbf{x}_j \tag{14.15}$$

$$=\; D_1 \sum_{i \in \mathbb{C}_1} \lambda_i \mathbf{x}_i - D_1 \sum_{j \in \mathbb{C}_2} \lambda_j \mathbf{x}_j \tag{14.16}$$

$$=\; D_1 \mathbf{p} - D_1 \mathbf{p} \tag{14.17}$$

$$=\; \mathbf{0}. \tag{14.18}$$

14.3.2 Convex Hull Representation

The first step to resolve the zero solution problem is to reformulate the original optimization problem (13.20). Since we just showed that the convex hull of the classes play the key role in the entire problem, we use the alternative dual formulation of (Bennett et al., 2000), who proved that hard margin SVM training (13.20) (and classification) can be described in terms of convex hulls:

If a solution exists, it can be found geometrically: (Bennett et al., 2000) showed that the maximal margin is given by the two closest points of the two convex hulls (see figure 14.11).

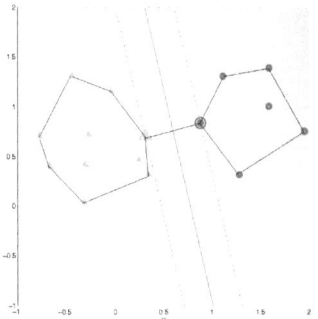

Figure 14.11: Convex hull interpretation for the hard margin SVM.

For the soft margin case (13.23), (Bennett et al., 2000) introduced the notion of reduced convex hulls (see Figure 14.12).

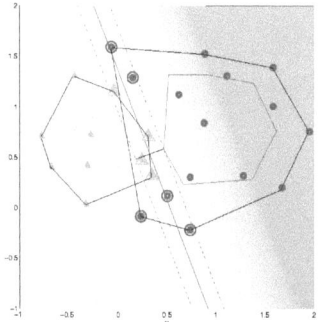

Figure 14.12: Reduced convex hull interpretation for the soft margin SVM.

The reduced convex hull is still lying around the center of gravity of the original convex hull. The reduction of the hulls is parameterized by D_1 and D_2.

Since the geometric interpretation does not change the original problem, we can extend theorem (1) to the convex hull representation. This is resumed in the following corollary:

Corollary 1 (Zero Solution In The Center Of Gravity Representation) *If the center of gravity* s_2
of class C_2 *is inside of the convex hull of class* C_1 *then it can be represented as*

$$s_2 = \sum_{i \in C_1} \lambda_i x_i \quad and \quad s_2 = \sum_{j \in C_2} \frac{1}{m_2} x_j$$

with $\lambda_i \geq 0$ *for all* $i \in C_1$ *and* $\sum_{i \in C_1} \lambda_i = 1$.

If additionally $D_1 \geq \lambda_{max} D_2 m_2$, *where* $\lambda_{max} = \max_{i \in C_1}\{\lambda_i\}$, *then* $w = 0$ *is a feasible solution*
for the primal problem.

Proof: Let class C_1 and class C_2 be as in (14.2), then the dual problem can be written as follows

$$\text{maximize} \quad \sum_{i \in C_1} \alpha_i + \sum_{i \in C_2} \alpha_i + \sum_{i \in C_1, j \in C_2} \alpha_i \alpha_j \langle x_i, x_j \rangle, \tag{14.19}$$

$$-\tfrac{1}{2} \sum_{i,j \in C_1} \alpha_i \alpha_j \langle x_i, x_j \rangle - \tfrac{1}{2} \sum_{i,j \in C_2} \alpha_i \alpha_j \langle x_i, x_j \rangle, \tag{14.20}$$

$$\text{subject to} \quad \sum_{i \in C_1} \alpha_i y_i + \sum_{i \in C_2} \alpha_i y_i = 0, \tag{14.21}$$

$$0 \leq \alpha_i \leq D_1 \text{ for all } i \in C_1, \tag{14.22}$$

$$0 \leq \alpha_j \leq D_2 \text{ for all } j \in C_2, \tag{14.23}$$

Let $\alpha_i = \lambda_i D_2 m_2 \leq \lambda_{max} D_2 m_2 \leq D_1$ for all $i \in C_1$ and $\alpha_j = D_2$ for all $j \in C_2$, then

$$\sum_{i \in C_1} \alpha_i y_i + \sum_{j \in C_2} \alpha_j y_j \quad = \quad \sum_{i \in C_1} \lambda_i D_2 m_2 - \sum_{j \in C_2} D_2 \tag{14.24}$$

$$= \quad D_2 m_2 \sum_{i \in C_1} \lambda_i - D_2 m_2 \tag{14.25}$$

$$= \quad D_2 m_2 - D_2 m_2 \tag{14.26}$$

$$= \quad 0. \tag{14.27}$$

Therefore $\alpha_i = \lambda_i D_2 m_2$ for all $i \in C_1$ and $\alpha_j = D_2$ for all $j \in C_2$ is a feasible solution for the
dual problem.
If we calculate the vector w with these values, we obtain:

$$w \quad = \quad \sum_{i \in C_1} \alpha_i x_i y_i + \sum_{j \in C_2} \alpha_j x_j y_j \tag{14.28}$$

$$= \quad \sum_{i \in C_1} \lambda_i D_2 m_2 x_i - \sum_{j \in C_2} D_2 x_j \tag{14.29}$$

$$= \quad D_2 m_2 \sum_{i \in C_1} \lambda_i x_i - D_2 m_2 s_2 \tag{14.30}$$

$$= \quad D_2 m_2 s_2 - D_2 m_2 s_2 \tag{14.31}$$

$$= \quad 0. \tag{14.32}$$

We obtain several insights on the zero solution problem from the geometric representation and corollary (1): first, the reduction of the convex hull (e.g. increasing the penalty term D_i) does not change
the center of gravity of the classes. Hence, we conclude that it is not enough to constrain only one of
the hulls - we rather need to adjust the penalties of both classes to avoid zero solutions.
Second, the **hard class** has to be chosen such that the center of the other class does not lie within its
convex hull.

We use these new insights to construct the so-called $H1$-SVM for our linear SVM nodes.

14.3.3 $H1$-**SVM**

For the construction of our SVM-Tree we design a novel linear SVM as node decision function. The name $H1$ indicates that we propose a hybrid, half hard and half soft margin SVM. The $H1$-SVM does not allow miss-classifications for the **hard class** $\mathbf{C}_k$, while the error for the **soft class** $\mathbf{C}_{\bar{k}}$ is optimized in a soft margin approach.

H1-SVM primal formulation: Let the classes be defined as in (14.2), the primal optimization problem for the $H1$ training is given as:

$$\underset{\mathbf{w} \in \mathcal{H}, b \in \mathbb{R}}{\text{minimize}} \quad \tau(\mathbf{w}) = \tfrac{1}{2}\|\mathbf{w}\|^2 - \sum_{i \in \mathbb{C}_k} y_i(\langle \mathbf{x}_i, \mathbf{w} \rangle + b), \tag{14.33}$$

$$\text{subject to} \quad y_i(\langle \mathbf{x}_i, \mathbf{w} \rangle + b) \geq 1 \text{ for all } i \in \mathbb{C}_k, \tag{14.34}$$

where $k = 1$ and $\bar{k} = 2$, or $k = 2$ and $\bar{k} = 1$.

The formulation in (14.3.3) provides the required hybrid behavior: the constraint $y_i(\langle \mathbf{w}, \mathbf{x}_i \rangle + b) \geq 1$ for all $i \in \mathbb{C}_k$ guaranties that all samples of the hard class are classified correctly, hence we ensure the hard margin. We introduce the additional soft margin for $\mathbf{C}_{\bar{k}}$ with the dual formulation:

H1-SVM dual formulation: The training of the $H1$-SVM can be formulated in terms of the following dual optimization problem:

$$\underset{\boldsymbol{\alpha} \in \mathbb{R}^m}{\text{maximize}} \quad W(\boldsymbol{\alpha}) = \sum_{i=1}^m \alpha_i - \tfrac{1}{2} \sum_{i,j=1}^m \alpha_i \alpha_j y_i y_j \langle \mathbf{x}_i, \mathbf{x}_j \rangle, \tag{14.35}$$

$$\text{subject to} \quad 0 \leq \alpha_i \leq C_i, \ i \in \mathbb{C}_k, \tag{14.36}$$

$$\alpha_j = 1, \ j \in \mathbb{C}_{\bar{k}}, \tag{14.37}$$

$$\sum_{i=1}^m \alpha_i y_i = 0, \tag{14.38}$$

where $k = 1$ and $\bar{k} = 2$, or $k = 2$ and $\bar{k} = 1$.

With this new definition of the SVM problem, the zero solution can only occur with a linear combination of the vector samples of the hard class. Without loss of generality, if the hard class is fixed to $\mathbf{C}_1$, then

$$\mathbf{w} \ = \ \sum_{i=1}^m \alpha_i y_i \mathbf{x}_i \tag{14.39}$$

$$= \ \sum_{i \in \mathbb{C}_1} \alpha_i \mathbf{x}_i - \sum_{i \in \mathbb{C}_2} \alpha_i \mathbf{x}_i \tag{14.40}$$

$$= \ \sum_{i \in \mathbb{C}_1} \alpha_i \mathbf{x}_i - \sum_{i \in \mathbb{C}_2} \mathbf{x}_i. \tag{14.41}$$

$$\tag{14.42}$$

If we define $\mathbf{z} = \sum_{i \in \mathbb{C}_2} \mathbf{x}_i$ and $|\mathbb{C}_1| \geq (n-1) = dim(\mathbf{z}) - 1$, then there exists a set of $\{\alpha_i\}, i \in \mathbb{C}_1, \alpha_i \neq 0$ such that

$$\mathbf{w} \ = \ \sum_{i \in \mathbb{C}_1} \alpha_i \mathbf{x}_i - \mathbf{z} = \mathbf{0}. \tag{14.43}$$

So, the number of zero solutions that are feasible in the $H1$-SVM Problem is a subset (strictly) smaller than the number of zero solutions in the original SVM Problem.

The introduction of the $H1$-SVM provides an effective learning algorithm for the linear decision nodes. The classification of samples is identical to standard SVMs. Even though the $H1$-SVM cannot completely avoid the occurrence of the zero solution, it strongly reduces the probability (Zapién et al., 2006).

Finding the best Hyperplane

Using the $H1$-SVM as linear decision function in the nodes of the SVM-Tree, we have to select the **hard class** for each node. This is done in a greedy fashion: we simply compute both possible models, and select the solution which reduces the training set the most.

This can be achieved in two simple steps: first, we compute the hyperplane normal **w** based on the α_i we obtain from (14.3.3):

$$\mathbf{w} = \sum_{i=1}^{m} \alpha_i y_i \mathbf{x}_i. \tag{14.44}$$

Second, we derive the offset b (see figure 14.13)

for hard class = 1 as

$$b = \frac{min_{i \in C_1} \langle \mathbf{w}, \mathbf{x}_i \rangle + max_{\{j \in C_2 \wedge \langle \mathbf{w}, \mathbf{x}_j \rangle < 0\}} \langle \mathbf{w}, \mathbf{x}_j \rangle}{2} \tag{14.45}$$

and for hard class = -1 as

$$b = \frac{max_{j \in C_2} \langle \mathbf{w}, \mathbf{x}_j \rangle + min_{\{i \in C_1 \wedge \langle \mathbf{w}, \mathbf{x}_i \rangle > 0\}} \langle \mathbf{w}, \mathbf{x}_i \rangle}{2} \tag{14.46}$$

and classify all training samples. We then pick the model which reduces the training set the most.

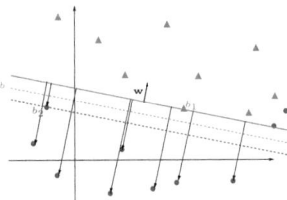

Figure 14.13: Search of threshold b for a non-linear problem.

Implementation

The implementation of the SVM-Tree with $H1$ nodes is a bit tricky. Especially the embedding of the $H1$ modifications into the standard SMO optimization (Keerthi et al., 1999) is not trivial.
However, a discussion of the implementation details is beyond the scope of this thesis. The interested reader may find an in-depth discussion in (Fehr and Zapién, 2007) and the C++ implementation in (Ronneberger and et al, 2004).

We show an evaluation of the SVM-Tree performance on standardized benchmark datasets in chapter 17 and apply the method to several applications shown in part III.

15 Markov Random Fields (MRF)

Support Vector Machines (see chapter 13) in combination with the SVM-Tree accelerated classification (see chapter 14) provide a powerful and fast classifier for our general *framework* (see section 1.2). However, for some applications, e.g. segmentation (see part III), it can be advantageous to base local decisions (e.g. voxel-wise classifications) not only on the local evidence, but to also take the distribution over the local neighborhood (of the voxel) into consideration.

Markov Random Fields (MRF) provide such a **contextual** classification ability, where the decision function $\Gamma_{MRF}(X_i, \mathcal{N}_i)$ classifies the sample (pattern or feature vector) $X_i \in \mathcal{X}$ based on the joint probability distribution over X_i and its neighbors $\mathcal{N}_i \subset \mathcal{X}$.

The remainder of this chapter is structured as follows: first we give a brief general introduction to Markov Random Fields based on the concept of probabilistic graph models (section 15.1). Then we discuss the construction of potential functions in section 15.3, before we take a closer look at the inference from MRFs in section 15.4. Finally, we introduce inference via Generalized Belief Propagation (GBP), a deterministic message passing inference algorithm which we speed-up in chapter 16.

15.1 Introduction

We begin our very brief review of Markov Random Fields and related methods with the introduction of probabilistic graph models which form the basis for the MRF subclass. The interested reader may refer to (Winkler, 2006) for a more detailed introduction.

15.1.1 Probabilistic Graph Models

Probabilistic graph models are commonly used to formalize and handle complex distributions over several random variables. There are different types of graphs which are commonly used, including "Directed Graphs", "Undirected Graphs" or "Factor Graphs" (Winkler, 2006). All of them have slightly different properties, but share the basic layout: The random variables are represented by nodes while the edges encode the probability of a set of variables.

The great advantage of the graph models is that their structure directly captures the conditional dependencies between variables. Recall, that the variable X is conditional independent of Y given V, if and only if

$$P(X|Y, V) = P(X|V). \tag{15.1}$$

If $P(X, Y) > 0$, then X is conditional independent of Y given V, if

$$P(X, Y|V) = P(X|V)P(Y|V). \tag{15.2}$$

The other advantage of graph models is that there already exist a wide range of algorithms for the inference of the joint and the marginal probability distributions which take advantage of the graph structure.

An in-depth description of the most common graph models can be found in (Winkler, 2006). Here, we limit our review to a short description of undirected graphs, which form the basis for the Markov Random Fields.

Undirected graphs: the probability distributions over a set of variables can be modeled in an undirected graph where the nodes representing the random variables are connected with undirected edges allowing cycles. The joint probability distribution can be represented as a factorisation over subsets of the variables (nodes):

$$P(\mathbf{x}) = \frac{1}{Z} \prod_i U_i(\mathbf{x}_{C_i}), \tag{15.3}$$

where $\mathbf{x}$ is a configuration of the set of all random variables $\mathbf{X}$ in the graph and $C_i \subset \mathbf{X}$ are subsets of variables called **cliques** with associated configurations $\mathbf{x}_{C_i}$. The cliques are usually defined by some local neighborhood property.

The so-called **potential functions** U_i operate on the cliques. Technically, the only constraint is that the U_i have to be non-negative, but in practice, the choice of an appropriate potential function is non-trivial since it dominates the inference results. Section 15.3 further discusses the design of the potential functions.

Finally, one needs a normalization (or so-called **partition function**) Z in order to normalize the probabilities to one:

$$Z = \sum_{\mathbf{x}} \prod_i U_i(\mathbf{x}_{C_i}). \tag{15.4}$$

We will later use the undirected model, combined with a markovian neighborhood definition and specially defined potential functions to construct Markov Random Fields.

15.2 Markov Random Fields

Markov Random Fields (MRF), also known as Markov Networks, are given by a random vector $\mathbf{X} := \{X_1, \ldots, X_n\}$ (with configuration $\mathbf{x}$) in the probability space $(\mathcal{X}, P)$ which fulfills the following properties:

Positivity: P on $\mathcal{X}$ is positive: $P(\mathbf{x}) > 0$

Local Markov Property: $P\Big(X_i = x_i | X_j = x_j, i \neq j\Big) = P\Big(X_i = x_i | X_j = x_j, X_j \in \mathcal{N}(X_i)\Big)$
where $\mathcal{N}$ is a neighborhood system which fullfills:

$$\mathcal{N}(X_i) \subset \mathbf{X}, \tag{15.5}$$
$$i \notin \mathcal{N}(X_i),$$
$$y \in \mathcal{N}(X_i) \text{ iff } i \in \mathcal{N}(X_j).$$

So, the dominating element of Markov Random Fields, compared to other probabilistic methods, is the restriction of the conditional dependencies to the local neighborhood, i.e. fulfilling the Markov property.

In most cases, the MRFs are expressed in terms of their joint probability distribution. This appears to be a rather complex problem, but thanks to the *Hammersley-Cifford theorem* this turns out to be quite easy in practice. *Hammersley-Cifford* (Winkler, 2006) showed that Markov Random Fields are theoretically equivalent to **Gibbs Random Fields**. We spare the theoretical details of this important relation and turn directly to the practical implications.

15.2.1 Gibbs Fields

Gibbs Random Fields are given by a random vector $\mathbf{X} := \{X_1, \ldots, X_n\}$ (with configuration $\mathbf{x}$) in the probability space $(\mathcal{X}, P)$ which fulfills the following properties:

Positivity: P on $\mathcal{X}$ is positive: $P(\mathbf{x}) > 0$

Gibbs (Boltzmann) Distribution: P is given by: $P(\mathbf{x}) = \frac{1}{Z}e^{-\beta E(\mathbf{x})}$ with

the partition function $Z = \sum_{\mathbf{x}} e^{-\beta E(\mathbf{x})}$

and $\beta = \frac{1}{kT}$

where E is the so-called energy function, T is the "temperature" parameter and k Boltzmann's constant.

Given this definition of Gibbs Fields and the undirected graph models (see 15.2), the *Hammersley-Cifford theorem* **allows the formulation of Markov Random Fields as an undirected graph model, where the potential functions are based on the Gibbs distribution**

$$U(\mathbf{x_{C_i}}) = \exp(-\beta E(\mathbf{x_{C_i}})) \tag{15.6}$$

and operate only on cliques $\mathbf{C}_i$ which are restricted to local markovian neighborhoods (as defined in 15.5).

With this formulation, one can directly apply the construction and inference methods from undirected graph models to MRFs. Hence, the construction of a MRF is essentially reduced to the design of a problem specific energy function $E(\mathbf{x_{C_i}})$ and the selection of an appropriate neighborhood.

15.3 Potential Functions

Usually we are not trying to find the problem specific energy function $E(\mathbf{x_{C_i}})$ for the entire Gibbs distribution directly. Instead, we rewrite the energy function as sum over *potentials U*:

$$E(\mathbf{x_{C_i}}) = \sum_{\mathbf{A} \subset \mathbf{C}_i} U(\mathbf{x_A}), \tag{15.7}$$

which act on sub-cliques $\mathbf{A} \subset \mathbf{C}_i$. In most applications, $\mathbf{A}$ is chosen in form of pairs, $\mathbf{A} = \{X_i, X_j\}$, $X_i, X_j \in \mathbf{C}_i$. We then write the energy function as a linearly weighted sum of pair-wise potentials:

$$E(\mathbf{x_{C_i}}) = \sum_{\{X_i, X_j\} \in \mathbf{C}_i} w_{ij} U(\{X_i, X_j\}). \tag{15.8}$$

This formulation allows to model energy functions for even difficult problems with rather easy to handle (and to design) potentials. However, this general solution does not yet address a subproblem which is especially interesting for image processing tasks: the "Labeling Problem".

15.3.1 The Labeling Problem

The so-called "Labeling Problem" is the fundamental problem behind most image processing and pattern recognition problems related to Markov Random Fields. In image segmentation, restoration or de-noising, we always face the same basic setup: at each site $X_i \in \mathbf{X}$ we have a feature vector $\mathbf{y}_i$ and a hidden scalar label x_i (e.g. representing the label in segmentation problems or the image gray-value in de-noising problems).

It should be noted that we are now using different variable names than before: while in previous chapters x denoted a feature vector with label y, we now use x to denote the hidden label of a variable with y observable features. This might be slightly confusing, but both notations form a strong standard within their communities such that the usage of either notation to the other field would cause even greater confusion.

The goal is to infer the most likely labeling from the joint probability distribution $P(\mathbf{y}, \mathbf{x})$. If we map this problem to (15.8) by introducing the index set $\mathcal{C}_i = \{1, \ldots, n\}$ for each clique $\mathbf{C}_i$ with $\forall j \in \mathcal{C}_i : (\mathbf{y}_j, x_j) \in \mathbf{C}_i$ where the i-th clique contains the neighbors of X_i, we obtain an energy function like:

$$E(\mathbf{y}, \mathbf{x}) = \sum_{X_i} w_i V(\mathbf{y}_i, x_i) + \sum_{j \in \mathcal{C}_i} w_{ij} U(x_i, x_j), \tag{15.9}$$

where $\sum_{X_i} w_i V(\mathbf{y}_i, x_i)$ is usually known as **data** or **node potential** and $\sum_{j \in \mathcal{C}_i} w_{ij} U(x_i, x_j)$ as **smoothness** or **edge potential**.

The addition of the node potentials enables us to infer local evidence for the labeling from X. This is useful when no initial labeling is given or the confidence in the labeling has to be differentiated individually for each site. Hence, the node potential acts more like a standard classifier, e.g. we use local confidence of SVMs as node potentials in some of our applications (see part III).

The edge potentials capture the markovian property. Even though, there are virtually unlimited possibilities to design the interaction of the neighbors during inference, two very simple models have been very successfully applied to a wide range of problems: the Ising and Pott's Model. Since we are applying derivations of these models in our applications, we briefly review both models.

15.3.2 Ising Model

The Ising model (Winkler, 2006) has been introduced for the prediction of magnetic fields in statistical physics. Given a field for a binary labeling problem with $x_{i,j} = \{-1, 1\}$, where -1 denotes antiferromagnetism and 1 ferromagnetism, the objective is to predict the state for each site.

Ising introduced a fairly simple model, which assumes that the state of a site is magnetically coupled to neighboring sites - hence, using the Markov property. Given the Gibbs framework (15.8), this leads to very simple potentials of the form:

$$U(x_i, x_j) = x_i x_j. \tag{15.10}$$

Regardless of its simplicity, the Ising model turned out not only to solve the ferromagnetism problem, but it also has been successfully applied to a wide range of other binary problems. It implies a piecewise constant prior which favors configurations with areas of locally constant labels - a property which is desirable for many applications.

15.3.3 Pott's Model

Pott's model is the direct extension of the Ising model to multi-label problems. The potential is chosen such that

$$U(x_i, x_j) = 2\delta(x_i, x_j) - 1, \tag{15.11}$$

where δ is the Kronecker Symbol.

In some cases it can be favorable to use a piecewise smooth prior instead of a constant prior. Then an adaption of Pott's model can be used, which has a potential of the form

$$U(x_i, x_j) = |x_i - x_j|,$$
(15.12)

that endorses smooth transition of the labels.

15.4 MRF Inference

Given a Markov Random Field with its problem specific energy functions, the common task for our labeling problems is to infer the hidden labels x from an observed feature configuration y. Before we review some selected inference algorithms, we have to discuss the quality measure for the estimation $\hat{x}$ of x. While there are several different estimates known from literature, such as "Marginal Posterior Mode (MPME)" or "Posterior Minimum Mean Squares (MMSE)" (Veksler, 1999)(Geman and Geman, 1984), we stick to the most popular "Maximum A Posteriori (MAP)" estimate.

15.4.1 Maximum A Posteriori (MAP) Estimate

Following the Bayesian Rule

$$P(x|y) = \frac{P(y|x)P(x)}{P(y)},$$
(15.13)

the MAP estimate $P(x|y)$ uses the distribution over the observed features $P(y|x)$ as well as given a priori knowledge on the labeling problem $P(x)$ to estimate x.

If we neglect the constant $P(y)$, we obtain the MAP estimate of x by

$$\hat{x} = \arg\max_x \Big(P(x|y) \Big) = \arg\max_x \Big(P(y|x)P(x) \Big).$$
(15.14)

Further, it can be shown that maximizing $P(x|y)$ is equivalent to minimizing the energy function $E(x, y_u)$ for unlabeled observations y_u when we use a Gibbs distribution for $P(x|y_u)$ (Winkler, 2006) and decompose $E(x, y_u)$ in its node and edge potentials (see 15.9):

$$P(x|y_u) = \frac{1}{Z_u} e^{-V(x,y_u)}$$
(15.15)

and $U(x)$ for $P(x)$.

15.4.2 Naive Inference

The main drawback of probabilistic models like Markov Random Fields is that a direct (naive) inference is usually computationally intractable. The reason for this can easily be seen by taking a look at the partition function (15.4): Since the number of possible configurations is growing exponentially with the number of nodes in a graph of arbitrary structure, the computation of the partition function Z, which is needed for an exact inference, becomes an **NP-Hard** problem.

15.4.3 Approximative Inference

There are several common strategies to approximately compute the inference on MRFs: **Monte Carlo** techniques try to approximate the exact distribution in Z by drawing random samples in a Markov Chain like approach. It can be shown (Winkler, 2006) that these sampling based methods eventually converge towards the exact inference results.

The most prominent examples for the sampling approach are the Gibbs Sampler (see section 15.4.5), the Metropolis algorithm (see section 15.4.4) and Simulated Annealing.

These sampling methods are very popular because they are rather easy to implement. But they usually suffer from slow convergence and the fact that they are non-deterministic. It is also difficult to determine how many iterations are actually needed and how good the resulting approximation actually is.

A deterministic alternative to Monte Carlo approximations which is especially suitable for binary segmentation problems like foreground/background problems, are the so-called **Graph Cut** algorithms (Kohli and Torr, 2005). It can be shown that it is possible to obtain the exact inference results for binary problems (where the configuration of the variables is bound to two different states) by reformulating the inference problem as min-cut problem on a graph. However, for non-binary labeling problems, only approximate graph cut solutions exist which additionally lose most of the great speed advantage this approach has in the binary case.

Since we usually have to deal with multi-label problems, we neglect the graph cut approach and turn to a third family of deterministic inference methods: **Message Passing** algorithms like the Belief Propagation (BP) (see section 15.4.6) and the Generalized Belief Propagation (GBP) (see section 15.4.7) which is more stable on cyclic graphs.

15.4.4 Metropolis

The Metropolis algorithm (also known as Metropolis-Hastings algorithm) uses a Markov Chain approach to approximate the inference target distribution $P(\mathbf{x})$ without needing to compute the normalizing partition function Z.

Starting from a random initialization $\mathbf{x}^0$, Metropolis computes a proposal density $Q(\mathbf{x}'; \mathbf{x}^t)$ in each approximation step. $Q(\mathbf{x}'|\mathbf{x}^t)$ is computed by use of the local densities $P(x_i^t)$ of randomly sampled variables X_i. Hence, only the label of a single variable X_i can be changed during one iteration. Additionally, the update is performed in a random manner: $x_i^{t+1} = x_i'$ only if

$$\alpha < \frac{P(x_i')Q(x_i^t|x_i')}{P(x_i^t)Q(x_i'|x_i^t)} \tag{15.16}$$

holds for the random $\alpha \in [0, 1]$, otherwise $x_i^{t+1} = x_i^t$.

The main drawback of the Metropolis algorithm is its slow convergence: it usually takes many iterations where each variable X_i has to be resampled several times before one can expect a reasonable approximation result.

15.4.5 Gibbs Sampling

The Gibbs Sampler is a special case of the Metropolis algorithm, where the random update rejection is neglected by setting $\alpha = 1$ and the proposal distribution $Q(\mathbf{x})$ is defined as local conditional distributions of the target P:

$$Q(x_i'|x_i^t) := P(x_i^t|\mathbf{x}^t/x_i^t). \tag{15.17}$$

The usage of conditionals on the target distribution for the computation of the proposal has the advantage that it is usually very easy to implement.

15.4.6 Belief Propagation (BP)

Belief Propagation (BP) is a deterministic inference algorithm which iteratively computes the marginal probabilities in a probabilistic graph model. It has been shown (Yedidia et al., 2001) that BP is able to compute the exact solution on undirected graph models without loops, i.e. tree-like graphs.

Inspired by very successful message-passing algorithms which were introduced in the context of Hidden Markov models, Belief Propagation uses messages between connected nodes to locally evaluate the marginal probabilities.

The term **belief** characterizes a temporal and localized approximation of the marginal probabilities. Belief Propagation then uses messages between nodes to update local beliefs based on the label probabilities propagated by neighboring nodes.

Before we begin our brief review of the definition of beliefs and messages, we rewrite the formulation of the joint probability function $P(x)$ in potential form. Plugging the Gibbs Distribution (15.6) into the formulation of the labeling problem (15.9), we introduce a compact notation for the **node potentials** $\phi_i(x_i)$ and **edge potentials** $\psi_{ij}(x_i, x_j)$:

$$\phi_i(x_i) := e^{w_i V(\mathbf{x}_i, y_i)} \tag{15.18}$$

$$\psi_{ij}(x_i, x_j) := e^{w_{ij} U(y_i, y_j)}. \tag{15.19}$$

Which leads to the potential form of the joint probability function:

$$P(x) = \prod_{X_i} \phi_i(x_i) \prod_{j \in \mathcal{C}_i} \psi_{ij}(x_i, x_j). \tag{15.20}$$

Further, for each node i with variable X_i, we denote the current belief by $b_i(x_i)$ and incoming messages from neighboring nodes $j \in \mathcal{C}_i$ by $m_{ji}(x_i)$.

Using (15.20) (Yedidia et al., 2001), the current belief in a node is then computed by

$$b_i(x_i) = Z \phi_i(x_i) \prod_{j \in \mathcal{C}_i} m_{ji}(x_i), \tag{15.21}$$

where Z normalizes the sum over all messages to 1.

The formulation of the messages is derived from the marginalization condition

$$b_i(x_i) = \sum_{j \in \mathcal{C}_i} b_{ij}(x_i, x_j), \tag{15.22}$$

which states that a single-node belief can be expressed in terms of the sum over all pair-wise beliefs with the members of the clique (see section 15.3). These pair-wise beliefs are computed (again using (15.20) (Yedidia et al., 2001)) as

$$b_{ij}(x_i, x_j) = Z \phi_i(x_i) \phi_j(x_j) \psi_{ij}(x_i, x_j) \prod_{h \in \mathcal{C}_i / j} m_{hi}(x_i) \prod_{g \in \mathcal{C}_j / i} m_{gj}(x_j). \tag{15.23}$$

Combining (15.21) and (15.23) with the MAP criterion (15.15), we obtain (Felzenszwalb and Huttenlocher, 2006) a maximum a-posteriori message update rule:

$$m_{ji}(x_i) = \arg\max_{x_j} \left(\phi_j(x_j) \psi_{ij}(x_i, x_j) \prod_{g \in \mathcal{C}_j / i} m_{gj}(x_j) \right), \tag{15.24}$$

Algorithm 4 BP inference

1: initialize $d = \infty$, $iter = 0$, set max_{iter} to some threshold
2: **for all** messages m_i **do**
3:     $m_i^{old} = 1$ *#initialize messages to 1*
4:     **for all** single node beliefs b_i **do**
5:         $b_i^{old} = 1$ *#initialize beliefs to 1*
6:     **end for**
7:     **while** $(d \geq \epsilon)$ and $(iter < max_{iter})$ **do**
8:         **for all** messages m_i **do**
9:             compute update m_i^{new} *#compute messages*
10:         **end for**
11:         $d = 0$
12:         **for all** single node beliefs b_i **do**
13:             compute b_i^{new} using updates m_i^{new} *#update beliefs*
14:             $d+ = |b_i^{new} - b_i^{old}|$
15:             $b_i^{old} = b_i^{new}$
16:         **end for**
17:         **for all** messages m_i **do**
18:             $m_i^{old} = m_i^{new}$ *#message update*
19:         **end for**
20:         $iter + +$
21:     **end while**
22:     **for all** nodes X_i **do**
23:         $x_i = \arg \subset k \max b_i(k)$ *#set labels*
24:     **end for**
25: **end for**

---

where each message $m_{ji}(x_i)$ contains a vector with the marginal probabilities for each possible label. An overview of the entire Belief Propagation procedure is given in algorithm 4.

For many applications, inference via Belief Propagation has proven to provide fast and accurate solutions on undirected probabilistic graph models without loops, refer to (Felzenszwalb and Huttenlocher, 2006) or (Tappen and Freeman, 2003). However, for graphs with loops, there is no guarantee that BP actually returns the correct solution or even converges.

Unfortunately, the graphs in our applications are usually extremely loopy, since we operate directly on volume grid representations. To cope with this common problem, two modifications to the standard BP have been introduced: **Loopy Belief Propagation** (Murphy et al., 1999) and **Generalized Belief Propagation (GBP)**(Yedidia et al., 2000). We chose the later approach, which we briefly review in section 15.4.7, before we derive several speed-up techniques for the very slow original GBP formulation in chapter 16.

15.4.7 Generalized Belief Propagation (GBP)

Generalized Belief Propagation (GBP) has been introduced by (Yedidia et al., 2000) to overcome the problems with the standard Belief Propagation (see section 15.4.6) algorithm on loopy graphs. GBP follows the intuition that the failure of the original Belief Propagation to converge to reasonable results in the presence of loops is caused by cyclic messages being passed around the loop over and over again. GBP tries to break up these "infinite" message loops between nodes by introducing additional

messages between regions of nodes. The basic idea is that this additional information stabilizes the local beliefs in loops over several iterations by propagating the beliefs of neighboring regions.
It should be noted that even though the Generalized Belief Propagation has empirically proven to deliver very good results on loopy graphs, there is absolutely no theoretical proof that GBP will converge to reasonable results.

The generalized version of the Belief Propagation still follows the basic setup of the original formulation with the addition of region messages. The formulation of these region messages is based on the notion of clusters, sub-regions and region graphs, which have to be defined first:

Clusters are defined as overlapping sub-sets of connected nodes in the graph. The cluster size is a design parameter and should be set such that clusters are large enough to capture the smallest loop in the graph but are not too large because the complexity of the GBP grows exponentially with the size of the clusters (Yedidia et al., 2000). Figure 15.1 illustrates clusters in a toy example: for our later applications on grid like graphs is a cluster size of 4 an obvious choice.

Sub-Regions are built upon the clusters. They are defined as the non-empty sub-sets of connected nodes in the graph that result from the intersection of clusters. Figure 15.1 shows all sub-regions of our toy example in the region graph.

Region Graphs are an important tool for the computation of the region messages. As Figure 15.1 illustrates, the structural dependencies of the sub-regions are encoded in an undirected and acyclic graph. Edges between sub-regions only exist between so-called **parent regions** P and **child regions** C where $C \subset P$. All regions D, that are connected by a direct path with P are called **descendant regions** and also hold $D \subset P$.

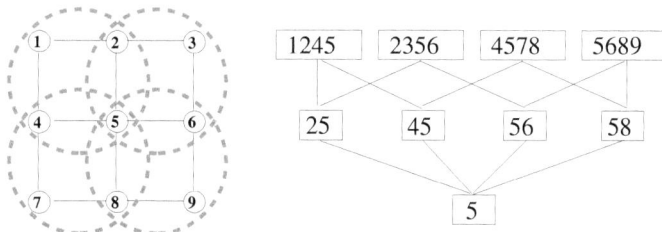

Figure 15.1: **Left:** Toy problem with a typical grid-like graph structure. The clusters (marked by red circles) have the form the smallest cycles in the graph. **Right:** Region graph of the toy problem.

Given these definitions, (Yedidia et al., 2000) derived the formulation of region beliefs based on the general maginalization condition (see 15.22):

$$b_R(\mathbf{x}_R) = Z\phi_R(\mathbf{x}_R)\Big(\prod_{P\in\mathcal{P}(R)} m_{PR}(\mathbf{x}_R)\Big)\Big(\prod_{D\in\mathcal{D}(R)}\prod_{P'\in\mathcal{P}(\mathcal{D})\varepsilon(R)} m_{P'D}(\mathbf{x}_D)\Big), \quad (15.25)$$

where k normalizes the sum of the beliefs to 1, $\mathcal{P}(R)$ is the set of parents of a region R, $\mathcal{D}(R)$ the set of descendants of R and $\varepsilon(R) = R \cup \mathcal{D}(R)$.
Intuitively, (15.25) states that the belief of a region R depends on the node potentials of the members of R (given by $\phi_R(\mathbf{x}_R)$) and all messages from R's parents as well as all messages from the parents of R's descendants. Figures 15.2 to 15.5 illustrate the computation of region beliefs on our toy example.

Notably, the computation of region messages for single node regions (see figure 15.2) is equivalent to the node beliefs in the standard Belief Propagation algorithm.

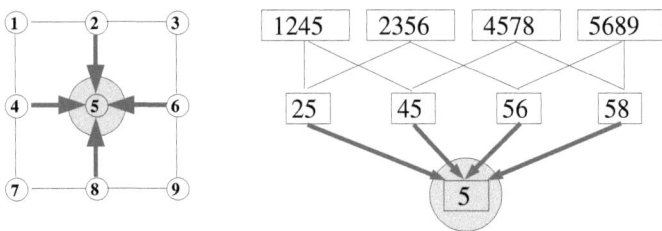

Figure 15.2: **Single node belief. Left:** Graph structure of our toy example. **Right:** the corresponding region graph. Blue edges denote single node messages into the single node belief region containing node 5. The belief is computed as given in (15.25): $b_5 = k\phi_5 m_{25} m_{65} m_{85} m_{45}$.

For the computation of the region messages, (Yedidia et al., 2000) introduced the following update rule:

$$m_{PR}(\mathbf{x}_R) = \frac{\sum\limits_{\mathbf{x}_{P/R}} \left(\phi_{P/R}(\mathbf{x}_{P/R}) \prod\limits_{(I,J)\in N(P,R)} m_{IJ}(x_J) \right)}{\prod\limits_{(I,J)\in D(P,R)} m_{IJ(x_J)}}, \tag{15.26}$$

where $N(P, R)$ denotes the set of all connected pairs of regions (I, J), such that $I \notin \varepsilon(P), J \in \varepsilon(P)/\varepsilon(R)$ and $D(P, R)$ defines the connected pairs of regions (I, J), that hold $I \in D(P)/\varepsilon(R), J \in \varepsilon(R)$.

The message updates (15.26) appear to be quite complex - and in deed, the computational complexity of the Generalized Belief Propagation is very high. However, a visualization of the message paths by use of the region graph (as given in figures 15.2 to 15.5) allows us to gain more insight into the behavior of the message and belief updates.

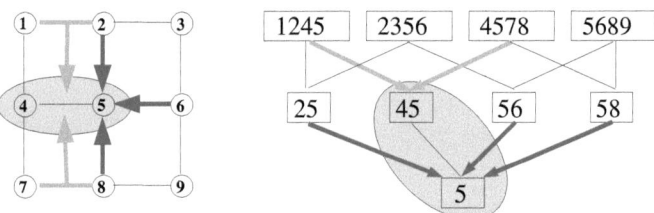

Figure 15.3: **Two node belief:** The belief for the region 45 is computed as in (15.25): $b_{45} = k\phi_4\phi_5\psi_{45}m_{25}m_{65}m_{85}m_{1245}m_{4578}$, where blue edges denote single node messages and green edges denote messages between regions.

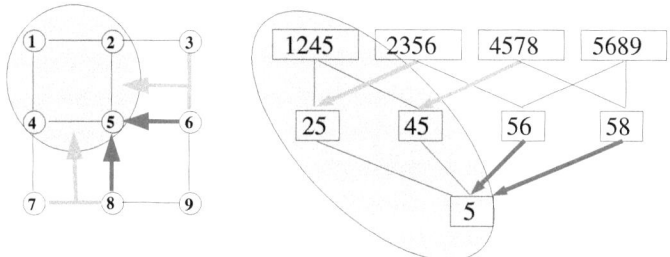

Figure 15.4: **Four node belief:** The belief for the region 1245 is computed as in (15.25): $b_{1245} = k\phi_1\phi_2\phi_4\phi_5\psi_{14}\psi_{12}\psi_{45}\psi_{25}m_{25}m_{65}m_{85}m_{3625}m_{4578}$, where blue edges denote single node messages and green edges denote messages between regions.

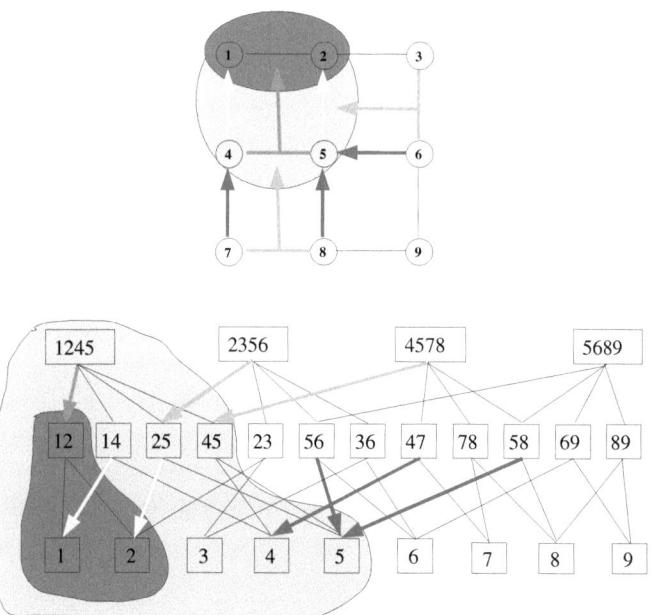

Figure 15.5: **GBP message update rule:** example message update for m_{4512} (red arrow), which propagates the belief from the light blue region (source) to the dark blue region (target). Following (15.26), $m_{4512} = phi_1\phi_2\phi_4\phi_5\psi_{14}\psi_{12}\psi_{45}\psi_{25}m_{47}m_{58}m_{56}m_{4578}m_{2356}$.

16 Speeding Up GBP Inference On MRF

Generalized Belief Propagation (GPB) (see section 15.4.7) provides us with a deterministic inference method which is usually able to cope with the loopy graph structure of the problems in our general *framework* (see section 1.2). The main drawback of GBP, as discussed in section 15.4.7, is its computational complexity.

In this chapter, we derive two speed-up techniques introduced in (Petersen et al., 2008) which take advantage of the loopy structure of our problems to achieve massive speed-ups for the GBP inference.

Related Work

There have been quite many publications tackling the problem of MRF inference speed, however we restrict our review on methods for the speed-up of Generalized Belief Propagation (see section 15.4.7). To the best of our knowledge, there are only two papers, (Shental et al., 2003) and (Kumar and Torr, 2006), that focus on speed-up techniques for the GBP algorithm. Both are guided by the same idea that several edge potentials (see section 15.3) in a MRF can be divided into *compatible* pairs of labels whose values are label-dependent and *incompatible* pairs of labels that all have the same value. As the number of compatible pairs of labels n_c is usually much smaller than the number of incompatible labels n_i, one can gain a speed-up of n_c/n_i by not computing redundant incompatible labels. (Shental et al., 2003) suggests this approach for the Ising model, and (Kumar and Torr, 2006) for the more general *robust truncated model*, comprising the piecewise constant prior and the piecewise smooth prior (Veksler, 1999). Thus, both techniques require a beneficial structure of the edge potentials for sparing redundant label configurations. In contrast, both our techniques accelerate the GBP algorithm on grid-like MRFs with arbitrary potential functions.

Our approach is substantially different: we introduce two different speed-up techniques which work independent of the underlying potential functions. We gain a massive speed-up by restricting the MRF to graphs with regular neighborhood structures, like 4 or 6−neighborhoods in 2D and 3D regular grids and exploiting redundancies in this regular structure. In practice, this constraint is not very problematic because the actual reason to use GBP is the loopy (grid-like) structure of the problems.

Our first method, called "Caching and Multiplication" (see section 16.1) uses smart caching strategies to minimize the number of messages which have to be computed.

Our second method is based on techniques known from standard BP and speeds up the MAP estimation for multi-label problems (see section 16.2).

16.1 Caching and Multiplication

Analyzing the messages that are computed within the same two- or four-node region, we notice that some messages appear repeatedly. As shown in figure 16.1, each cluster message computation involves four of the eight surrounding edge messages and three of the four surrounding cluster messages. Remarkably, the selection of the messages is not arbitrary but follows a simple pattern. In a cluster message m_{stuv} for instance, where s and t are the source nodes, and u and v are the target nodes, node potentials ϕ are only defined for the source nodes, while edge potentials ψ demand that at least one source node is involved. Similarly, incoming edge messages lead from outside the basic cluster to a source node of m_{stuv}, while incoming cluster messages demand that at least one of its source nodes has to be a source node of m_{stuv}.

Also in edge messages, source nodes depend on data potentials and incoming edge messages, whereas pairwise node regions rely on edge potentials and incoming cluster messages. We subsume related factors of the message update rules into *cache products* and benefit in two ways:

1. *Caching*: Some cache products appear in several message update rules. We gain a speed-up if we cache the messages and use them for multiple message computations (see figure 16.1).

2. *Multiplication Order*: The multiplication order of the potentials and incoming messages plays a vital role. Node potentials and edge messages are represented by k-dimensional *vectors*, whereas edge potentials and cluster messages correspond to $k \times k$ *matrices*. The cache products are factors of either vector or matrix form, which means that we need less computations than in the original formula where vectors and matrices are interleaved.

16.1.1 Caching and Multiplication in 2D

Edge messages in 2D

If we subsume all edge message factors that depend on the same source node s into a cache product P_s, we obtain

$$P_s = \phi_s m_{as} m_{bs} m_{cs}, \tag{16.1}$$

whereas edge message factors that depend on two nodes s and u can be summarized as a cache product P_{su}

$$P_{su} = \psi_{su} m_{bdsu} m_{cesu}. \tag{16.2}$$

Combining both cache products, we can rewrite (15.24) as

$$m_{su}(x_u) = \max_{x_s} P_s P_{su}. \tag{16.3}$$

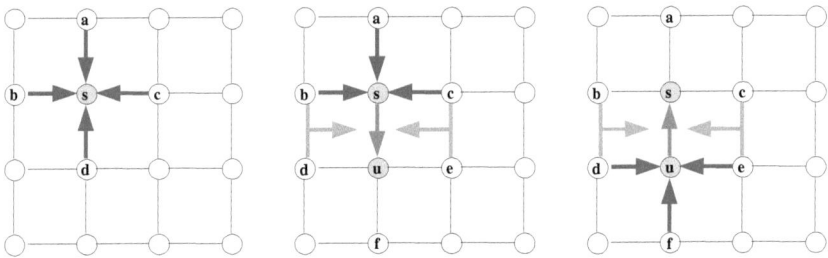

Figure 16.1: **Left**: A diagram of the messages that influence the single-node belief at site s in a two-dimensional grid. **Center** and **right**: All edge messages (red) that are contained in the same two-node belief region $R = \{s, u\}$ (gray nodes). Note that the cluster messages from edges to edges are identical in both figures.

Cluster messages in 2D

By analogy to the case of edge messages, we can define cache products within the message update rule for cluster messages. For instance, if we compute the message update rule for the first cluster message of figure 16.2, the required cache products for source nodes are given by

$$P_s = \phi_s m_{as} m_{cs}, \qquad P_t = \phi_t m_{bt} m_{dt} \qquad (16.4)$$

and the cache products for pairs of nodes can be written as

$$P_{st} = \psi_{st} m_{abst}, \qquad P_{su} = \psi_{su} m_{cesu}, \qquad P_{tv} = \psi_{tv} m_{dftv}. \qquad (16.5)$$

Substituting these expressions into (15.25), we obtain

$$m_{stuv}(x_u, x_v) = (m_{su} m_{tv})^{-1} \max_{x_s, x_t} P_s P_t P_{st} P_{su} P_{tv}. \qquad (16.6)$$

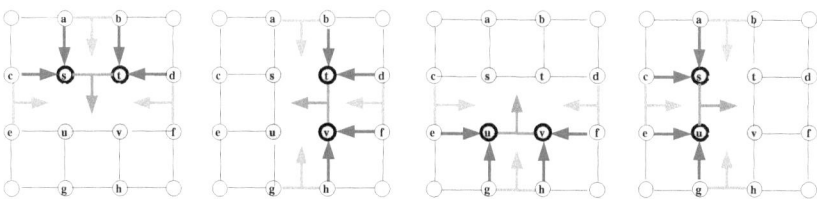

Figure 16.2: A diagram of all cluster messages that are contained in the same four-node belief region $R = \{s, t, u, v\}$ (gray nodes). Blue edges on the grid lines stand for edge messages in the nominator, whereas yellow edges are those in the denominator of the corresponding message update rule. Green messages in the center of the grid cells denote cluster messages that influence the value of the red cluster message. We can observe that the same messages appear within several figures.

16.1.2 Caching and Multiplication in 3D

We can extend the caching and multiplication technique to 3D grids with a six-connected neighborhood system. The only difference is that the products of nodes and edges involve more terms than in the two-dimensional case, thereby increasing the speed-up.

Edge Messages in 3D

The cache product over the source variable of edge messages is computed by

$$P_s = \phi_s m_{as} m_{cs} m_{ds} m_{es} m_{is} \qquad (16.7)$$

and the corresponding product over the pairs of nodes is described by

$$P_{su} = \psi_{su} m_{absu} m_{dfsu} m_{egsu} m_{ijsu} \qquad (16.8)$$

Using these definitions of the cache products, the 3D version has the same form as in the 2D case (see formula (16.3)).

Cluster Messages in 3D

For cluster messages, we define the cache products for the source nodes as

$$P_s = \phi_s m_{as} m_{es} m_{gs} m_{ms} \tag{16.9}$$

and the cache products on pairs of nodes as

$$P_{st} = \psi_{st} m_{abst} m_{efst} m_{mnst}. \tag{16.10}$$

The explicit expression in (15.25) transforms to the same as in the 2D case (see (16.6)).

16.2 Accelerating MAP Estimation

According to (16.6) the GBP algorithm grows with the power of four in the number of labels, since the computation of a cluster message requires the traversal of all label combinations of x_s and x_t for each combination of x_u and x_v. Compared to edge messages that require quadratic computation time (see (16.3)), the update rule for cluster messages consumes most of the time for inference problems with multiple labels. In this section, we therefore pursue the question if it is necessary to explore all possible label combinations of x_s and x_t for determining the maximum.

In the spirit of (Felzenszwalb and Huttenlocher, 2006), (Kumar and Torr, 2006) and (Kumar et al., 2005), we sort the terms of (16.6) by *source variables* x_s and x_t, yielding

$$m_{stuv}(x_u, x_v) = (m_{su} m_{tv})^{-1} \max_{x_s, x_t} \left(P_{st} M_{su} M_{tv} \right) \tag{16.11}$$

where we define

$$M_{su} = P_s P_{su}, \qquad M_{tv} = P_t P_{tv}.$$

We observe that the maximum message value is likely to consist of relatively large factors P_{st}, M_{su} and M_{tv}. Thus, for each combination of x_u and x_v the basic idea is to start at the maximum values of M_{su} and M_{tv} in the respective columns and then systematically decrease the factors until the product of both entries and the corresponding value in P_{st} is assured to be maximal. Thus, we have to answer two questions:

(1) How do we traverse the label combinations for x_s and x_t such that the product of M_{su} and M_{tv} decreases monotonically?

(2) Under which conditions can we terminate the search for the maximum?

Traversal Order

We have to proceed for each combination of x_u and x_v separately. Assume we set $x_u = u$ and $x_v = v$. Then we obtain the maximum product of the first two factors in (16.11) by determining the maximum entry s_{max} in the u-th column of M_{su} and the maximum entry t_{max} in the v-th column of M_{tv}. We multiply this product with the entry at position (s_{max}, t_{max}) in P_{st} and store the result as the first *temporary* maximum product value r_{max}. Suppose that the entry (s_{max}, t_{max}) is the i_{left} biggest value of all entries in P_{st}. Then, all combinations of x_s and x_t whose entry in P_{st} is smaller than the i_{left} biggest value of P_{st} are not eligible to be the *final* maximum product value. For this reason we can save time by just computing the products for combinations of x_s and x_t with a bigger value than the i_{left} biggest value of P_{st}.

Unfortunately, our speed-up is relatively small if i_{left} is large. For decreasing i_{left}, we examime which label combination of x_s and x_t leads to the next biggest product of M_{su} and M_{tv}. We *sort* M_{su}

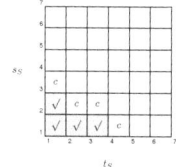

Figure 16.3: Visualization of the candidates for the next combination of s_S and s_T. Visited combinations are marked with a tick on dark gray background. The light gray fields with a c denote possible candidates for the maximal unvisited combination. White fields are unvisited and are not eligible as the next possible combination.

and M_{tv} column by column and refer to them as S_{su} and S_{tv}. Then s_{max} and t_{max} correspond to the positions $(1, u)$ in S_{su} and $(1, v)$ in S_{tv}, and the candidates for the next biggest combination have to be either $(1, u)$ in S_{su} and $(2, v)$ in S_{tv} or $(2, u)$ in S_{su} and $(1, v)$ in S_{tv}. We compute both products and take the bigger one. In general, the set of candidates for the next biggest product value of M_{su} and M_{tv} constitutes from label combinations for x_s and x_t that are adjacent to the already visited. Compare with figure 16.3 where s_S and t_S refer to the row positions in S_{su} and S_{tv}.

Thus, we gradually determine the next biggest products of M_{su} and M_{tv} and multiply it with the corresponding entry of s and t in P_{st}. We compare the result with the temporary maximum product value r_{max} and replace it if the new value is bigger. In this case, we also update i_{left}. This pattern is repeated until i_{left} is considerably small, i.e. smaller than a predefined threshold β. Once i_{left} falls below β, we can trigger the traversal of less than i_{left} combinations whose entries in P_{st} are bigger than the entry of the current maximum product value $(s_{\text{max}}, t_{\text{max}})$.

Termination conditions

We have found the maximum product if any of the following two conditions is satisfied:

1. We have visited all entries in P_{st} that are bigger than the entry at position (s_{max}, t_{max}) in P_{st}.

2. The product of M_{su} and M_{tv}, multiplied with the maximal unvisited entry in P_{st}, is smaller than r_{max}.

16.3 Discussion

The evaluation of our speed-up techniques on a benchmark setting in section 17.2 shows the huge potential of the introduced methods - especially for 3D grids. However, even with speed-ups of up to factor 100, GBP remains to be a rather expensive method. Hence, an application of GBP inference on large volume data is still not advisable, but we will show in part III, for most applications it is possible to use cheap non-deterministic methods to initialize the data for a final small and local GBP inference.

17 Experiments

In this chapter, we provide the results of benchmark evaluations of our proposed classification speed-up algorithms. Section 17.1 shows the possible speed-ups using our SVM-Tree algorithm from section 14.

Section 17.2 gives benchmark results for our two algorithms from section 16 for the fast GBP inference of MRFs.

17.1 SVM-Trees

In order to show the validity and classification accuracy of our algorithm, we performed a series of experiments on standard benchmark data-sets (Zapién et al., 2006)(Fehr et al., 2007)(Fehr and Zapién, 2007). In this series of experiments, we compare our tree of linear $H1$-SVMs with a standard non-linear SVM using a RBF kernel. The data has been split into training and test sets, normalized to minimum and maximum feature values and we applied the One-vs-One multi-class algorithm for the multi-class problems.

Tables for each dataset are presented with the number of features of each dataset, the number of training and testing samples used, the number of required SVs or hyperplanes depending on the method, training and classification time[1] (hh:mm:ss). Finally, the classification accuracy is shown.

Speed-up comparison with similar works is difficult to state since most publications (see related work) used datasets with less than 1000 samples, where the training and testing time are negligible compared to the size of our datasets.

17.1.1 DNA Dataset

DNA	RBF-SVM	H1-SVM
Nr. Features	180	180
Nr. Train Samples	1330	1330
Nr. SVs or Hyperplanes	798	3
Training Time	00:02.35	00:01.84
Nr. Test Samples	1446	1446
Correctly Classified Samples	1354	1305
Classification Time	00:06.70	00:01.86
Classif. Accurancy %	93.64 %	90.25 %

Table 17.1: Results for the DNA dataset.

---

[1]These experiments were run in a computer with a P4, 2.8 GHz and 1G in Ram.

This dataset contains features from DNA sequences (Brazdil and J.Gama, 2006). Splice junctions are points on a DNA sequence at which "superfluous" DNA is removed during the process of protein creation in higher organisms. The problem given in this dataset is to locate the boundaries between exons (the parts of the DNA sequence retained after splicing) and introns (the parts of the DNA sequence that are spliced out). This problem consists of two subtasks: recognizing exon/intron boundaries (referred to as EI sites) and recognizing intron/exon boundaries (IE sites). From the given data, we randomly created two sets with the same proportion of elements of each class. One third of the observations were used for the training set and the rest as testing set.

17.1.2 Faces Dataset

This dataset of face and non-face images can be found in (Carbonetto, 2005). The objective is to determine if an image contains a face or not. From the original dataset, two sets were randomly created with the same proportion of elements of each class. Two thirds of the observations were used for the training set and the rest as testing set.

Faces	RBF-SVM	H1-SVM
Nr. Features	576	576
Nr. Train Samples	9172	9172
Nr. SVs or Hyperplanes	2206	4
Training Time	14:55.23	10:55.70
Nr. Test Samples	4262	4262
Corretly Classified Samples	4082	3879
Classification Time	03:13.60	00:14.73
Classif. Accurancy %	95.78 %	91.01 %

Table 17.2: Results for the Faces dataset.

17.1.3 Fourclass Dataset

This is a artificial 2D dataset from (Ho and Kleinberg, 1996). The test and the training samples were randomly generated; one third of the population became training samples.

Fourclass	RBF-SVM	H1-SVM
Nr. Features	2	2
Nr. Train Samples	287	287
Nr. SVs or Hyperplanes	150	16
Training Time	00:00.10	00:00.18
Nr. Test Samples	618	618
Corretly Classified Samples	498	573
Classification Time	00:00.08	00:00.05
Classif. Accurancy %	80.58 %	92.72 %

Table 17.3: Results for the Fourclass dataset.

17.1.4 USPS Dataset

The USPS data is a database for handwritten text recognition research (Hull, 1994), the training set contains 2007 examples and the test set 7291 examples.

USPS	RBF-SVM	H1-SVM
Nr. Features	256	256
Nr. Train Samples	18063	18063
Nr. SVs or Hyperplanes	3597	49
Training Time	00:44.74	00:22.70
Nr. Test Samples	7291	7291
Corretly Classified Samples	6986	6836
Classification Time	01:58.59	00:19.99
Classif. Accurancy %	95.82 %	93.76 %

Table 17.4: Results for the Usps dataset.

17.1.5 Discussion

We proposed a method for fast SVM classification via SVM-Trees with linear $H1$ nodes. Compared to non-linear SVM and speed-up methods, our experiments showed a very competitive speed-up while achieving reasonable classification results (loosing only marginally when we apply the non-linear extension compared to non-linear methods). Especially if our initial assumption holds that large problems can be split in mainly easy and only a few hard problems, our algorithm achieves very good results. The advantage of this approach clearly lies in its simplicity since no parameter has to be tuned.

17.2 Fast MRF GBP

We estimate the effect of the accelerated MAP computation with two experiments[2]: First, we measure the speed-up for different numbers of labels on a 8×8 grid-like MRF, where we use the Potts model

---

[2]All experiments are conducted on a 3 GHz CPU with 2 GB RAM. The caching and multiplication technique is enabled.

♯ Labels	Standard [s]	MAP accelerated [s]	Speed-up
8	0.03	0.05	0.61
16	0.15	0.15	1.03
32	1.21	0.59	2.05
64	15.43	2.92	5.28
128	243.03	19.29	12.60
256	4845.19	183.36	26.42

Figure 17.1: The average iteration time of the standard and the accelerated MAP implementation for various label sizes.

(see section 15.3.3) (Winkler, 2006) for the edge potentials. In figure 17.1, we show how the average runtime per iteration varies between the standard implementation and our technique. Note that the runtime in the first iterations is often much higher than in later iterations. The reason could be that the message values contain more candidate maxima, which have to be evaluated in our optimized algorithm. After several iterations, edge messages seem to attribute relatively high probabilities to a small number of labels.

Second, we demonstrate the effectiveness of our technique for other potentials by computing the average runtime of 100 random edge potentials for various sizes of k (see figure 17.2). Opposed to the first experiment, we do not evaluate the computation cost of the whole GBP algorithm, but solely the elapsed time for computing the MAP estimate for cluster messages. Figure 17.2 shows the ratio of these runtimes. We can observe that the speed-up of our implementation grows almost linearly.

While we always benefit from using cache products, we recommend to use the second optimization technique solely for label sizes bigger than 15. For smaller labels sizes, the computational overhead per combination outweighs the reduced number of visited combinations.

Our experiments show that the Caching and Multiplication technique improves on the standard implementation roughly by factor 10. Several optimizations contribute to this result. First, we gain most of the speed-up by exploiting cache products that inherently use a beneficial multiplication order. Second, compared to the standard form of the message update rule in (Yedidia, 2004), the direct evaluation of the message update rules avoids the initial recursive traversal of the region graph for determining all incoming messages in the formulas. And finally, we do not have to evaluate the variable order of factors before multiplication.

An additional benefit of the caching and multiplication technique is that we can reduce the storage costs, since we do not have to store references from a message to its dependent messages.

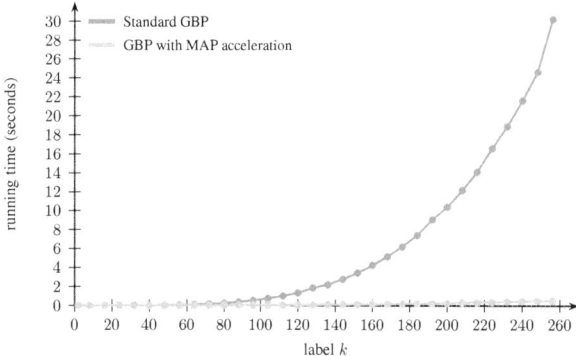

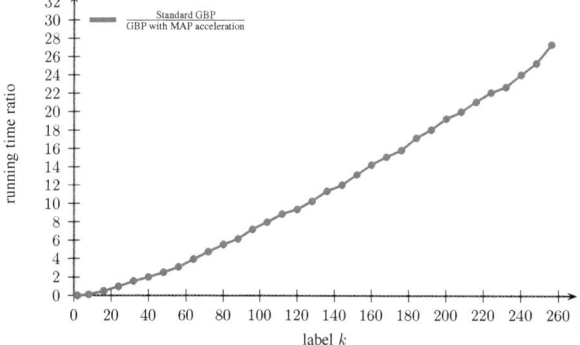

Figure 17.2: **Top**: Runtime as a function of the number of labels k. **Bottom**: Ratio of standard GBP to MAP accelerated GBP as a function of k.

Part III

Applications

18 Introduction

In this third and final part of the thesis, we present three quite different applications for our 3D image analysis *framework*:

Cell Classification: In chapter 19, we apply our *framework* to automatically segment and classify different cell types in dense 3D confocal laser scanning microscope (LSM) tissue recordings. The goal of this application is to establish a quantitative high-throughput analysis of tissue samples in order to gain statistics on the cooccurrence of certain cell types during physiological processes.

Spine Detection: Neuronal spines play an important role in many neuro-physiological processes. In chapter 20, we applied our *framework* to automatically detect and count spines in 3D volume data recorded by an confocal laser scanning microscope (LSM).

3D Shape Retrieval: Finally, in chapter 21, we apply our *framework* to 3D shape retrieval, which is a common problem when searching in large databases of 3D objects like protein databases or 3D object collections. We evaluated our novel approach of local 3D shape descriptors, which is motivated by the "Bag of Features" approach form 2D image retrieval, on the "Princeton Shape Benchmark".

Since two of our applications use that which has been obtained from 3D confocal laser scanning microscopes (LSM), we give a very brief roundup of this imaging technique. A complete reference on 3D microscopy can be found in (Pawley, 1995). Additionally, (Ronneberger, 2008) addresses the aspects of 3D microscopy from an image processing/pattern recognition point of view.

18.1 Data Acquisition by 3D Microscopy

Our data is recorded by Confocal Laser Scanning Microscopy (LSM), which is a special 3D method based on fluorescent microscopy.

18.1.1 Fluorescent Microscopy

Definition: Fluorescence is a luminescence phenomenon in which a molecule absorbs a high-energy photon and re-emits another in a lower state of energy (longer wave-length).

Fluorescent microscopy takes advantage of the fluorescence effect in order to image details of the specimen, which hardly could be retrieved by common light microscopy. Most light microscopes can be used for fluorescent microscopy, all it takes is a special light source and some filters.
Since most fluorescent substances are mostly excited by rather short-wave emissions, the light source usually has a wave-length in the blue to ultra violet spectrum, but other frequencies are also possible.
The light is projected by a dichroic mirror from the source onto (or through) the probe. The excited fluorescent molecules then emit photons themselves, which are collected by the objective lens. The dichroic mirror has the property of reflecting only certain frequencies and letting others pass. Hence, the light emitted by the fluorescent, with its shorter wavelength, can pass the mirror and reach the CCD

camera or the ocular.

Since most probes are not auto-fluorescent, one uses anti-body or transgenic markers to couple biological structures with fluorescent molecules. A further advantage of this approach is that one can selectively mark structures of interest while other structures remain invisible.

Fluorescent Anti-Body Markers

One convenient way to place fluorescent markers is to couple them with anti-bodys which dock to the target structure. There are countless fluorescent marker/anti-body combinations for many different structures available, some of which are quite toxic and can be used to fixate a current biological stage while others can be applied to living organisms. Two of these were used in some of our applications:

BrdU: This chemical is a base analog of thymidine, with the thymine substituted by bromouracil. By substituting for thymidine during DNA replication, BrdU is incorporated in newly synthesized DNA. Hence, BrdU antibodies linked to fluorescent molecules are used to visualize active DNA in living cells.

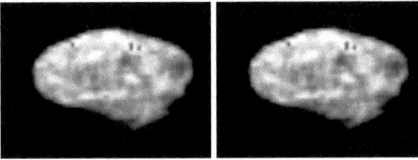

Figure 18.1: An LSM recorded nucleus marked with BrdU. Left in pseudo coloration, right in grayscale.

YoPro: Binds to the DNA double helix. This works with inactive or dead cells, as well as with active ones. YoPro is usually used to visualize the entire nuclei of cells.

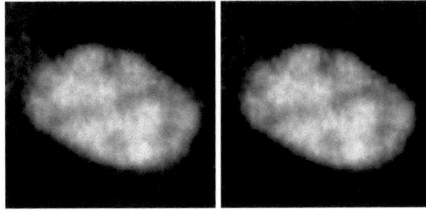

Figure 18.2: An LSM recorded erythrocyte nucleus marked with YoPro. Left in pseudo coloration, right in gray scale.

Transgenic Fluorescent Markers

Another method is to directly embed a "fluorescence gene" into the DNA. This causes an artificial auto-fluorescence which can be targeted at specific structures or gene expressions or at the complete anatomic structure. The advantage of the transgenic method is that one can avoid permanent bleaching effects (see section 18.1.3) which is needed when a probe has to be observed over the time.

GFP: The green fluorescent protein (GFP) from the sea pansy has a single major excitation peak at 498 nm. In cell and molecular biology, the GFP gene is frequently used as a reporter of gene expressions or to visualize anatomic structures. Figure 18.3 shows an example recording of neuronal structures from a transgenic mouse.

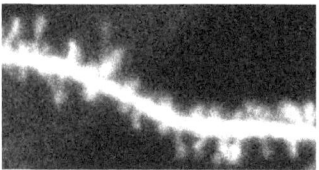

Figure 18.3: Example recording of neuronal structures from a transgenic mouse (GFP) as gray-scale image.

The advantage of fluorescent microscopy is that only previously marked structures are imaged and reflections of the exciting light from unmarked structures are filtered by the dichroic splitter (Pawley, 1995).

One major drawback of conventional fluorescent microscopy is that it is a quite sensitive technique. In thicker probes, underlying and overlying structures outshine those in focus and cause huge background noise eventually covering much of the requested detail.

To avoid this problem, confocal laser scanning microscopy is used instead.

18.1.2 Confocal Laser Scanning Microscopy (LSM)

The use of lasers as light source for fluorescent microscopy has several advantages compared to other kinds of exciting light. First, lasers beam only in one predetermined direction, can be focused to a single point with very high resolution, and have a fixed wavelength (Pawley, 1995). Most laser scanning microscopes (LSM) have more than one laser with different wavelengths. So, different stainings can be applied simultaneously and recorded in different channels. Just like ordinary light, the laser beam is reflected by the dichroic mirror and projected through the objective onto the probe. Unlike in conventional microscopy, the laser only exposes one point in the x-y-coordinate of the specimen at a time. By moving the beam over the probe line by line, the image is scanned and then reassembled.

The actual "trick" of laser scanning microscopes is that it is also possible to control the position of the focal plane in direction of the z-axis. This is achieved by use of the **pinhole**.

The light emitted from the probe is collected by the objective and passes the dichroic mirror. Before reaching the photomultiplier, which is the actual imaging medium, beams have to pass the pinhole. Fig. 18.4 shows, how only focused paths and such close to them are able to pass the pinhole. Other defocused paths are hardly mapped.

By moving the probe in the z-axis, a series of focal images can be recorded slice by slice, where the pinhole size determines the thickness.

18.1.3 Imaging Problems

Even though laser scanning microscopes are able to produce high-resolution image stacks with many favorable properties, there are still some quite challenging imaging problems:

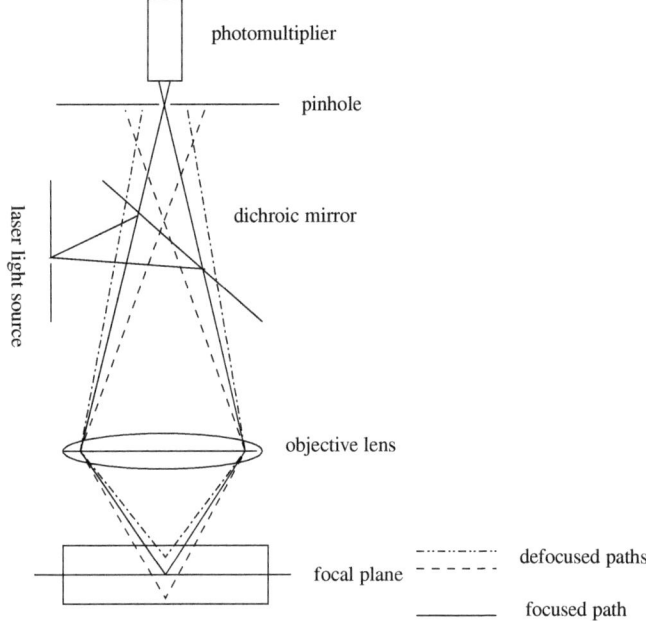

Figure 18.4: Schematic view of a confocal laser scanning microscope (Pawley, 1995)

Reduced z-Resolution: The resolution in direction of the z-axis of a LSM recording is usually not as high as for the x-y-planes. This results in a non-cubic voxel resolution and a strong blur along z-direction on the point spread function (PSF). The different spatial resolution cause major problems, especially when we try to extract rotation invariant features. Section 4.1.3 describes how we cope with this problem.

Absorption: Another common problem is that the emitting fluorescent light is absorbed by higher layers of the specimen. Depending on the optical density of the probe, this leads to the phenomenon that the intensity of the recorded data is decreasing in z-direction. Hence, absorption is one of the reasons why gray-scale invariance is an important property of our features.

Bleaching: A further cause of unstable recording intensities is the so-called bleaching effect: the fluorescent molecules can only emit a certain number of photons. After photons have been emitted, the fluorescence effect fades-out. While auto-fluorescence recovers after some time, the usual markers are loosing their ability permanently.

Laser/Specimen Interaction: Finally, we also have to face the problem that the design of the biological experiment prevents an "optimal" image quality. The typical example is that one needs to avoid an interaction between the imaging device and the probe. Especially living organisms (like in chapter 20) tend to react on the laser light and heat. Hence, we often have to reduce the laser intensity, causing additional noise and darker images.

We try to cope with most of these problems by using our combination of invariant features and learning methods. We explicitly abstain from the common approach of using **deconvolution** methods. The main reason is that our method achieves good results without an expensive deconvolution. Additionally, we have the "feeling" (so far we have not gathered any empirical data that would prove this "feeling") that the available deconvolution methods are not sufficient to deliver beneficial results for our data. The reason for that might be that even if one calibrates the deconvolution by measuring the point spread function for each microscope, the interaction of the lasers and emitting light with the individual specimens alters the PSF in each and every single recording.

19 Simultaneous Segmentation and Classification of Cell Nuclei in Dense Tissue Samples

19.1 Introduction

The first application for our combination of local invariant features and learning methods is stated in the emerging field of biological image analysis. Recent approaches in biological research, especially in *System Biology*, are establishing novel quantitative evaluation methods which try move the traditionally used qualitative descriptions of biological observations towards a more formal quantitative modelling. One technical side-effect of this new quantitative biology is the raising demand of (semi)-automatic image analysis systems. Since many commonly used biological observation techniques are based on the visual evaluation and the analysis of biological processes based on reliable quantitative measurements require the acquisition of rather large data sets, it is obvious that the demand for an alternative to tedious and expensive manual evaluations by automatic systems is vastly growing.

A large portion of the images which have to be analyzed are obtained from various microscopy techniques. Most commonly, image analysis problems are stated in the domain of 2D, possibly multi-channel (see section 2.2.1) images from standard imaging techniques, such as transmitted light, incident light, darkfield or fluorescent microscopy (see section 18.1.1). By now, research on (semi)-automatic analysis methods in this 2D domain has been carrying on for over two decades. The results which have been achieved so far are twofold: on one hand, there have been some great advances in algorithmic solutions to many key problems such as the *Watershed* algorithm (Beucher, 1991), *Level Sets* (Sethian, 1996) or *Snakes* (Michael et al., 1988) for segmentation problems and the adaption of powerful learning techniques like *Support Vector Machines* (Schölkopf and Smola, 2002) or *Boosting* (Schapire, 2002) for the classification of biological structures. On the other hand, there are still so many open problems that only a few simple automatic analysis tasks could be considered to be solved to the extent that would match a manual evaluation.
A major aspect of the remaining problems, besides the huge intra class variations one has to face in biological systems and the often poor imaging quality, is the fact that most biological systems are not bound to a 2D environment. Hence, it is obvious that one cannot actually expect to solve analysis problems of often anisotropic 3D structures by means of 2D imaging. This common argument has recently been confirmed by a comparative study which showed the advantages of a 3D approach (Meyer et al., 2008).

Recent technological advances in the field of 3D microscopy (see section 18.1 for an introduction of 3D microscopy techniques) allow the recording of real 3D volumetric images of biological structures. This development directly implies the need of novel algorithms which take advantage of the full 3D information.
However, moving from 2D to 3D does not only have advantages, but also comes along with some new problems: Besides some issues concerning the image quality of 3D volume recordings (see section

18.1.3 for details), one has to deal with a strong increase in the data size of the recordings and the additional computational complexity in three dimensions which causes many approved 2D methods to be too expensive for many applications.

Another common problem of biological image analysis, which is further increased in the case of 3D data, is the fact that many algorithms that are actually solving a given problem have been designed using a highly specific model of the target structures. This largely inhibits the direct application of these methods to even closely related problems. In general, this can be seen as one of the major limiting factors in current biological image analysis methods because it requires the costly and time consuming development of individual solutions for every new problem setting.

In this context, we emphasize the need for more generic solutions, which are able to adapt to a wider range of different problems. Our approach towards such a generic modelling is driven by learning methods. In combination with our local invariant features, we are able to present a novel approach which provides a generic *framework* for the solution of different analysis tasks on quite different 3D data sets.

We evaluate our approach on two different biological applications: the automatic simultaneous segmentation and classification of cell nuclei in dense tissue samples which is presented in this chapter, and the automatic detecting of neuronal spines presented in chapter 20.

19.1.1 Segmentation and Classification of Cell Nuclei

In biological and medical research as well as in histopathologic diagnosis, the localization and classification of cells is an everyday business. A vast number of research techniques and treatment methods require detailed information on the amount, type, localization and state of cells in a given probe of tissue or dilution.

Locating, classifying and analyzing cells is not a simple task: its very time consuming, and in most cases a human expert is needed. Although there are various methods around, which perform quite well for simple tasks like counting or the segmentation of single cells in dilution, the very same tasks remain largely unsolved when the nuclei are located in dense tissue.

A major problem of the cell classification in dense tissue probes is the segmentation. In order to achieve good classification results, supervised-learning classifiers rely on properly segmented training samples and classification probes. However, a proper segmentation is hard to realize without higher semantic knowledge about the object to segment. On the other hand, the use of a-priori knowledge and manual segmentations are exactly what we are trying to avoid in the design of a generic automatic approach.

For this reason, we chose to use a learning based segmentation algorithm, which is capable of performing segmentation and classification simultaneously. Using our local invariant features from part I, which are extracted from the surrounding neighborhood of each voxel, we apply an interactive training procedure to train support-vector machine and MRF models (see part II). Once these models have been obtained for the requested cells types, the segmentation and classification of unknown data sets can then be performed automatically without any further human interaction.

19.1.2 Contributions

The methods presented in this chapter resulted in a number of publications and contributed to several different novel results. On the biological side, our algorithms were used to investigate anatomical structures involved in the physiological processes during angiogenesis (see section 19.2 for details). Using our quantitative image analysis results for cell counting or the co-location analysis of cell types, helped to gain several novel biological findings which resulted from our cooperations with research partners[1] in the biological field: (Kurz et al., 2007) (Kurz et al., 2006) (Sauer et al., 2006) (Kurz et al., 2005a) (Kurz et al., 2005b).

A key result of the biological application of our methods has been introduced in (Kurz et al., 2008), where it has been shown that it is possible to differentiate several cell types using only a single antibody marker (see section 18.1.1 for a brief introduction on fluorescent markers). This technical result could lead to the use of a novel time saving staining procedure which eventually could be used for many biological experiments.

On the pattern recognition side, we investigated the performance of our local features and introduced several additional biological applications for our methods: (Fehr et al., 2005) (Ronneberger et al., 2005) (Fehr et al., 2006) (Schilling et al., 2007) (Wicklein, 2006) (Fehr, 2005) (Fehr, 2007b) (Fehr and Burkhardt, 2007a).

19.1.3 Related Work

There have been countless publications on automatic segmentation and classification of cells in 2D data sets. However, we restrict our review of related work to methods which use the full 3D information to segment (and classify) cell nuclei in dense tissue.

The most popular method for the segmentation of nuclei is to apply one of the 3D versions of the (seeded) watershed algorithm (Beucher, 1991). A typical example of such an approach is shown in (Lin et al., 2007).

The approach presented in (Li et al., 2007) also only provides a segmentation of the nuclei. The method is quite similar to our $1v$-Feature (see section 9.1) and uses a diffusion smoothing of the 3D gradient field combined with a Hough like detector for spherical structures.

Another approach that is closely related to our $1v$-Feature is the method presented in (Schulz et al., 2006), which uses a Haar framework to detect spherical cell structures by integrating over local gradient directions.

Finally, there has been a notable 2D cell segmentation approach: (Conrad et al., 2004) implements a segmentation by classification, using various local 2D features, such as 2D Haar-Features (Schulz-Mirbach, 1995b), moments (Flusser, 1998) or Haralick Texture Features (Haralick, 1979).

19.2 Biological Background

The experiments presented in this chapter were all performed on 3D volumetric data samples of chicken embryo chorioallantoic membrane (CAM) probes recorded by a confocal laser scanning microscope (LSM) (also see section 18.1.2 for a description of the LSM technique). The data (along with manual annotations) has been kindly provided by the group of H. Kurz from the Institute of Anatomy I at the University of Freiburg.

It should be noted that our proposed method is not bound to CAM data, but could be directly applied to any other 3D LSM recordings of cell nuclei in dense tissue data. We chose to base the presentation of our methods on the sample CAM application because of the availability of large annotated data samples (see section 19.4.1).

The CAM is a widely used model for angiogenesis (the formation and growth of blood vessels) research. For the quantitative investigation of angiogenesis at cellular level, an automatic localization and identification of the different cell types is crucial. Understanding angiogenesis has been found

---

[1]Special thanks to Prof. Kurz and his team for the very fruitful cooperation.

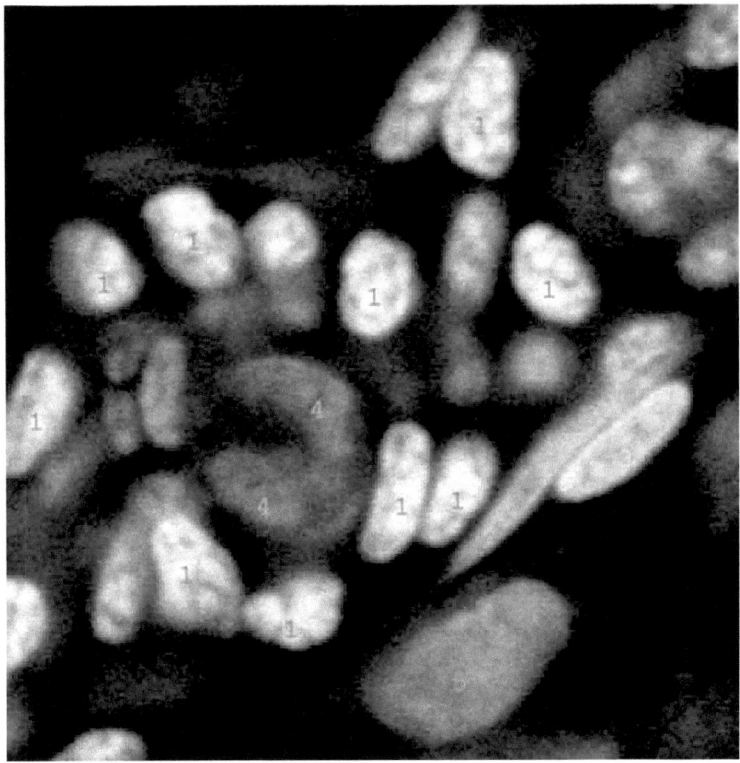

Figure 19.1: Sample CAM data. The xy-slice shows a typical cross-section of a capillary. The majority of cells which can be found in the recordings belongs to one of the following categories: 1. erythrocyte (**Ery**), 2. endothelial cell (**EC**), 3. pericyte (**PC**), 4. fibroblast (**FB**), 5. macrophage (**MΦ**).

key to treatment of many frequent diseases, including cancer and heart ischemia. The samples were prepared as described in (Kurz et al., 2002)(Kurz et al., 2005c) and treated with YoPro-1 and SMACy3 fluorescent markers (see section 18.1.1).

19.2.1 Cell Types

Figure 19.1 shows an xy-slice from an LSM recording of a typical capillary cross-section. The "red blood cells" (erythrocytes, marked by [1]) lie inside the capillary. Note that the applied markers only stain the cell nuclei. Hence, the boundaries of the capillary, which are formed by the endothelial cells [2], are not captured by this imaging technique. Other cell types that play a role in the investigation of angiogenesis are pericytes [3], fibroblasts [4] and macrophages [5].

19.3 Algorithm

Our approach for the simultaneous segmentation and classification of cell nuclei in dense tissue samples is divided into two parts: an off-line training part and the on-line automatic evaluation part.

In the off-line part, we apply a training scheme which iteratively interacts with a human expert. This allows us to model the experts decision function in terms of an optimized combination of local features and SVM kernel functions. Given such a model, we are able to apply an automatic on-line evaluation of unknown data sets which have been recorded under the same conditions as the training set. The entire approach follows our general *framework* as shown in figure 1.1.

19.3.1 Iterative Training.

The heart of the iterative training procedure is our interactive annotation tool (see figure 19.2). The tool provides different 2D slice views (ortho-views) and various annotation tools which allow a human expert to mark positive and negative examples for a set of pre-defined cell types and a background class.

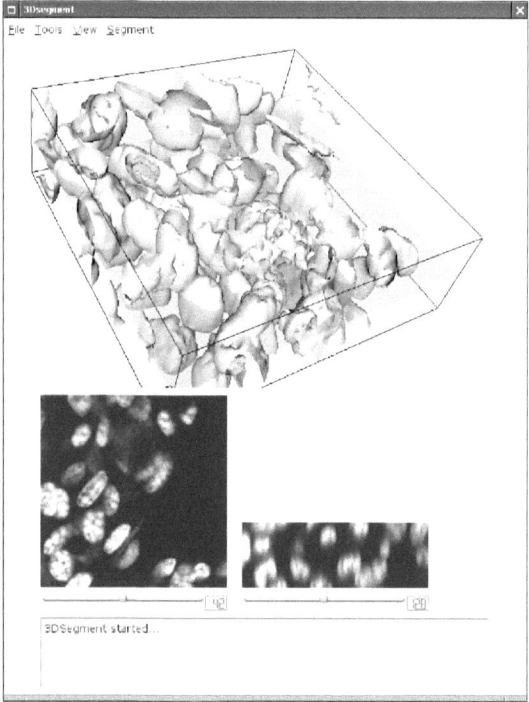

Figure 19.2: Screen-shot of the software-tool used for the iterative training of the cell segmentation and classification model. The human expert uses the xy- and yz-slices to locally and sparsely annotate the training data. The 3D reconstruction is used for the 3D navigation in the volume data.

In the initial iteration step, the expert is asked to give some very sparse examples, i.e. to mark several cell nuclei by a single point. Then, our algorithm computes a first model, and provides an initial evaluation of the entire data set based on this model (see section 19.3.2 for the details of this evaluation). In the following iterations, the expert then adds additional sparse samples to correct the remaining errors. Figures 19.3 and 19.4 show some examples of intermediate training results.

As the model converges towards a smaller training error, we stop the iterative procedure after a predefined number of steps in order to avoid overfitting problems (see section 12.1).

In the following paragraphs, we give an in-depth discussion of these computation steps:

Feature Extraction and Selection. The first step in each iteration is to extract a large number of local features centered at the positions of the given label markers (from this and all previous iterations). The computed features cover a wide range of feature types and heuristic parameter combinations which are defined prior to the off-line training.

Since the classification of cell types is mainly based on their (3D) texture, we apply many of the features presented in part I (refer to sections in brackets): $\mathcal{SH}_{abs}$ (5.1), $\mathcal{SH}_{phase}$ (5.2,) $\mathcal{SH}_{corr}$ (5.3), $\mathcal{SH}_{bispectrum}$ (5.4), 2p-Haar (7.1), 3p-Haar (7.2), $\mathcal{VH}_{abs}$ (8.1) and $\mathcal{VH}_{autocorr}$ (8.2).

Using the SIMBA (see section 10.2) feature selection algorithm, we rank all of the extracted features in terms of their separability of the given training samples. We then use the top 50 features for the further modeling.

SVM Training/Classification. The previous computation step provides a 50 dimensional feature vector for each manually labeled example voxel marked by the expert. This data is used to train an SVM (see chapter 13). We apply a grid search over the kernel parameters for RBF- (13.44) and Histogram-Intersection (13.46) kernels, using cross-validation (12.3) to find the most suitable SVM model.

Then, we apply our fast SVM classification methods (see chapter 14) to perform a voxel-wise classification of the entire training volume. Figures 19.3 and 19.4 show two examples of the convergences of our training procedure over several iterations.

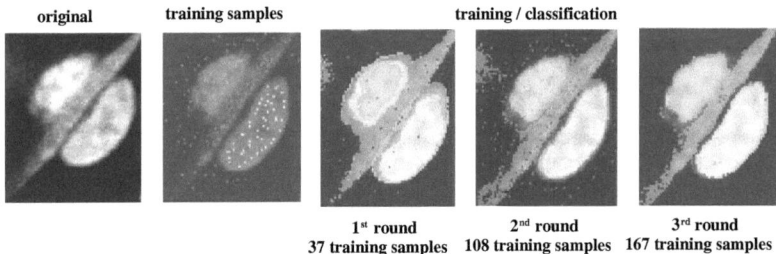

original	training samples	training / classification

	1st round	2nd round	3rd round
	37 training samples	108 training samples	167 training samples

Figure 19.3: Example for the convergences of our training procedure over several iterations. Shown on a local sub-volume of a larger CAM data set which contains three different cell types.

MRF Post-Processing. In the final step, we use the resulting probability map of the SVM classification confidence as node potentials (see section 15.3) of a Markov Random Field (see chapter 15.2). We apply the Pott's Model (15.11) for the edge potentials (see section 15.3) to obtain a smoothing of the voxel-wise classification.

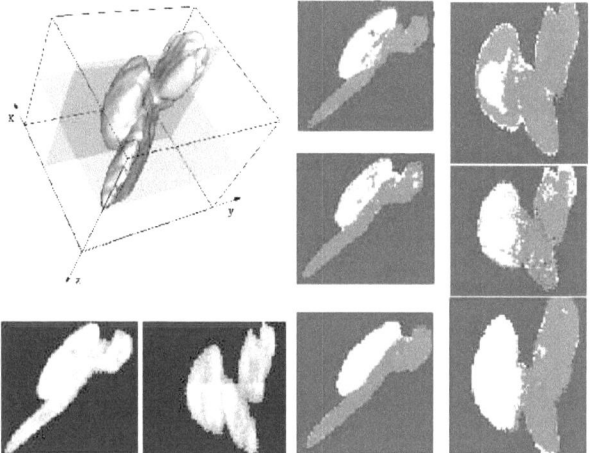

Figure 19.4: Another example showing intermediate results during the training. **Left column:** input data, 3D reconstruction, xy- and yz-slice views. **Center column:** xy-slices of the intermediate results after the 1st, 2nd and 3rd iteration. **Right column:** yz-slices of the same iterations.

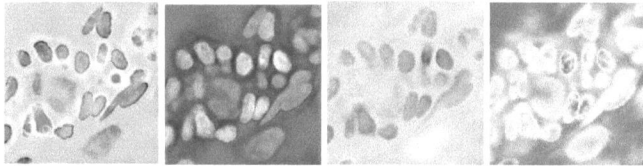

Figure 19.5: Intermediate results during a iteration of the iterative training procedure, xy-slices of the voxel-wise SVM confidence for different cell types (high gray values indicate high confidence). **From left to right:** background class, erythrocytes, marcophages, endothelia cells.

19.3.2 Automatic 3D Image Analysis

After we have obtained the models for the local features and their global interaction, we use these and simply run the feature extraction, classification and post-processing steps on unknown data sets. This can be done fully automatically without any further human interaction, as long as the characteristics of the data are not changing: i.e. the microscope parameters are the same and the preparation of the biological probes lies within the variance of the training data. In practice, this results in the need to retrain the models for each microscope and staining procedure.

In order to speed-up the evaluation, we usually apply fast SVM classification (see chapter 14) and fast MRF inference (see chapter 16).

19.4 Experimental Evaluation

We evaluate our segmentation and classification approach on a manually labeled database of cell nuclei in dense tissue.

19.4.1 Nuclei Database

The database consists of 236 nuclei samples divided into 5 different classes (erythrocyte, endothelia cells, pericyte, fibroblast and macrophage). The samples were recorded from tissue probes of chicken chorioallantoic membrane (see section 19.2) which were treated as described in (Kurz et al., 2002). Human experts manually segmented and labeled the sample nuclei recordings to obtain a voxel-wise ground truth labeling.

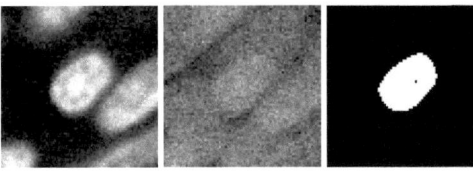

Figure 19.6: Slice of a sample 3D database entry (erythrocyte). Left: YoPro stained channel. Center: SNAAlexa stained channel. Right: ground truth segmentation and label. More examples of this database can be found in appendix C.

We randomly split the database into two equally large train and test sets. Limiting the number of training iterations to 5, we simulated the interactive labeling process by using the ground truth information to randomly label 100 of the remaining miss- or unclassified voxels.
The size of the feature vectors was set to 50. Table 19.1 shows the results of a voxel-wise classification / segmentation using our approach.

type	voxel-wise recognition rate (true positive)
Erythrocyte	93,3%
Endothelial cell	84,6%
Pericyte	91,1%
Fibroblast	79,8%
Macrophage	88,6%
Background	94,1%

Table 19.1: Results of the voxel-wise classification (segmentation) against the human ground truth the database.

It should be noted that the "ground truth" as given by human experts does not reflect an irrevocable established truth. Even for the expert, it is very hard to fix the boundary of a nucleus down to a single voxel. Hence, it is rather unlikely that two experts would give the very same annotation. As a result, we can hardly expect any algorithm to provide a 100% accuracy for the given benchmark.

One reason for the varying performance on the different cell classes, besides that some classes appear to be more difficult to separate than others, could be the fact that the number of available training samples also underlies strong variations. While erythrocytes (for which the approach has the best performance) are overrepresented, there are only few samples of fibroblast (worst performance) contained in the database.

19.5 Conclusions and Outlook

We showed that our generic approach of combining local features with learning is able to use the manually given information from the human expert to infer a powerful model for the segmentation and classification of cell nuclei in dense 3D tissue data. Our approach did not use any a-priory knowledge about the cell segmentation problem. This allows the conclusion (together with the results for the spine detection in the next chapter 20) that in fact, our proposed generic method can be easily adapted to various different problems - simply by retraining the model.

For the future development, we suggest to enhance the existing methods by semi-supervised learning techniques. This potentially could speed-up the convergence of the training phase while prohibiting a manually enforced overfitting.

20 Neuronal Spine Detection

Before we introduce the second biological application for our *framework*, it should be noted that the here presented detection of neuronal spines practically applies the very same algorithmic concept as we use for the cell nuclei classification. Hence, reader may first refer to chapter 19.

20.1 Introduction

The main motivation to include the spine detection problem as an independent application is two-fold: First, it is one of our prime examples supporting the claim that our proposed *framework* is indeed generic enough to solve quite different problems such as the nuclei segmentation and the spine detection by simply retraining the underlying model parameters. Second, it also nicely suits as a showcase for our highly specific np- and nv-Features (see sections 7.3 and 9.3).

From an algorithmic point of view, the detection of neuronal spines in 3D data is an object or keypoint detection problem. The task is to obtain a reliable and reproducible detection (and count) of rather small, anisotropic structures in large data volumes. Figure 20.1 gives an example of the problem setting in a 3D volume. The arrows indicate the manually annotated positions of spines.

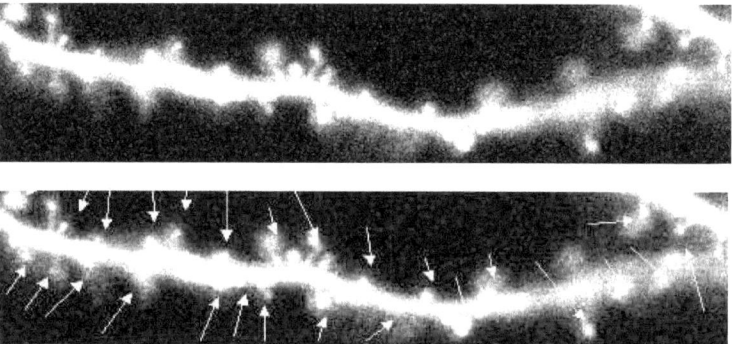

Figure 20.1: **Top:** Sample xy-slice from a 3D volume recording of a neuronal dendrite. **Bottom:** The arrows indicate the location of so-called spines.

Figure 20.1 already gives some indications of the challenges we have to face approaching this problem. Major difficulties arise from the fact that the target structures are very small (given the resolution of the available data). Hence, the discrete sampling of the original signal is quite sparse and the information of a single spine is concentrated in only a few voxels. Another difficulty stems from the high intra class variation of the spines. Biologically, there exist different categories of spines which are additionally occurring in different development stages. This leads to a wide spectrum of different visual appearances of spines.

20.1.1 Related Work

Even though, the automatic detection of dendrite spines appears to be a common problem, there have not been many proposals for algorithmic solutions. Most publications on this topic are focusing on biological aspects, rather than the technical and algorithmic questions.

The methods presented in (A. Rodriguez et al., 2003) focus on the deconvolution and stitching of large neuron recordings where the dendrites are spread over several recorded tiles. The authors also propose semi automatic spine detection algorithms, which use manual seed points to initialize a local spine segmentation via simple thresholding.

In (Weaver et al., 2004), the authors proposed to skeletonize the dendrite and then to apply two adaptive thresholds in local tiles around the short branches of the skeleton in order to detect the spines.

A very similar approach has been suggested by (Cheng et al., 2007). They also use a skeletonization to extract the dendrite backbone and use the local signal to noise ratio (SNR) to initialize an adaptive local thresholding.

The most sophisticated approach so far has been presented by (Koh et al., 2002). They also propose to use a skeletonization, but are then using local geometric spine models instead of simple thresholds. These models use local geometric parameterizations in terms of distances and angles to describe spines.

A general problem, which is shared by all of the presented publications is that they are either only providing qualitative evaluations of their methods or are not making the data publicly available. Hence, it is very hard to compare the performance of any of these methods with each other or with novel approaches.

20.2 Biological Background

Neuronal spines are anatomic structures located at the dendrites of neurons. Figure 20.3 shows an overview of a neuron cell. The dendrites, which are originating from the cell body, carry the spines (see figures 20.1).

Spines are an anatomical indicator of neuronal activity, because the synapses of incoming neuronal connections are located at the tip of the spines. The synapses themselves are too small to be imaged by standard confocal microscopes. However, spines are degenerating if their synapses loose neuronal connections, and are re-growing if new connections are established. Hence, the spines are a good indicator for the degree of neuronal connections.

Due to this property, the spine density has become an important parameter in empiric models for many anatomical and physiological research areas, such as Alzheimer's and Parkinson's disease. A common approach is to count the number spines in predefined segments of dendrites before and after the injection of a lesion or application of a treatment. As for most 3D image analysis tasks in biological applications, this tedious and time consuming counting of the spines over several time steps is done manually. An automatic evaluation of the spine count would be a very useful tool for wide areas of neuronal research.

Imaging: The imaging routine for the dendrite recordings differs in several aspects from the recordings of the nuclei data (see section 19.2). The main difference is that we have several recordings of the same probe over time. The biological material is still alive. Since most of the fluorescent anti-body

markers (see section 18.1.1) are highly toxic, GFP markers (see section 18.1.1) are used in this case. The samples used in our experiments were obtained of transgenic GFP mouse embryos.
An additional advantage of GFP is that the probes are recovering from bleaching effects (the data is recorded in time steps of several days).

However, there are also two additional imaging problems compared to the nuclei recordings: the z-resolution is only one third of the xy-resolution and the dendrite by itself has an unpleasant optical property: it acts like a lens, causing a strong blur in the lower layers of the recordings. Figure 20.2 shows an example for this problem.

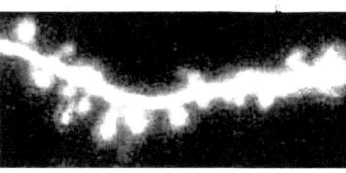 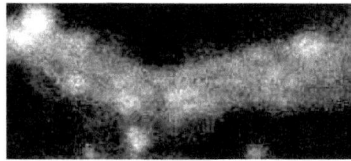

Figure 20.2: Example for strong blur in the lower layers of the dendrite recordings which are caused by the lens effect of the spine itself. **Left:** upper layer, no blurring. **Right:** problems in a lower layer.

20.3 Finding Dendrite Segments

An important subtask for an automatic 4D counting of neuronal spines is to find the same dendrite segments in each time step. Since the neurons are still alive, this is not a trivial task. While the cell body itself is hardly moving, are the dendrites able to change their position and shape - much like the "branches of a tree are moving in the wind".

The standard approach to identify the same dendrite segments over time is to count the number of spines between two bifurcations. Hence, we need to detect these bifurcations in order to find the correct segments. Figure 20.3 shows a maximum intensity projection of an entire neuronal "dendrite tree" and a manual annotation of a segmentation.

20.3.1 Algorithm

Since the dendrites in the overview recordings of the neurons are not showing any texture, it turns out to be very hard to reliably detect the bifurcations by use of scalar features. For this reason, we base our approach on the 3D gradient vector field extracted from the scalar input data and use our $\mathcal{VH}_{abs}$-Features (see section 8.1) to detect the Y-shaped bifurcations.

Obtaining a smooth 3D vector field: Our first step for the detection of the bifurcations is to compute the 3D gradients in each voxel. We then apply a very conservative thresholding based on the gradient magnitude, which only removes background clutter. The next step is to normalize all vectors in the remaining field to the magnitude 1. Hence, we are completely neglecting the magnitude and just rely on the gradient directions. Finally, we apply the Gradient Vector Flow (GVF) algorithm (Xu and Prince, 1997) with only 10 iteration in order to slightly smooth the field. Figure 20.4 shows an example GVF smoothed field.

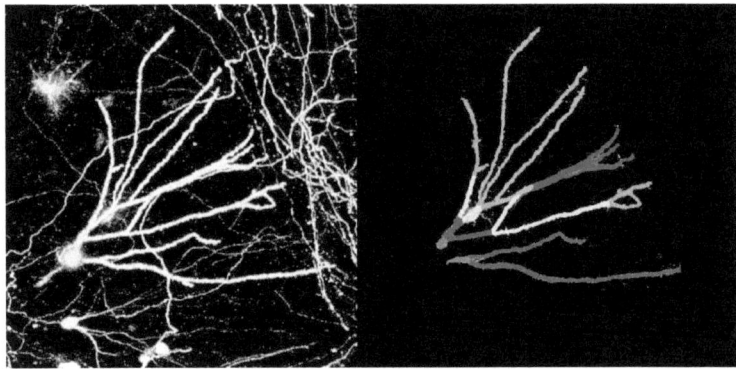

Figure 20.3: Global overview of a complete neuron recording at lower magnification.
Left: 2D maximum intensity projection of a 3D LSM recording of a complete neuron. The round structure in the lower left is the cell body (soma), which is the origin of the dendrite "sprouting". The thinner structures are dendrites from neighboring neurons (which potentially can intersect with each other).
Right: Manual annotation of so-called dendrite segments. The spines are counted segment by segment. Given 4D recordings where the dendrites are moving over time, we have to identify the segments in each time step to perform a reliable re-counting of the spines.

Computing $\mathcal{VH}_{abs}$-Features: Given the smoothed and normalized 3D vector field, we use our $\mathcal{VH}_{abs}$-Features (see section 8.1) in our standard iterative *framework* (as in the case of the cell nuclei segmentation) to detect the bifurcations. Figure 20.4 shows an example detection result.

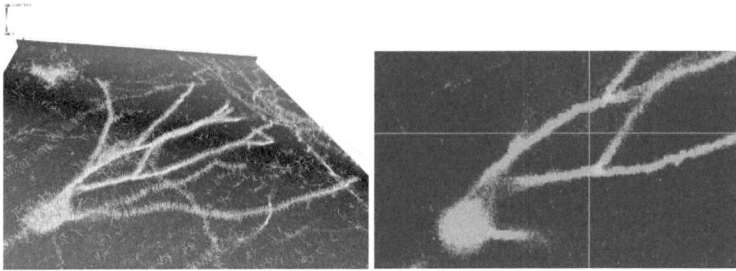

Figure 20.4: **Left:** Sparse visualization of the resulting 3D vector field after we applied the Gradient Vector Flow algorithm. **Right:** Visualization of an example test result of the bifurcation detection based on the $\mathcal{VH}_{abs}$-Feature.

20.4 Algorithm: Detecting Spines

Once we have isolated the dendrite segments using the previous algorithm, we are theoretically able to obtain 4D LSM recordings of matching segments at a higher resolution. However, in the course of the work presented in this thesis, this step has not been performed in practice. The detection results we show here have all been obtained from single 3D recordings of manually segmented dendrite segments. The main reason for this limitation is that the microscope hardware for 4D recordings has not yet been available for our experimental setup.

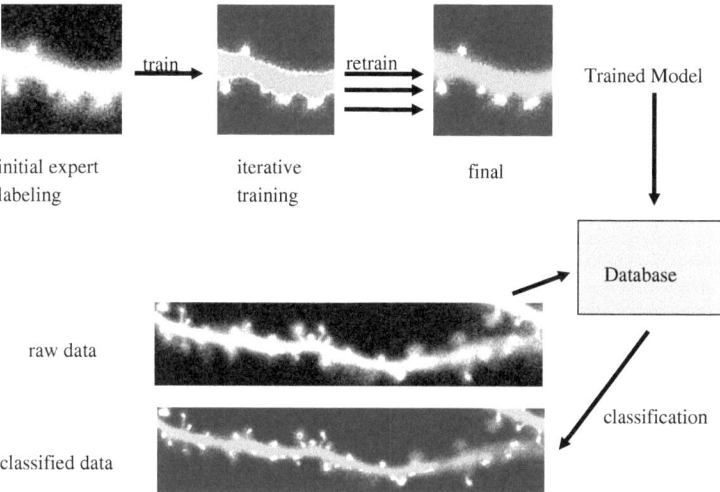

Figure 20.5: Overview of the iterative training procedure for the detection of neuronal spines for example data. Refer to figure 1.1 for an schematic overview of the training and test procedure.

As mentioned before, our approach for the detection of spines is following the same scheme as for the nuclei classification. In fact, we are using the very same implementation of our iterative *framework* to solve both problems, simply by re-training the underlying model. The only difference is that we use some a-priory knowledge and constrain the *framework* to general texture features in the case of the nuclei segmentation (see chapter 19) and to highly specific np, nv and $1v$-Features for the spine detection.

Since the details of our iterative *framework* have been discussed in section 19.3, we keep the description of the algorithms very brief and focus on the changes that have been made to perform the spine counting. Figure 20.5 gives an additional overview of the iterative *framework* with a sample visualization for the spine detection task.

20.4.1 Training

The training of the underlying model of our *framework* is performed with our interactive annotation tool (see figure 19.2), where a human expert iteratively annotates and corrects the temporary results on a set of training samples until the model converges to a stable and reliable training result. In each iteration, the training procedure runs through the following steps:

Learning and selecting features: In each iteration, we use the current and previous annotations to extract local np, nv and $1v$-Features. It is reasonable to rely on these highly specific features since we are solely pursuing a detection task (instead of a texture based volume segmentation as in the case of the cell nuclei). The use of the vectorial nv and $1v$-Features is motivated by the observation that the spines are hardly having any texture and the shape is the dominating factor in the description of the spine. Using vectorial features on a GVF generated vector field allows us to gain additional information on the local shape and structure which is not directly present in the raw gray-scale data.

While we use our *data driven feature design* (see chapter 10.3) to infer highly specialized features for the detection of the spines, we use the $1v$-Feature as indicator for the tube-like structure of the dendrite samples.

Using the SIMBA (see section 10.2) feature selection algorithm, we rank all of the extracted features in terms of their separability of the given training samples. We then use the top 35 features for the further modelling.

Voxel-wise classification: Given the feature design, we use the annotated samples to train an SVM (see chapter 13 and section 19.3.1). In the next step, we extract all 35 features at every voxel in the training data and use the SVM model to perform a voxel-wise classification. Figure 20.6 shows some intermediate results of this voxel-wise SVM classification.

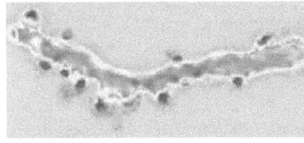 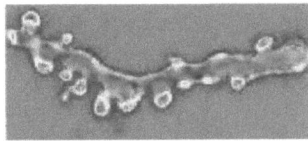

Figure 20.6: Intermediate results of the voxel-wise SVM classification. **Left:** pseudo coloration of the SVM decision confidence for the dendrite class. **Right:** decision confidence for the spine class.

MRF post-processing: In the next step, we use the resulting probability map of the SVM classification confidence as node potentials (see section 15.3) of a Markov Random Field (see chapter 15.2). We apply the Pott's Model (15.11) for the edge potentials (see section 15.3) to obtain a smoothing of the voxel-wise classification. Figure 20.7 shows an example how the MRF removes small outliers and smooths the class boundaries.

 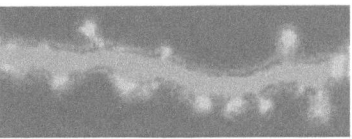

Figure 20.7: MRF post-processing of the voxel-wise SVM results. **Left:** sample result before the MRF post-processing. **Right:** same sample after the post-processing.

Counting: The actual counting of the spines is finally performed by the use of a simple connected component labeling algorithm.

20.4.2 Automatic Evaluation

After we have obtained the models for the local features and their global interaction, we use these models and simply run the feature extraction, classification and post-processing steps on unknown data sets. This can be done fully automatically without any further human interaction, as long as the characteristics of the data are not changing: i.e. the microscope parameters are the same and the preparation of the biological probes lies within the variance of the training data.

In order to speed-up the evaluation, we usually apply fast SVM classification (see chapter 14) and fast MRF inference (see chapter 16). Additionally, we use a simple but very conservatively selected threshold to remove large background areas prior to the actual evaluation. This reduces the computational complexity of the an automatic evaluation of a typical $256 \times 128 \times 16$ test sample to about 10 seconds.

20.5 Experimental Evaluation

The performance of our spine detection approach has been evaluated during the master thesis of Matthias Asal (Asal, 2008). The neuron data and ground truth annotation has been kindly provided by the group of Prof. Deller, Institute for Neuro-Anatomy at the University of Frankfurt, Germany. Special thanks to Andreas Vlachos for the fruitful cooperation.

Setup: The experiments have been conducted on a series of data sets which were obtained from LSM recordings of 10 different mouse individuals. We used three of these sets for the iterative training, and the rest for the actual evaluation. A manual ground truth annotation has been provided for all samples.

Results: In this series of experiments, our approach achieves a true-positive detection rate of 81% of the manually annotated spines. Notably, our method has at the same time a false-positive rate of 0%. Hence, the 19% error rate of our method is solely caused by false-negative errors. The main reason for this problem is given by the fact that our generic algorithm is not able to separate closely interlaced spines. Even if we correctly detect all spines, out method counts touching spines as a single detection. Figure 20.8 shows some examples for these problems.

Compared to other approaches, our 81% detection rate is slightly above the results presented in (Koh et al., 2002), where 80% have been reported. However, since the experiments were not conducted on the same data sets, it is very hard to compare both results: i.e. our data appears to have a much denser spine population than the data used in (Koh et al., 2002). Hence, we could expect better results on their data since sparse spines are less likely to be connected.

20.6 Conclusions and Outlook

The main aspect of the entire spine detection approach is that we were able to show that we can easily adapt our generic *framework* to novel problems - simply by retraining the underlying model. As for the spine detection task itself, we were able to show that our generic method is well in the range of non-generic, highly specialized approaches.

The remaining false-negative errors are solely caused by the fact that our algorithms are not yet able to handle connected spines. First approaches towards an automatic splitting of the spines have already been presented in (Wicklein, 2006) and (Asal, 2008). In both cases, we tried to add additional potential constraints into the MRF post-processing. Although theses methods provide some promising results, they are still too expensive for a practical application and require further investigations.

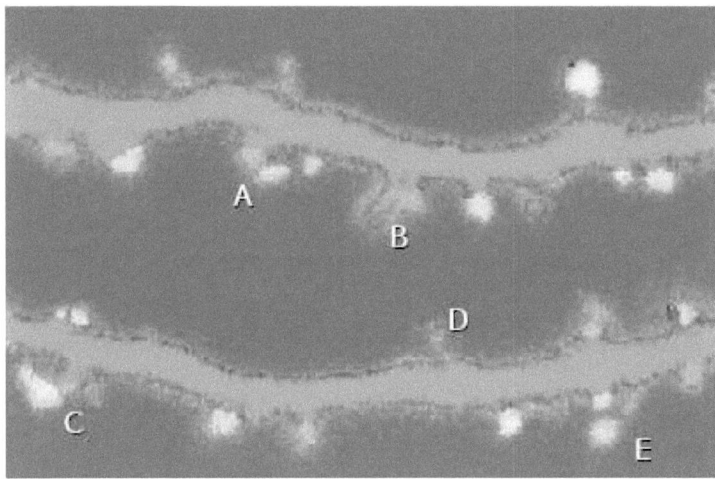

Figure 20.8: Example spine detection results taken from (Asal, 2008). Sample xy-plane of a detection result. A good detection of connected spines is given by the results at **A** and **E**, while the spines at **B** and **C** are counted as one spine and contribute to the false-negative errors. **D** is not an error, the detection simply lies in another z-plane.

Finally, we also suggest to look into additional preprocessing steps, e.g. deconvolution of the data. It also could be helpful to record the samples twice, top-down and bottom-up, and to use a registration of both recordings in order to overcome the lens effects in lower z-slices of the 3D data.

21 3D Shape Retrieval

The last application for our local 3D features presented in this thesis is slightly different than the previous two. Most of the difficulties we face in biological image analysis, like poor imaging quality and the need to localize unsegmented objects in strongly structured backgrounds, are not occurring in most retrieval tasks. However, one usually still has to deal with high intra class variations and most often with a new, even more difficult problem: the semantic classification of objects.

We have chosen the 3D shape retrieval problem as additional application for our *framework* because it is another practically relevant, interesting and challenging problem, which we can use to endorse the flexibility and description power of our local 3D features.

This chapter is structured as follows: first, we give a brief introduction to the shape retrieval problem (see 21.1) and review related work, before we motivate the use of local features and adapt the "Bag of Features" concept from 2D image retrieval in section 21.2. Section 21.3 introduces the Princeton Shape Benchmark (PSB), before we give a detailed algorithmic description of our approach in section 21.4. Finally, we show the results of the evaluation of our methods in section 21.5.

21.1 Introduction

The retrieval of digitized 3D objects is a rising topic. Similar to 2D image retrieval, which recently has become a very popular research topic, the constantly growing size of available 3D data from artificial 3D CAD models to 3D scans of real world objects triggers the need for effective search methods. However, the existing data is usually not annotated and a manual annotation is practically infeasible. Hence, a text based search approach is hardly possible. Results for the search problem in 2D images led to the "query by example" approach in order to cope with the missing annotation. This approach is a classical retrieval problem.

There have been several practically important applications for 3D object retrieval, such as retrieving 3D protein structures from very large databases in bio-informatics and computational chemistry (Reisert and Burkhardt, 2006) or the retrieval of 3D objects from depth images (laser range scans) in robot navigation (Wolf et al., 2005).

We apply our methods to a more academic problem setting given by the Princeton Shape Benchmark (PSB) (Shilane et al., 2004) (see section 21.3) which has become the standard benchmark in 3D shape retrieval.

Even though many digitized 3D objects are associated with a color or even with surface textures, the shape of an object is its dominant characterizing feature. Hence, 3D object retrieval is mostly reduced to a 3D shape retrieval problem.

The object shape is digitized in various formats of polygons, triangle meshes or volume data. Our methods, as most others, operate on volume data since it is easier to handle and rather simple to render other formats to a volume representation.

Typically, the retrieval is performed on databases containing single segmented object shapes which may vary in scale, translation and especially in rotation.

21.1.1 Related Work

There have been numerous publications on 3D shape retrieval for different tasks and applications. We limit our brief review of related work to methods which have been applied to the Princeton Shape Benchmark (see section 21.3) and thus can be compared to our results later on.

The very basic **Global Shape Histogram (SHAPEHIST)** computes the distance for each point on the surface of the shape to all other points on the surface and stores the results in a histogram. As the results in table 21.10 show, the discriminative power of this approach is rather limited and SHAPEHIST is clearly not able to cope with the large semantic intra class variations in the PSB.

The **Global Shell Histogram (SECSHELL)** (Ankerst et al., 1999) divides an object in spherical shells and sectors located around the center of mass and generates histograms over the subdivisions which are combined to one global object feature.

The **Spherical Extent Function (EXT)** (Saupe and Vranic, 2001a) projects the distance of the object center to each point of the object surface onto the enclosing outer sphere. The resulting spherical distance map is then expanded in Spherical Harmonics from which the $\mathcal{SH}_{abs}$ (see chapter 5.1) feature is extracted.

The **Radialized Spherical Extent Function (REXT)** (Vranic, 2003) extends the (EXT) approach by computing the $\mathcal{SH}_{abs}$ feature on the harmonic expansion of the signal on several concentric spheres with increasing radii located around the object center.

The **Spherical Harmonic Descriptor (SHD)** (Kazhdan et al., 2003) is very similar to (REXT), it also computes $\mathcal{SH}_{abs}$ over several radii, but organizes the results in a 2D histogram.

Finally, we have to mention the **Light Field Descriptor (LDF)** (Chen et al., 2003), which uses multiple 2D views of 3D shapes. Rotation invariance is achieved by a collection of 100 2D views per object, which are rendered orthogonal to the outer enclosing sphere of the object. Then a set of 2D features (mostly geometric and Zernike moments) is computed for each 2D view. Currently, LDF is the best performing approach on the PSB.

The (EXT), (REXT) and (SHD) methods use Spherical Harmonic representations but rely on the weak $\mathcal{SH}_{abs}$ feature (see chapter 5.1) to obtain rotation invariance.

All of these methods have in common that they try to model an object shape at a global level which has the disadvantage that the assumption that objects of the same class are sharing the same base shape is not always adequate - especially when one considers more semantic groupings with high intra-class variance.

We try to overcome this problem by describing objects as collection of local parts (see section 21.2). To our knowledge, due to the lack of discriminative local features, this has not been done before. The only exception is our own preliminary work in (Fehr and Burkhardt, 2007b) which uses histograms over locally computed $2p$ and $3p$-Haar features (see chapters 7.1 and 7.2). The promising results in (Fehr and Burkhardt, 2007b) (see table 21.10) led to our approach using local patches for 3D shape retrieval (Streicher, 2008).

Special thanks to Alexander Streicher, who implemented all the nice visualization tools used throughout this chapter during his master thesis (Streicher, 2008).

21.2 3D Shape Retrieval with Local Patches

Our approach is a direct 3D extension of the very successful "Bag of Features" concept (see section 21.2.1), which has been introduced for 2D image retrieval. Our ability to effectively represent local 3D information, to register it via fast and accurate local correlation and to compute very discriminative local rotation invariant 3D features allows us to simply replace all 2D specific components of the "Bag of Features" concept by their 3D counterparts and map the concept one to one onto 3D.

21.2.1 The "Bag of Features" Concept

One "state of the art" approach in modern 2D image retrieval is commonly known under the name "Bag of Features (BoF)" (Mikolajczyk et al., 2005)(Sivic et al., 2005). The method of BoF is largely inspired by the "Bag of Words" (Blei et al., 2003) concept which has been used in text retrieval for quite some time.

Even though there are countless variations of retrieval algorithms emerging under the label "Bag of Features" (Mikolajczyk et al., 2005)(Sivic et al., 2005) and it is hard to capture *the* actual BoF algorithm, there is a common concept which is shared by all of theses methods. The central aspects are the usage of **local features** and their representation by a so-called **codebook** (Jurie and Triggs, 2005).

Local Features: The central aspect of the "Bag of Features" concept is to move away from a global image description and to represent images as a collection of local properties. These local properties are derived in form of (invariant) **image features**, e.g. the very popular SIFT features (Lowe, 2004), which are computed on small sub-images called **patches**. The patches, are simply small rectangular regions which are extracted around **interest points** (see section 21.4.2).

Codebook Representation: the second main aspect of the "Bag of Features" concept is the way images are represented as collections of local features and how two or more of these representations can be compared. The basic idea here is to use a class independent **clustering** over the feature representations of all patches (from all training samples). The representatives of the resulting clusters are then used as entries of a unified (class independent) **codebook**. Each patch is then mapped against the entries of this codebook, such that an image is represented as the **histogram** over the best codebook matches of its patches.

The similarity of images can then be obtained by comparing the BoF histograms, e.g. by histogram intersection (Siggelkow, 2002) (see section 13.5.1).

Figure 21.1 gives a schematic overview of the computation steps in the codebook generation and retrieval stage of the 'Bag of Features" concept.

21.3 The Princeton Shape Benchmark (PSB)

The Princeton Shape Benchmark (PSB) (Shilane et al., 2004) has become one of the standard evaluation benchmarks in 3D shape retrieval. The PSB not only provides a set of 3D shape models which were collected from various publicly available internet sources, but it also comes with pre-defined training and test sets as well as a set of standardized evaluation tools. This makes the results for the PSB very comparable.

Data: The PSB contains 1814 shape models which come in a triangular mesh format. The models are organized in four different semantic abstraction levels, *base, coarse1, coarse2 and coarse3*. At the *base* level, objects are grouped in very differentiated classes, e.g. *"F117 Fighter Jet"*, *"Biplane"* or *"Balloon"*. At higher levels, these classes are combined to more and more semantic classes like *"Commercial Plane"* or *"Fighter Jet"* at *coarse1* or all together in *"Aircraft"* at *coarse2*. Finally, *coarse3*

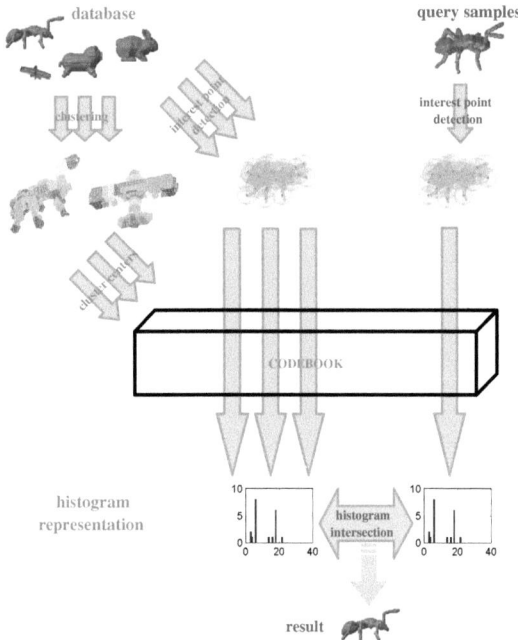

Figure 21.1: Schematic overview of the "Bag of Features" concept.

only distinguishes between "*natural*" and "*human made*" objects.

At all levels, the PSB provides pre-defined training and test sets, where the test sets may contain classes which are not present during training. Figure 21.2 shows examples for classes in the Princeton Shape Benchmark. More examples can be found in appendix B.

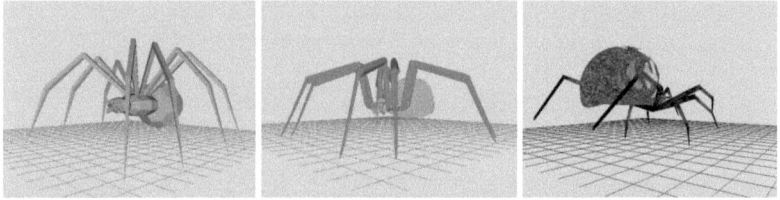

Figure 21.2: Example "spider" class from the Princeton Shape Benchmark (PSB).

Evaluation Tools: The PSB also provides a set of standardized tools, performance measures and graph plots for a comparable evaluation of the results:

Nearest Neighbor (NN): The nearest neighbor measure applies a simple $k = 1$ k-nearest neighbor classifier (Bishop, 2006) to return the most similar object from the database for a given query.

Since the NN-measure considers only the best match to test the quality of retrieval algorithms, it is not very suitable to evaluate the performance for actual search tasks where the user usually expects a list of retrieval results.

Precision Recall Graph (ROC): To cope with the limitations of the NN-measure, the PSB also provides a tool for the generation of precision recall graphs, with

$$\text{Precision:} \qquad \frac{|R \cap P|}{|R|} \qquad\qquad (21.1)$$

$$\text{Recall:} \qquad \frac{|R \cap P|}{|P|}, \qquad\qquad (21.2)$$

where R is the number of "relevant" results of P answers to a query using a k-nearest neighbor classifier (Bishop, 2006).

A precision score of 1 indicates that every result retrieved by a search was relevant (but says nothing about whether all relevant documents were retrieved) whereas a recall score of 1 means that all relevant documents were retrieved by the search (but says nothing about how many irrelevant documents were also retrieved). The combination of both measures in a 2D Precision Recall Graph is the standard quality measure for retrieval tasks.

21.4 Algorithm

Our approach directly follows the "Bag of Features" scheme (see figure 21.1). With the exception of the preprocessing in section 21.4.1 and an extension to the codebook histograms by a localization of the object parts in section 21.2, we walk through the BoF pipeline step by step and replace 2D specific algorithms with our own 3D methods.

21.4.1 Preprocessing

Prior to the actual BoF pipeline, we apply a series of preprocessing steps to the objects in the PSB database: primarily, we have to render the objects from triangular mesh format to a volume representation. We use this rendering step to align each object in the geometric center of the volume and to normalize the object size to a fixed height of the object bounding box. Thus, we obtain translation and scale invariant volume representations of the models.

The rendering itself is performed in a very simple fashion: given the normals of the triangulated object surface, we determine for each voxel in the target volume if it lies within the object boundaries. Voxels inside the object are set to 1, outside to 0.

Figure 21.3 shows an example of the preprocessing results for different normalizations of the object size. The selection of the size parameter is a tradeoff between the presentation of object details and computational complexity.

21.4.2 Interest Point Detection

The next step, the first of the actual BoF pipeline, is to determine the location of the local patches. In the original 2D setting, where the objects of interest are located in more or less cluttered scenes, the so-call detection of interest points is a crucial step: important parts of the target objects should not be missed, while the overall number of interest points directly affects the computational complexity, so that one tries to avoid large numbers of false positive points.

There are quite many different interest point detectors for 2D image retrieval available, like the "Differential of Gaussian" (Mikolajczyk and Schmid, 2004) or "Laplacian" (Mikolajczyk and Schmid, 2004), just to name two prominent examples. Most of the 2D methods have in common that the patches are

Figure 21.3: Preprocessing of the PSB models: The 3D triangular mesh models are rendered to a volume representation such that the voxels inside the objects are set to 1 and outside to 0. The objects are centered and normalized to a fixed scale. From **left** to **right**: the rendered objects of sizes 32, 64 and 256 clearly show an increase in the level of detail.

placed at regions of the image "where something is happening", e.g. at edges and corners.

For our 3D case, the selection of interest points is by far less crucial since we already have segmented objects. However, the number of extracted patches is still an important factor for the computational complexity. Hence, a simple equidistant sampling on the object surface might produce too many patches or leave out characteristic positions on the shape when choosing a sparser sampling.

Following the edge and corner characteristic of the 2D detectors, we use the $\mathcal{SH}_{phase}$ feature (see chapter 5.2), which responses to changes in signals over several concentric spheres - hence, $\mathcal{SH}_{phase}$ can be interpreted as 3D corner detector.

We manually select a threshold on the $\mathcal{SH}_{phase}$ response and place interest points in the center of the remaining regions. Figure 21.4 shows the results of an equidistant and a $\mathcal{SH}_{phase}$ interest point detection.

Figure 21.4: Interest point detection on 3D shapes (sample ant model) [1]. **Left**: equidistant sampling and **right** points detected by $\mathcal{SH}_{phase}$.

21.4.3 Extracting Local Patches

The next step is to extract the local patches p at the location of the interest points. In contrast to the original 2D case, where the patches are rectangular areas, we extract spherical patches that are centered in the respective interest points.

---

[1]Thanks to A. Streicher for the Matlab visualization tool.

Given the volume rendering of a model X and interest points at positions $\mathbf{x}$, the associated patches are then represented by a series of m concentric spherical neighborhoods $X|_{\mathcal{S}[r_i](\mathbf{x})}$ (see definition in 4.1) at different radii $r_i \in \{r_1, \ldots, r_m\}$. We then expand the local patches radius by radius in Spherical Harmonics. Hence, we define a patch p as collection of radius-wise harmonic expansions up to some upper band $l = b_{max}$ around $\mathbf{x}$:

$$p(\mathbf{x}) := \left\{ \mathcal{SH}\left(X|_{\mathcal{S}[r_1](\mathbf{x})}\right)^l, \ldots, \mathcal{SH}\left(X|_{\mathcal{S}[r_m](\mathbf{x})}\right)^l \right\}. \tag{21.3}$$

Figure 21.5 illustrates the patch extraction.

Figure 21.5: Extracting spherical patches at the interest points: **left**: detected interest points, **right**: extraction of spherical neighborhoods (patches) around the interest points.

The motivation to use spherical instead of rectangular patches is obvious considering that we need to obtain full rotation invariance, which often times can be neglected in the case of 2D image retrieval.

21.4.4 Generating the Codebook

While the preprocessing, interest point detection and patch extraction has to be done for all training and query objects, we now turn to the off-line training procedure which is only performed on the training set. The training itself has two different stages: first, we have to generate a problem specific but class independent codebook of local patches, which is done via clustering, and then, we have to represent the training samples in terms of histograms over the codebook.

Clustering After the extraction of the patches, we use a simple k-means clustering (Bishop, 2006) to obtain k patch clusters. The key for the clustering is the choice of the similarity function d: we apply our fast and accurate correlation (see chapter 3.4) for the Spherical Harmonic domain to measure the similarity of two patches in a rotation invariant way. More precisely, we use the normalized cross-correlation (3.57) over all radii at once (see section 3.4.6) to obtain a partitioning of the patches into k clusters:

$$d\left(p(\mathbf{x_i}), p(\mathbf{x_j})\right) := p(\mathbf{x_i}) \# p(\mathbf{x_j}). \tag{21.4}$$

In order to reduce the computational complexity, we do not apply the clustering on all patches from all training samples. Our experiments showed (see section 21.5) that it is sufficient to use a small random subset of t training samples to generate a stable set of clusters.

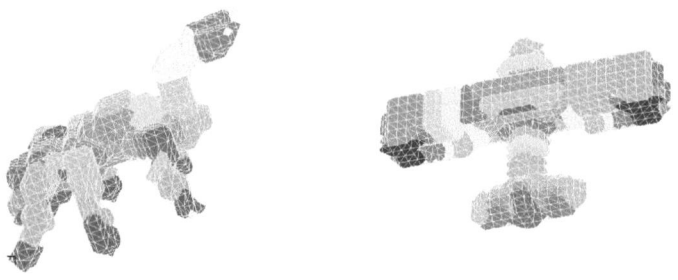

Figure 21.6: Example clustering results where patches were extracted at all object voxels.

Figure 21.7: Example clustering results where patches were extracted at combined $\mathcal{SH}_{phase}$ and equidistant interest points.

It should be noted that the class label of the training samples is completely neglected during the clustering since our goal is to obtain a general, class independent representation of local patches in the codebook. Figures 21.6 and 21.7 show example results of the clustering.

The final step towards the generation of the codebook is based on the previous clustering. Essentially, each of the k clusters is represented by one of its member patches, which is stored as an entry in the codebook. Clusters with only a few members may be neglected.

The task is now to select the appropriate representative for each cluster: the naive way would be to simply use the cluster center, e.g. the patch which has the largest similarity with all other cluster members. This approach works sufficiently well, but to gain an even better performance, we compute an artificial generalized cluster representative.

Generalized codebook entries: we follow the same basic idea that we used for the np and nv data driven feature selection in chapter 10.3. First, we select a reference patch for each cluster like in the naive approach. Then, we use the rotation parameters from the correlation matrices between the reference patch and the other cluster members which we obtained during the clustering and register all cluster members to the reference (see 3.4.4 and 10.3).

After the registration, we transform all members back to the spatial domain, radius by radius. Hence, we obtain a discrete 3D volume grid representation of spherical surfaces for each considered radius.

Then, we compute the voxel-wise variance $\sigma(r, \Phi_i, \Theta_i)$ at fixed voxel position Φ_i, Θ_i over all cluster members. Finally, we locate regions on the surfaces that have a locally stable low variance and set the reference patch at these positions to 1 or 0 otherwise (see figure 21.8).

This way, we obtain an artificial cluster representative, which contains only the dominant structures of the cluster. Finally, we radius-wise transform the representative back to the harmonic domain and use it as codebook entry for this cluster.

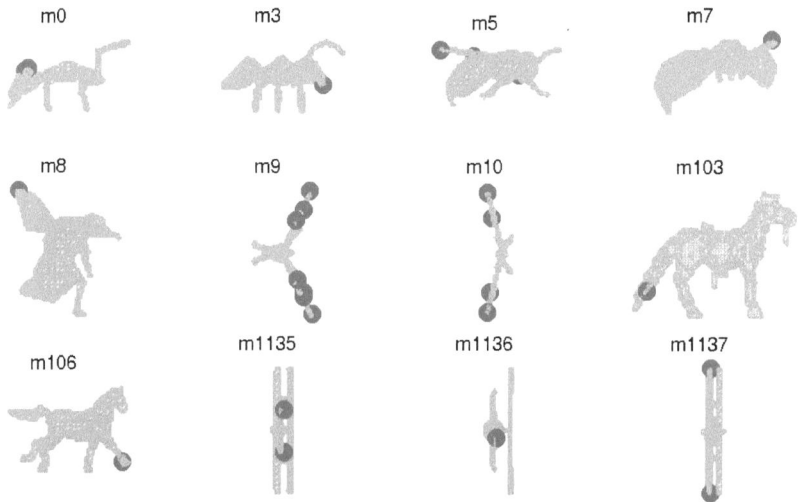

Figure 21.8: Sample generalized codebook entry: the figure illustrates the location (blue circle) of a sample codebook entry on several different objects.

21.4.5 Retrieval by Feature Histograms

After we learned the codebook based on a small subsection of the training samples, we can pursue the BoF approach without further changes.

As in the original "Bag of Features" concept, all of the training samples are represented as histograms over the codebook entries. We simply use our fast normalized cross-correlation (3.57) to match all patches of an object with the codebook and rise the count of the histogram bin associated with the best match. Figure 21.9 illustrates a example codebook histogram representation of an object.

Retrieval Query: Given a query object, we perform the preprocessing, interest point detection and patch extraction steps and then compute its codebook histogram representation just as we do it for the training data. We then use a histogram intersection (as defined for the SVM Histogram Intersection Kernel in section 13.5.1) as similarity measure to find the best matches in the training data.

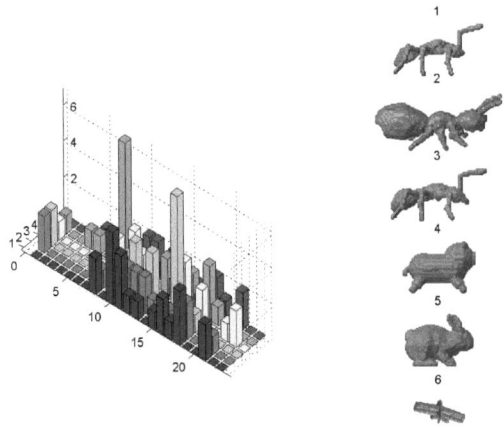

Figure 21.9: Sample "Bag of Features" representation for a selection of 3D shape models. Each model is represented by a histogram over the generalized codebook entries.

21.4.6 Parameter Selection

The major drawback of the entire BoF framework is that we have quite a lot of open parameters which need to be adjusted: the number of interest points, the m radii within a patch and the maximum band b_{max} of their harmonic expansion and the size of the codebook, just to name the most important ones. Unfortunately, it turns out to be quite tedious to manually select these parameters appropriately.

21.5 Experimental Evaluation

We evaluate our proposed approach on the standard PSB experimental setup, as described in (Shilane et al., 2004). We use the *base* scheme (see section 21.3 and appendix B), where the 1814 shapes of the PSB are split into equally large training and test sets.

- We use a rendering normalized to the size of 64 voxels on the longest edge of the bounding box (see 21.4.1).

- The codebook is built from a random selection of 5% of the available training samples (more samples simply increase the training time without notable a effect on the later recognition rate).

- 5 different radii, with $r \in \{4, 6, 8, 10, 12\}$ are used to compute the codebook.

- The harmonic expansion is limited to $b_{max} = 5$.

- And the codebook size k is set to 150 bins, using a combined codebook for all radii.

Given these parameters, we obtained the following results for our approach on the PSB *base* test set: table 21.10 shows the $k = 1$ nearest neighbor results of our method compared to the results known from literature.

Features	PSB *base* level
LFD	$65.7\%^{\dagger}(61.9\%)^{*}$
BoF with $\mathcal{SH}_{corr}$	**62.4%**
REXT	$60.2\%^{\dagger}$
SHD	$55.6\%^{\dagger}(52.3\%)^{*}$
EXT	$54.9\%^{\dagger}$
SECSHELL	$54.6\%^{\dagger}$
BoF with $\mathcal{SH}_{abs}$	54.5%

Figure 21.10: Results for the 3D shape retrieval on the PSB. Results taken from the literature are marked with †, results from our own implementations are marked with ∗. Unfortunately, we were not able to exactly reproduce the results given in the literature. This could be caused by a different initial rendering, which is not discussed in the given literature.

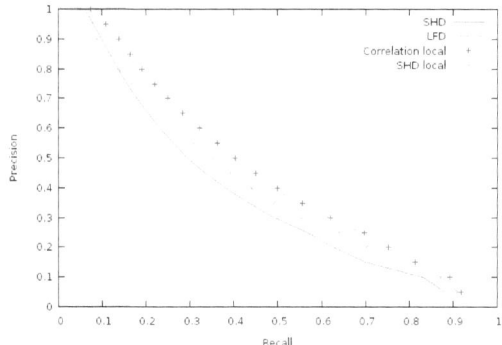

Figure 21.11: Precision recall graph for our approach on the PSB *base* test set.

21.6 Conclusions and Outlook

The experiments showed that our approach achieves competitive results on the difficult PSB. The main drawback of our method is that we cannot be sure if the given results are actually representing the global optimum of what can be achieved with our method or if we are stuck in a local maximum of the parameter space. Due to the large number of parameters, we face the problem that the maximum search in the parameter space turns out to be quite tedious.

A possible further extension of our histogram approach could be to localize the patch positions. Similar to the 2D approach in (Leibe and Schiele, 2003), we could increase the discrimination power by replacing the global histogram with a localized patch histogram.
One possible idea in this direction could be to project the number of the associated histogram bin at the location of each interest point onto a surrounding sphere. One could then use the harmonic representations of these projections to compare objects.

22 Conclusions and Outlook

In this thesis, we have presented a novel generic approach towards an automatic analysis of 3D images. Our central concept, the combination of local invariant features with learning techniques into a unified *framework* has shown its flexibility and performance for a wide range of different applications.

The key contributions of our work are the theoretical derivation and algorithmic implementation of several novel local invariant 3D features, novel supervised learning techniques for a data driven adaption of these features to new problems, as well as several methods to speed-up the classification and inference using Support Vector Machines and Markov Random Fields.

Combining theses methods, we were able to obtain a generic and powerful *framework* for 3D image analysis. The prime example for this claim is the fact that we are using the very same algorithm to solve the cell nuclei segmentation and classification (*see* capter 19) and the spine detection (see chapter 20). We simply train the underlying model of our *framework* with different data. We were able to show that our generic approach is flexible enough to obtain solutions, which are even out-performing non-generic and highly specialized methods in some cases.

22.1 Outlook

Despite the very promising results we have obtained so far, our proposed *framework* and its underlying methods and theories still leave room for further improvements, extensions and novel ideas.

While we are convinced that our general approach realizes a potentially powerful solution to a wide range of 3D image analysis problems, we also feel that the content of this thesis is just founding a basis towards generic volume analysis. This should encourage further developments of the entire approach and especially of some of the individual methods.

3D Invariant Features. Even though, the design of fast local invariant 3D volume features is one of the main contributions of this thesis and has been covered in-depth, there are still some open issues remaining.

The first issue is speed. Our proposed feature method could be even faster, if the underlying $\mathcal{SH}$- and $\mathcal{VH}$-Transformations, which make up a large portion of the computational complexity, could be computed more efficiently. There have been some approaches towards an FFT like fast $\mathcal{SH}$-Transformation (see section 4.1.6). However, these methods suffer from an initially large computational overhead that only pays off for transformations with high expansion bands (about $b_{max} > 15$). In our case, where the harmonic transformations are made at the small radii, we hardly use expansions beyond the 8th band. Hence, a fast $\mathcal{SH}$-Transformation for strongly band-limited signals would be a beneficial research topic.

Another vital issue is the investigation of features that are invariant (or at least robust) toward additional transformations. So far, we only covered the basic rotation and gray-scale transformations. For many practically relevant applications, it would be very helpful to be also able to cope with local deformations. One idea to address this problem could be to infer the nature of such deformations by finding corresponding pairs of local key points, implicitly capturing local deformations. This possible approach is directly linked to a potential further global modelling.

Global Modelling. Our global modelling of the interaction and alignment of local image properties (captured by the invariant features) leaves plenty of room for further improvement. So far, we only have applied quite simple MRF models to capture the global interaction of local properties. It is likely that an increase of contextual information could further improve the flexibility and performance of the *framework*.

A possible approach in this direction could be the use of graph based methods similar to the 2D methods in (Peloschek et al., 2007), where features were not only extracted at local positions, but also along the graph edges connecting these positions.

Learning. Finally, there are several possibilities to improve the learning methods used within the *framework*. A potential way to increase the convergence of the iterative learning procedure could be the use of semi-supervised learning techniques that are able to gain additional information from the majority of unlabeled data points. Benefitting from this information, the initial training errors could be reduced, thus leading to a faster convergence.

Another concern is the classification speed. While our fast SVM and MRF methods provide some of the needed speed-up, one could easily think of many further approaches for a faster classification: from importance sampling methods to speed-up MRF inference to the use of faster alternatives for the local SVM classification.

Part IV

Appendices

A Artificial 3D Volume Texture Database

The following tables show a few sample images of xy-slices taken from the training samples of our artificial 3D volume texture database.

A.0.1 Texture Generation

The volume textures were generated from 2D texture samples which were taken from the **BFT texture data base** provided by the University of Bonn (*http://btf.cs.uni-bonn.de/download.html*). Figure A.1 gives an overview of our very simple volume texture generation process.

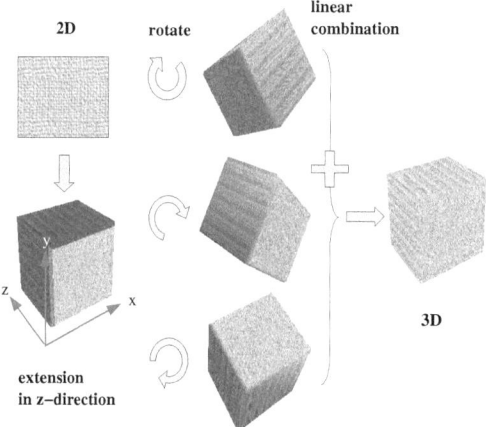

Figure A.1: Generation of the volume texture database: in a first step, we extend 2D texture images X from the **BFT texture data base** into volumes V, such that $\forall z : V(x, y, z) = X(x, y)$. We then generate volume textures VT as linear combinations of arbitrary rotations of these volumes: $VT := \alpha_1 \mathcal{R}_1 V_1 + \cdots + \alpha_n \mathcal{R}_n V_n$.

The number of linear combinations n, as well as the rotations $\mathcal{R}_i$ and factors $\alpha_i \in [0, 1]$ are chosen randomly.

A.0.2 Base Textures

The database contains 10 "base samples" for each of the six different textures (*texture 1-6*), all of which have a normalized average gray-value. These "base samples" are used to generate separate training and test sets using arbitrary rotations and additive gray-value changes.

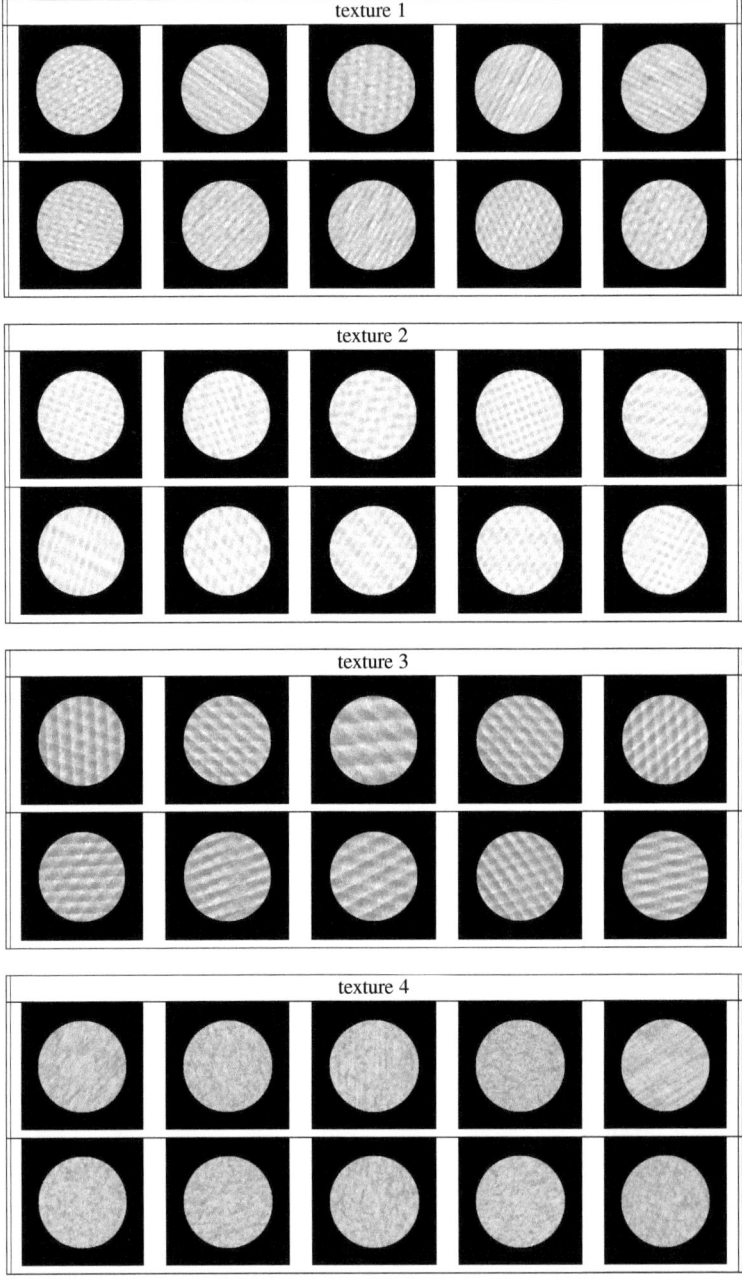

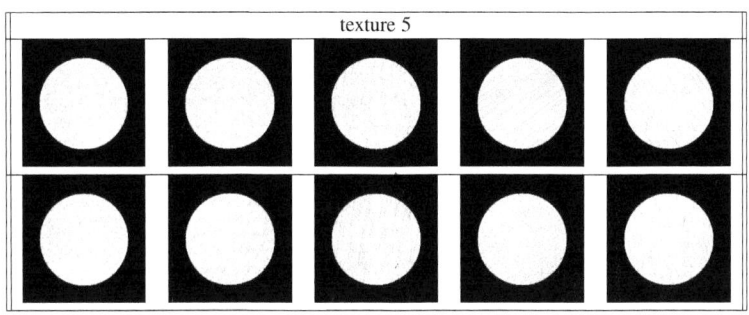

texture 5

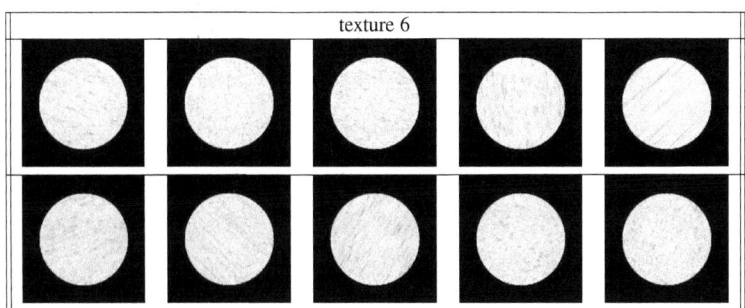

texture 6

A.0.3 Texture Segmentation

Given the "base samples" of the 3D volume textures, we generated a simple texture segmentation benchmark. One half of the "base samples" was used to build 60 labeled training samples (see figure A.3) and the other half was used for the test samples.

The 200 test samples consist of random combinations of two textures with a ground-truth labeling, where each the textures was rotated randomly and subject to an additive gray-value change (see figure A.2).

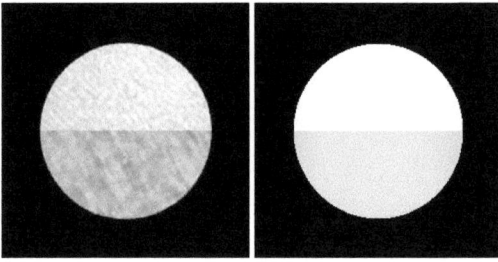

Figure A.2: Test sample. **Left:** the xy-slice shows how two randomly selected textures are combined in one test sample. **Right:** ground-truth labeling.

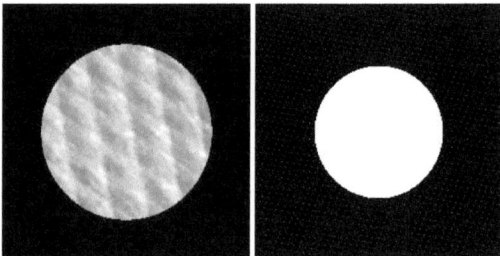

Figure A.3: Training sample. **Left:** the xy-slice shows the volume texture of a training sample. **Right:** ground-truth labeling.

B The Princeton Shape Benchmark (PSB)

The PSB contains 1814 shape models which come in a triangular mesh format. The models are organized in four different semantic abstraction levels, *base, coarse1, coarse2 and coarse3*. At the *base* level, objects are grouped in very differentiated classes, e.g. *"F117 Fighter Jet"*, *"Biplane"* or *"Balloon"*. At higher levels, these classes are combined to more and more semantic classes like *"Commercial Plane"* or *"Fighter Jet"* at *coarse1* or all together in *"Aircraft"* at *coarse2*. Finally, *coarse3* only distinguishes between *"natural"* and *"human made"* objects.

We illustrate some examples of the PSB objects in the next tables. For a better visual impression, we use the original mesh representation given by the PSB. This is in contrast to our experiments, where we used volume renderings of the shape information, neglecting the color and texture information. Each table shows some examples from a class of a higher level and some more examples from some of its base level sub-classes.

Level: Coarse1	Aircraft
Level: Base	Sub-Classes of Aircraft
fighter jet	
biplane	

Level: Coarse1	Car
Level: Base	Sub-Classes of Car
sports car	
sedan	

Level: Coarse1	Building			
Level: Base	Sub-Classes of Building			
home				
castle				

Level: Coarse2	Animal			
Level: Base	Sub-Sub-Classes of Animal			
human				
spider				

Level: Coarse2	Furniture			
Level: Base	Sub-Sub-Classes of Furniture			
table				
couch				

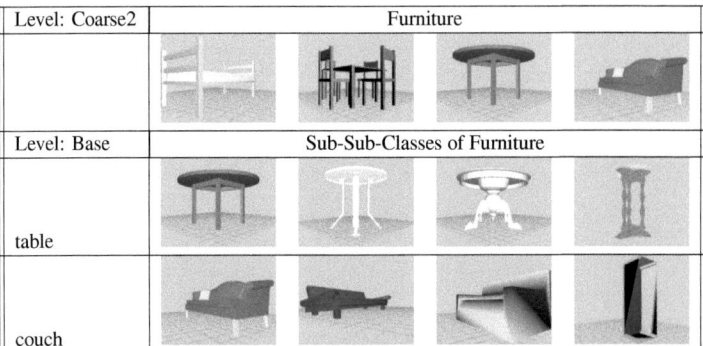

C Cell Nuclei Database

The database consists of 236 nuclei samples divided in 5 different target classes: erythrocyte (ery), endothelia cells (endo), epithelia cells (epithel), fibroblast (fb) and macrophages (lc-nseg) as well as some additional samples of cell types which can be found in the context of the target types (mono) and (pc-svmc). The samples were recored with an LSM from tissue probes of chicken chorioallantoic membrane (see section 19.2) which were treated as described in (Kurz et al., 2002). Human experts manually segmented and labeled the sample nuclei recordings to obtain a voxel-wise ground truth labeling.

The following tables show sample images of xy-planes taken at the central z-coordinates of the manually created segmentation mask and the two recorded channels.

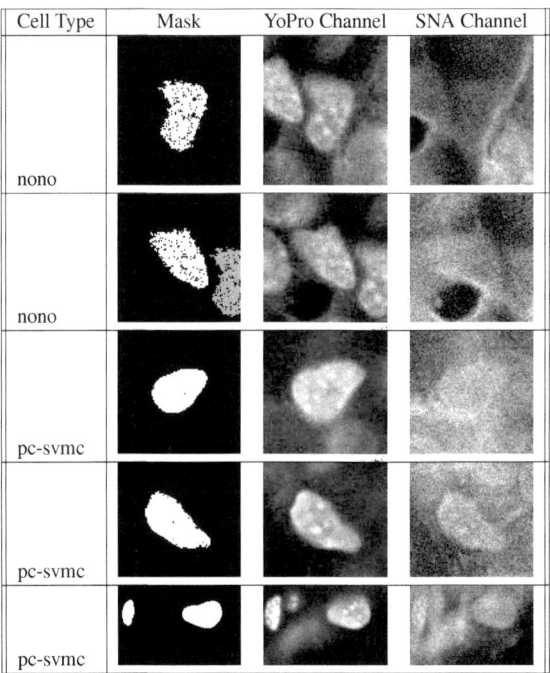

Cell Type	Mask	YoPro Channel	SNA Channel

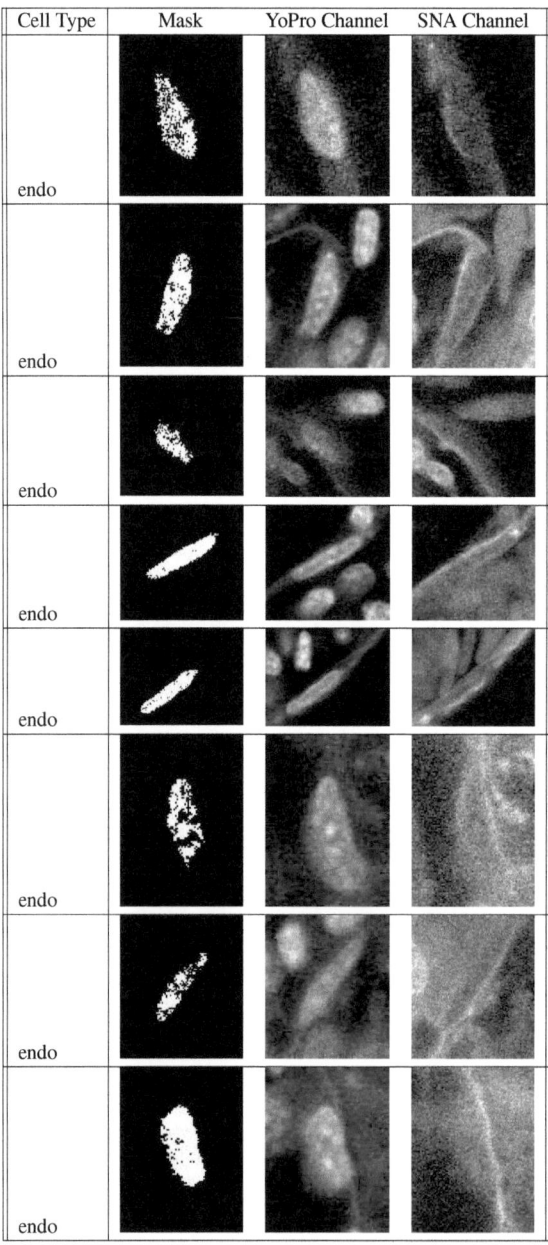

endo

endo

endo

endo

endo

endo

endo

endo

Cell Type	Mask	YoPro Channel	SNA Channel
epithel			
epithel			
epithel			
epithel			
epithel			
epithel			
epithel			
epithel			

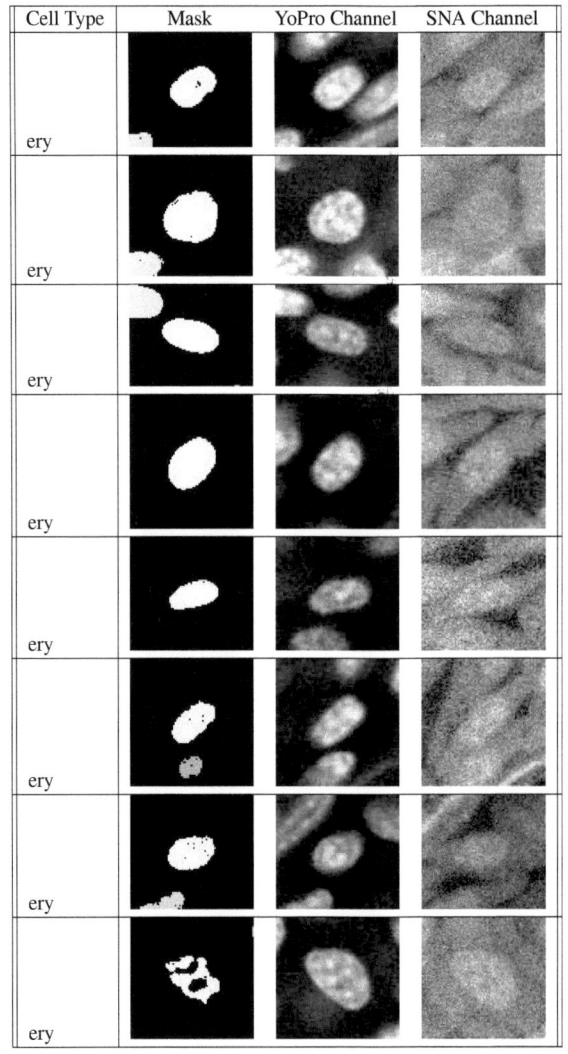

Cell Type	Mask	YoPro Channel	SNA Channel
ery			
ery			
ery			
ery			
ery			
ery			
ery			
ery			

Cell Type	Mask	YoPro Channel	SNA Channel
fb			
fb			
fb			
fb			
fb			
fb			
fb			
fb			

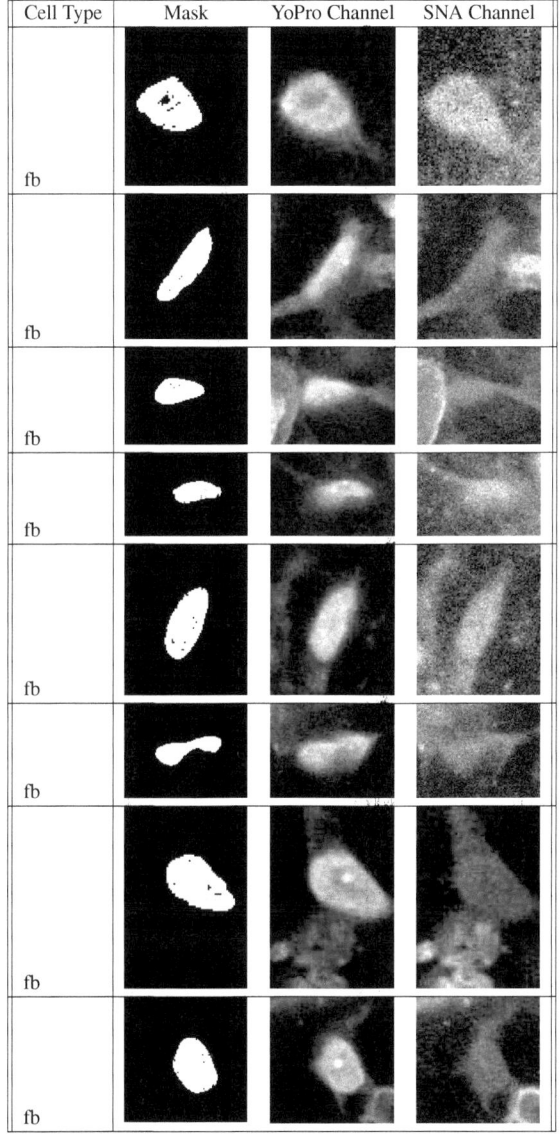

Cell Type	Mask	YoPro Channel	SNA Channel
lc-nseg			
lc-nseg			
lc-nseg			
lc-nseg			
lc-nseg			
lc-nseg			
lc-nseg			
lc-nseg			

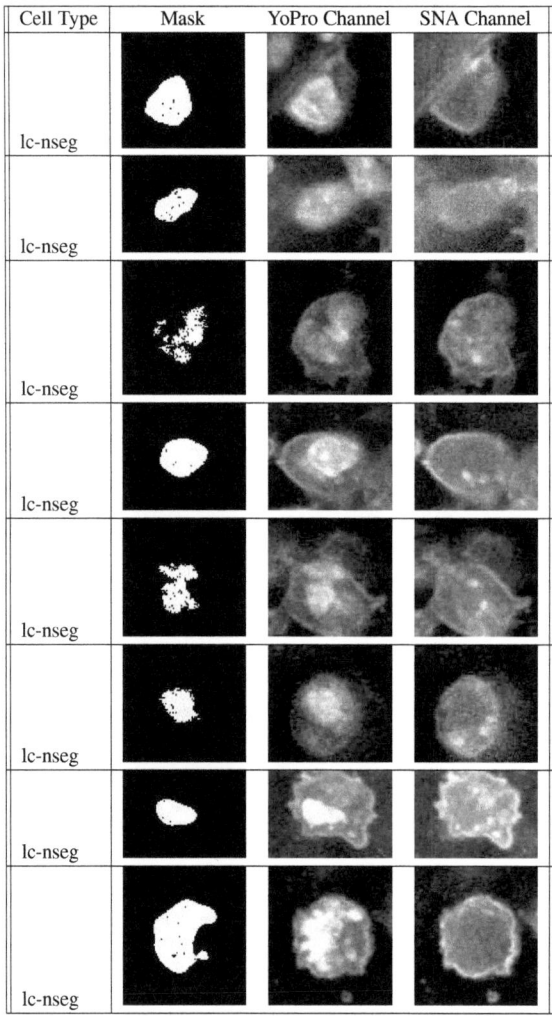

List of Figures

List of Figures

242

List of Tables

List of Tables

Bibliography

K. K. A. Rodriguez, D. Ehlenberger et al. Automated reconstruction of three-dimensional neuronal morphology from laser scanning microscopy images. *Science Methods*, 30:94–105, 2003.

M. Ankerst, G. Kastenmueller, H. Kriegel, and T. Seidl. Nearest neighbor classification in 3d protein databases. In *in Proc. ISMB*, 1999.

K. Arbter, W. Snyder, H. Burkhardt, and G. Hirzinger. Application of Affine-Invariant Fourier Descriptors to 3-D Objects. *IEEE Trans. on Pattern Analysis and Machine Intelligence*, PAMI-12(7): 640–647, 1990.

M. Asal. *Segmentierung und Klassifikation von Dendritischen Spines in 3D Volumendaten*. University of Freiburg, Masterthesis, supervised by J. Fehr and H. Burkhardt., 2008.

R. Barrera, G. Estevez, and J. Giraldo. Vector spherical harmonics and their application to magnetostatic. *Eur. J. Phys.*, 6:287–294, 1985.

K. P. Bennett, N. Cristianini, J. Shawe-Taylor, and D. Wu. Enlarging the margins in perceptron decision trees. *Machine Learning*, 41(3):295–313, 2000.

S. Beucher. The watershed transformation applied to image segmentation, 1991.

C. M. Bishop. *Pattern Recognition and Machine Learning (Information Science and Statistics)*. Springer, August 2006. ISBN 0387310738.

D. Blei, A. Ng, and M. Jordan. Latent dirichlet allocation. *J. Mach. Learn. Res.*, 3:993–1022, 2003.

B. E. Boser, I. Guyon, and V. Vapnik. A training algorithm for optimal margin classifiers. In I. D. Haussler, editor, *Computational Learing Theory*, pages 144–152, 1992.

P. Brazdil and J.Gama. Statlog datasets. http://www.liacc.up.pt/ML/statlog/datasets.html, 2006.

L. Breiman. Random forests. *Machine Learning*, 45 (1):5–32, 2001.

D. Brink and G. Satchler. *Angular Momentum, Second Edition*. Clarendon Press, Oxford, 1968.

G. Burel and H. Henoco. Determination of the orientation of 3d objects using spherical harmonics. *Graph. Models Image Process.*, 57(5):400–408, 1995. ISSN 1077-3169.

C. J. C. Burges and B. Schölkopf. Improving speed and accuracy of support vector learning machines. In M. J. M. Mozer and T. Petsche, editors, *Advances in Neural Information Processing Systems 9*, pages 375–381. MIT Press, Cambridge, MA, 1997.

H. Burkhardt. *Transformationen zur Lage Invarianten Merkmalsgewinnung*. VDI-Fortschritt-Bericht, Reihe 10 (Angewandte Informatik), Nr. 7, VDI-Verlag Düsseldorf, 1979.

H. Burkhardt and S. Siggelkow. Invariant features in pattern recognition - fundamentals and applications. *In Kotropoulos, C., Pitas, I., editors, Nonlinear Model-Based Image/Video Processing ans Analysis*, pages 269–3007, 2001.

N. Canterakis. 3d zernike moments and zernike affine invariants for 3d image analysis and recognition. In *11th Scandinavian Conf. on Image Analysis*, 1999.

P. Carbonetto. Faces datasets. http://www.cs.ubc.ca/ pcarbo/, 2005.

C. C. Chang and C. J. Lin. A library for support vector machines. http://www.csie.ntu.edu.tw/ cjlin/libsvm/, 2005.

D.-Y. Chen, M. Ouhyoung, X.-P. Tian, and Y.-T. Shen. On visual similarity based 3d model retrieval. In *Computer Graphics Forum*, pages 223–232, 2003.

J. Cheng, X. Zhou, E. Miller, R. Witt, et al. A novel computational approach for automatic dendrite spines detection in two-photon laser scan microscopy. *Journal of Neuroscience Methods*, 165:122–134, 2007.

C. Conrad, H. Erfle, P. Warnat, N. Daigle, T. Lörch, J. Ellenberg, R. Pepperok, and R. Eils. Automatik identification of subcellular phenotypes on human cell arrays. *Genom Research*, 14:1130–1136, 2004.

C. Cortes and V. Vapnik. Support-vector networks. *Machine Learning Journal*, 20:273–297, 1995.

R. A. Crowther. The molecular replacement method. In M. Rossmann, editor, *Gordon and Breach, New York*, pages 173–178, 1972.

H. Cundy and A. Rollett. *Mathematical Models*. Oxford Univ. Press, 2nd ed., 1961.

P. K. D. Healy Jr., D. Rockmore and S. Moore. Ffts for the 2-sphere - improvements and variations. *The Journal of Fourier Analysis and Applications*, 9(4):341–385, 2003.

T. Downs, K. E. Gates, and A. Masters. Exact simplification of support vector solutions. *Machine Learning*, 2:293–297, 2001.

J. Fehr. Rotational invariant uniform local binary patterns for full 3d volume texture analysis. In *Proc. FinSig 2007*, 2007a.

J. Fehr. Selbstlernende segmentierung und klassifikation von zellkernen in 3d volumendaten basierend auf grauwertinvarianten. In *Workshop "Quantitative Bildanalyse", FH Darmstadt.*, 2005.

J. Fehr. Lernen im kontext der bildanalyse. In *Workshop "Quantitative Bildanalyse", FH Darmstadt.*, 2007b.

J. Fehr and H. Burkhardt. Rotational invariant uniform local binary patterns for full 3d volume texture analysis. In *Proc. ICPR 2008 (to apear)*, 2008.

J. Fehr and H. Burkhardt. Invariant local features for 3d biomedical image analysis. In *Proceedings of the Workshop on Image Analysis and in Vivo Pharmachology (IAVP), 12-14 April 2007,Roskilde, Denmark*, 2007a.

J. Fehr and H. Burkhardt. Harmonic shape histograms for 3d shape classification and retrieval. In *IAPR Workshop on Machine Vision Applications (MVA2007)*, Tokyo, Japan, 2007b.

J. Fehr and H. Burkhardt. Phase based 3d texture features. In *Proceedings of the DAGM 2006, Springer LNCS 4174, pp 263-272*, 2006.

J. Fehr and K. Zapién. Fast support vector machine classification of very largedatasets. Internal report 2/07, IIF-LMB, University Freiburg, march 2007.

J. Fehr, O. Ronneberger, H. Kurz, and H. Burkhardt. Self-learning segmentation and classification of cell-nuclei in 3d volumetric data using voxel-wise gray scale invariants. *Proceedings of the 27th DAGM Symposium, in number 3663 LNCS, Springer, Vienna, Austria, 30.8 - 2.9. 2005.*, 2005.

J. Fehr, H. Kurz, C. Sauer, O. Ronneberger, and H. Burkhardt. Identifikation von zellen in intaktem gewebe - selbst-lernende segmentierung und klassifikation von zellkernen in 3d volumendaten mittels voxel-weiser grauwertinvarianten. In *Handels H. Ehrhardt J. Editors, Informatik Aktuell, Bildverarbeitung fÃijr die Medizin 2006, Hamburg 19. - 21.3.06*, pages 368–373. Springer-Verlag, 2006.

J. Fehr, K. Zapien, and H. Burkhardt. Fast support vector machine classification of very large datasets. In *Post-Proceedings of the GfKl Conference, Data Analysis, Machine Learning, and Applications*, University of Freiburg, Germany, 2007. LNCS, Springer.

J. Fehr, O. Ronneberger, J. Schulz, T. Schmidt, M. Reisert, and H. Burkhardt. Invariance via group-integration: A feature framework for 3d biomedical image analysis. In *proceeding of the special session on Invariance And Robustness at the International Conference on Computer Graphics and Imaging (CGIM 2008), Innsbruck, Austria*, 2008.

P. F. Felzenszwalb and D. P. Huttenlocher. Efficient belief propagation for early vision. *Int. J. Comput. Vision*, 70(1):41–54, 2006. ISSN 0920-5691.

J. Flusser. Effective boundary-based calculation of object moments. In *IVCNZ*, pages 369–374, 1998.

M. Frigo and S. G. Johnson. The design and implementation of FFTW3. *Proceedings of the IEEE*, 93 (2):216–231, 2005. special issue on "Program Generation, Optimization, and Platform Adaptation".

S. Geman and D. Geman. Stochastic relaxation, gibbs distributions and the bayesian restoration of images. *IEEE Transactions on Pattern Analysis and Machine Intelligence*, 6(6):721–741, November 1984.

R. Gilad-Bachrach, A. Navot, and N. Tishby. Margin based feature selection - theory and algorithms. In *ICML '04: Proceedings of the twenty-first international conference on Machine learning*, page 43, New York, NY, USA, 2004. ACM. ISBN 1-58113-828-5.

H. Groemer. *Geometric Applications of Fourier Series and Spherical Harmonics*. Cambridge University Press, 1996.

I. Guyon, B. Boser, and V. Vapnik. Automatic capacity tuning of very large VC-dimension classifiers. In S. J. Hanson, J. D. Cowan, and C. L. Giles, editors, *Advances in Neural Information Processing Systems*, volume 5, pages 147–155. Morgan Kaufmann, San Mateo, CA, 1993.

R. Haralick. Statistical and structural approaches to texture. *Proc. IEEE*, 67,5:786–804, 1979.

D. Healy, D. Rockmore, P. Kostelec, and S. Moore. Ffts for the 2-sphere - improvements and variations. *Journal of Fourier Analysis and Applications*, 9:4:341–385, 2003.

E. Hill. The theory of vector spherical harmonics. *Am. J. Phys.*, 22:211–214, 1954.

T. K. Ho and E. M. Kleinberg. Building projectable classifiers of arbitrary complexity. In *Proceedings of the 13th International Conference on Pattern Recognition*. Vienna, Austria, 1996.

P. Hough. Method and means for recognising complex patterns. *Technical report, U.S. Patent No. 3069654*, 1962.

C. Hsu and C. Lin. A comparison of methods for multi-class support vector machines, 2001.

J. J. Hull. A database for handwritten text recognition research, 1994.

F. Jurie and B. Triggs. Creating efficient codebooks for visual recognition. In *ICCV '05: Proceedings of the Tenth IEEE International Conference on Computer Vision (ICCV'05) Volume 1*, pages 604–610. IEEE Computer Society, 2005.

Y. Kangl, K. Morooka1, and H. Nagahashi. Scale invariant texture analysis using multi-scale local autocorrelation features. In *Scale Space and PDE Methods in Computer Vision, LNCS 3459*, 2005.

M. Kazhdan. Rotation invariant spherical harmonic representation of 3d shape descriptors. *Symp. on Geom. Process.*, 2003.

M. Kazhdan, T. Funkhouser, and S. Rusinkiewicz. Rotation invariant spherical harmonic representation of 3d shape descriptors. In *Symposium on Geometry Processing*, 2003.

S. Keerthi, S. Shevade, C. Bhattacharyya, and K. Murthy. Improvements to platt's smo algorithm for svm classifier design, 1999.

A. Koh, W. Lindquist, K. Zito, et al. An image analysis algorithm for dendritic spines. *Neural Computation*, 14:1283–1310, 2002.

R. Kohavi. A study of cross-validation and bootstrap for accuracy estimation and model selection. In *Fourteenth International Joint Conference on Artificial Intelligence*, pages 1137–1143, 1995.

P. Kohli and P. H. S. Torr. Effciently solving dynamic markov random fields using graph cuts. In *ICCV '05: Proceedings of the Tenth IEEE International Conference on Computer Vision*, pages 922–929, Washington, DC, USA, 2005. IEEE Computer Society. ISBN 0-7695-2334-X-02.

R. Kondor. A complete set of rotationally and translationally invariant features for images. *CoRR*, abs/cs/0701127, 2007.

J. A. Kovacs and W. Wriggers. Fast rotational matching. *Acta Crystallogr*, (58):1282–1286, 2002.

H. A. Kropatsch W., Sablatnig R., editor. *Over-Complete Wavelet Approximation of a Support Vector Machine for Efficient Classification*, 2005. Proceedings of the 27th DAGM Symposium, Vienna.

M. P. Kumar and P. H. S. Torr. *Fast Memory-Efficient Generalized Belief Propagation*, volume 3954/2006 of *Lecture Notes in Computer Science*, pages 451–463. Springer Berlin / Heidelberg, 2006. ISBN 978-3-540-33838-3.

M. P. Kumar, P. H. S. Torr, and A. Zisserman. Obj cut. In *Computer Vision and Pattern Recognition, 2005. CVPR 2005. IEEE Computer Society Conference on*, volume 1, pages 18–25 vol. 1, 2005.

H. Kurz, J. Fehr, S. Winnik, M. Moser, O. Ronneberger, and H. Burkhardt. Dynamics of vascular cells in their social conbooktitle: quantitative 3-d-analysis of vascular growth and remodeling and new insights into mechanisms of angiogenesis. In *Proceedings of the Jahrestagung der AnatoInProceedingshen Gesellschaft, Freiburg, 7 - 10 April*, 2005a.

H. Kurz, O. Ronneberger, J. Fehr, R. Baumgartner, J. Korn, and H. Burkhardt. Automatic classification of cell nuclei and cells during embryonic vascular development. *Ann Anat*, 187:130ff, 2005b.

H. Kurz, C. Sauer, J. Fehr, O. Ronneberger, and H. Burkhardt. Automated identification of large numbers of cells in intact tissues as a highthroughput approach in morphology. In *Proceedings of the Jahrestagung der AnatoInProceedingshen Gesellschaft, Freiburg, 7 - 10 April*, 2006.

H. Kurz, J. Fehr, R. Nitschke, and H. Burkhardt. Two types of perivascular cells in the chorioallantoic membrane capillary plexus. In *Proceedings of the 24. Arbeitstagung Anat Ges, Sept 26-28, Würzburg*, 2007.

H. Kurz, J. Fehr, R. Nitschke, and H. Burkhardt. Pericytes in the mature chorioallantoic membrane capillary plexus contain desmin and alpha-smooth muscle actin: relevance for non-sprouting angiogenesis. *Journal of Histochemistry and Cell Biology*, 2008.

H. Kurz et al. Automatic classification of cell nuclei and cells during embryonic vascular development. *Ann Anat 2005; 187 (Suppl): 130.*, 2005c.

H. Kurz et al. Pericytes in experimental mda-mb231 tumor angiogenesis. *Histochem Cell Biol*, pages 117:527–534, 2002.

C. Lampert and M. B. Blaschko. A multiple kernel learning approach to joint multi-class object detection. In *Pattern Recognition: Proceedings of the 30th DAGM Symposium*, pages 31–40. Springer, 2008.

B. Leibe and B. Schiele. Interleaved object categorization and segmentation. In *British Machine Vision Conference (BMVC'03), Norwich, UK, Sept. 9-11*, 2003.

R. Lenz. *Group theoretical methods in Image Processing*. Springer Verlag, Lecture Notes, 1990.

G. Li, T. Liu, A. Tarokh, J. Nie, L. Guo, A. Mara, S. Holley, and S. Wong. 3d cell nuclei segmentation based on gradient tracking. *Cell Biology*, 8:40ff, 2007.

G. Lin, M. Chawla, K. Olson, C. Barnes, et al. A multi-model approach to simultaneous segmentation and classification of heterogeneous populations of cell nuclei in 3d confocal microscope images. *Cytometry*, 71A:724–736, 2007.

K. Lin and C. Lin. A study on reduced support vector machines, 2003.

S. R. Lin H. and A. L., editors. *Speeding Up Multi-class SVM Evaluation by PCA and Feature Selection*, 2005. 2005 SIAM Workshop, Newport Beach, CA.

R. Linsker. Self-organization in a perceptual network. *IEEE Computer*, 19:153–158, 1988.

A. Lohmann, D. Mendlovic, and G. Shabtay. Significance of phase and amplitude in the fourier domain. *J. Opt. Soc. Am.*, 14:2901–2904, 1997.

D. Lowe. Distinctive image features from scale-invariant keypoints. *International Journal of Computer Vision*, 60:91–110, 2004.

T. Mäenpää and M. Pietikäinen. Texture analysis with local binary patterns. In C. Chen and P. Wang, editors, *Handbook of Pattern Recognition and Computer Vision*, chapter Texture analysis with local binary patterns., pages 197–216. World Scientific, 2005.

T. Mäenpää, T. Ojala, M. Pietikäinen, and M. Soriano. Robust texture classification by subsets of local binary patterns. In *Proc. 15th International Conference on Pattern Recognition, Barcelona, Spain*, 2000.

A. Makadia and K. Daniilidis. Rotation recovery from spherical images without correspondences. *IEEE Transactions on Pattern Analysis and Machine Intelligence*, 28(7), 2006.

A. Makadia and K. Daniilidis. Direct 3d-rotation estimation from spherical images via a generalized shift theorem. In *IEEE Conference on Computer Vision and Pattern Recognition, Madison*, 2003.

A. Makadia, L. Sorgi, and K. Daniilidis. Rotation estimation from spherical images. In *International Conference on Pattern Recognition, Cambridge*, 2004.

M. Meyer, M. Fauver, J. Rahn, et al. Automatic cell analysis in 2d and 3d: a comparitive study. *Pattern Recognition*, 2008.

K. Michael, W. Andrew, and T. Demetri. Snakes: Active contour models. *International Journal of Computer Vision*, V1(4):321–331, January 1988.

K. Mikolajczyk and C. Schmid. Scale and affine invariant interest point detectors. *International Journal of Computer Vision*, 60(1):63–86, 2004.

K. Mikolajczyk, B. Leibe, and B. Schiele. Local features for object class recognition. In *ICCV '05: Proceedings of the Tenth IEEE International Conference on Computer Vision*, pages 1792–1799. IEEE Computer Society, 2005.

K. Murphy, Y. Weiss, and M. Jordan. Loopy belief propagation for approximate inference: An empirical study. In *Proceedings of the 15th Annual Conference on Uncertainty in Artificial Intelligence (UAI-99)*, pages 467–47, San Francisco, CA, 1999. Morgan Kaufmann.

J. Nocedal and S. Wright. *Numerical Optimization*. Springer Series in Operations Research. Springer-Verlag New York, Inc., 1999.

M. Novotni. 3d zernike descriptors for content based shape retrieval. In *In The 8th ACM Symposium on Solid Modeling and Applications*, pages 216–225. ACM Press, 2003.

H. Nyquist. Certain topics in telegraph transmission theory. *Trans. AIEE*, 47:617–644, 1928.

J. B. Pawley, editor. *Handbook of Biological Confocal Microscopy*. Plenum Press, New York, 1995.

P. Peloschek, G. Langs, M. Weber, J. Sailer, M. Reisegger, H. Imhof, H. Bischof, and F. Kainberger. An Automatic Model-based System for Joint Space Measurements on Hand Radiographs: Initial Experience. *Radiology*, page 2452061281, 2007.

K. Petersen, J. Fehr, and H. Burkhardt. Fast general belief propagation for map estimation on 2d and 3d grid-like markov random fields. In *Proceedings of the DAGM 2008*, pages 41–50, München, Germany, 2008. LNCS, Springer.

M. Reisert. Efficient tensor voting with 3d tensorial harmonics. In *Albert-Ludwigs-University Freiburg, Internal Report 2, February 2008*, 2008.

M. Reisert and H. Burkhardt. Efficient tensor voting with 3d tensorial harmonics. In *CVPR Workshop on Tensors, 2008, Anchorage, Alaska*, 2008.

M. Reisert and H. Burkhardt. Irreducible group representation for 3d shape description. In *Proceedings of the 28th Pattern Recognition Symposium of the German Association for Pattern Recognition (DAGM 2006), Berlin, Germany*, pages 132–142. LNCS, Springer, 2006.

O. Ronneberger. *3D Invariants for Automated Pollen Recognition*. Dissertation, University of Freiburg, 2008.

O. Ronneberger and et al. Svm template library. http://lmb.informatik.uni-freiburg.de/lmbsoft/libsvmtl/index.en.html, 2004.

O. Ronneberger and J. Fehr. Voxel-wise gray scale invariants for simultaneous segmentation and classification. In *Proceedings of the 27th DAGM Symposium, in number 3663 LNCS, Springer, Vienna, Austria,*, 2005.

O. Ronneberger, H. Burkhardt, and E. Schultz. General-purpose object recognition in 3d volume data sets using gray-scale invariants - classifacation of airborne pollen-grains recorded with a confocal laser scanning microscope. In *Proceedings of the 16th International Conference on Pattern Recognition, Quebec, Canada*, 2002.

O. Ronneberger, J. Fehr, and H. Burkhardt. Voxel-wise gray scale invariants for simultaneous segmentation and classification – theory and application to cell-nuclei in 3d volumetric data. Internal report 2/05, IIF-LMB, University Freiburg, april 2005.

M. Rose. *Elementary Theory of Angular Momentum*. Dover Publications, 1957.

C. Sauer, J. Fehr, O. Ronneberger, H. Burkhardt, K. Sandau, and H. Kurz. Automated identification of large cell numbers in intact tissues - self-learning segmentation, classification, and quantification of cell nuclei in 3-d volume data via voxel-based gray scale invariants. In *Proceedings of the Jahrestagung der AnatoInProceedingshen Gesellschaft, Freiburg, 7 - 10 April*, 2006.

D. Saupe and D. V. Vranic. 3d model retrieval with spherical harmonics and moments. In *DAGM 2001*, pages 392–397, 2001a.

D. Saupe and D. V. Vranic. 3d model retrieval with spherical harmonics and moments. In *Proceedings of the 23rd DAGM-Symposium on Pattern Recognition*, pages 392–397, London, UK, 2001b. Springer-Verlag. ISBN 3-540-42596-9.

M. Schael. Invariant 3D Features. Technical Report 4/97, Albert-Ludwigs-Universität, Freiburg, Institut für Informatik, 1997.

M. Schael and S. Siggelkow. Invariant grey-scale features for 3d sensor-data. In *Proceedings of the International Conference on Pattern Recognition, volume 2, Barcelona, Spain*, pages 531–535, 2000.

R. E. Schapire. Msri workshop on nonlinear estimation and classification. the boosting approach to machine learning an overview, 2002.

R. Schilling, J. Fehr, R. Spörle, H. Burkhardt, B. Herrmann, M. Vingron, and A. Schliep. Comparison of whole mouse embryos by non-linear image registration. In *Proceedings of the German Conference on Bioinformatics, Potsdam, September 26-28*, 2007.

P. Schröder and W. Sweldens. Spherical wavelets: efficiently representing functions on the sphere. In *SIGGRAPH '95: Proceedings of the 22nd annual conference on Computer graphics and interactive techniques*, pages 161–172, New York, NY, USA, 1995. ACM. ISBN 0-89791-701-4.

P. Schröder and W. Sweldens. Spherical wavelets: Texture processing. In P. Hanrahan and W. Purgathofer, editors, *Rendering Techniques '95*. Springer Verlag, Wien, New York, August 1995.

J. Schulz, T. Schmidt, R. Ronneberger, H. Burkhardt, T. Pasternak, A. Dovzhenko, and K. Palme. Fast scalar and vectorial grayscale based invariant features for 3d cell nuclei localization and classification. In *Proceedings of the 28th Pattern Recognition Symposium of the German Association for Pattern Recognition (DAGM 2006), Berlin, Germany*, 2006.

H. Schulz-Mirbach. *Anwendung von Invarianzprinzipien zur Merkmalgewinnung in der Mustererkennung.* PhD thesis, Technische Universität Hamburg-Harburg, 1995a. Reihe 10, Nr. 372, VDI-Verlag.

H. Schulz-Mirbach. Invariant features for grey scale images. In F. K. G. Sager, S. Posch, editor, *17. DAGM-Symposium Mustererkennung,* pages 1–14, 1995b.

B. Schölkopf and A. Smola. *Learning with Kernels.* The MIT Press, Cambridge, MA, USA, 2002.

J. Sethian. *Level Set Methods: Evolving Interfaces in Geometry.* Cambridge University Press, 1996.

N. Shental, A. Zomet, T. Hertz, and Y. Weiss. Learning and inferring image segmentations using the gbp typical cut algorithm. In *ICCV '03: Proceedings of the Ninth IEEE International Conference on Computer Vision,* page 1243, Washington, DC, USA, 2003. IEEE Computer Society. ISBN 0-7695-1950-4.

P. Shilane, P. Min, M. Kazhdan, and T. Funkhouser. The princeton shape benchmark. In *Shape Modeling International, Genova, Italy,* 2004.

S. Siggelkow. *Feature Historgrams for Content-Based Image Retrieval.* PhD thesis, Albert-Ludwigs-Universität Freiburg, 2002.

J. Sivic, B. C. Russell, A. A. Efros, A. Zisserman, and W. T. Freeman. Discovering objects and their location in images. In *Computer Vision, 2005. ICCV 2005. Tenth IEEE International Conference on,* volume 1, pages 370–377 Vol. 1, 2005.

A. Streicher. *3D Shape Retrieval mit lokalen Merkmalen.* University of Freiburg, Masterthesis, supervised by J. Fehr and H. Burkhardt., 2008.

M. F. Tappen and W. T. Freeman. Comparison of graph cuts with belief propagation for stereo, using identical mrf parameters. In *ICCV '03: Proceedings of the Ninth IEEE International Conference on Computer Vision,* page 900, Washington, DC, USA, 2003. IEEE Computer Society. ISBN 0-7695-1950-4.

M. Tinkham. *Group Theory and Quantum Mechanics.* Dover Publications, 1992.

S. Trapani and J. Navaza. Calculation of spherical harmonics and wigner d functions by fft. applications to fast rotational matching in molecular replacement and implementation into amore. *Acta Crystallogr,* 62:262–269, 2006.

V. Vapnik. *The Nature of Statistical Learning Theory.* New York: Springer Verlag, 1995.

N. Vasconecelos. Feature selection by maximum marginal diversity: optimality and implications for visual recognition. In *Proceedings of IEEE Conf. on Computer Vision and Pattern Recogniton, Madison, USA,* 2003.

O. Veksler. *Efficient graph-based energy minimization methods in computer vision.* PhD thesis, Cornell University, August 1999.

D. V. Vranic. An improvement of rotation invariant 3d shape descriptor based on functions on concentric spheres. In *IEEE International Conference on Image Processing (ICIP 2003),* volume 3, pages 757–760, 2003.

C. Weaver, P. Hof, S. Wearne, et al. Automated algorithms for multiscale morphometry of neuronal dendrites. *Neural Computation,* 16:1353–1383, 2004.

S. Wenndt and S. Shamsunder. Bispectrum features for robust speaker identification. *Acoustics, Speech, and Signal Processing, IEEE International Conference on*, 2:1095, 1997.

J. Wicklein. *Segmentierung biologischer Strukturen in 3D Volumen Daten mit assoziativen Markov-Netzwerken*. University of Freiburg, Masterthesis, supervised by J. Fehr and H. Burkhardt., 2006.

G. Winkler. *Image Analysis, Random Fields and Markov Chain Monte Carlo Methods*. Springer, February 2006.

J. Wolf, W. Burgard, and H. Burkhardt. Robust vision-based localization by combining an image retrieval system with Monte Carlo localization. *IEEE Transactions on Robotics*, 21(2), 2005.

C. Xu and J. Prince. Gradient vector flow: A new external force for snakes. In *Proc. IEEE Conf. on Comp. Vis. Patt. Recog. (CVPR), Los Alamitos*, pages 66–71, 1997.

H. Yang and Y. Wang. A lbp-based face recognition method with hamming distance constraint. In *ICIG '07: Proceedings of the Fourth International Conference on Image and Graphics*, pages 645–649, Washington, DC, USA, 2007. IEEE Computer Society. ISBN 0-7695-2929-1.

L. Yaroslavsky. Boundary effect free and adaptive discrete signal sinc-interpolation algorithms for signal and image resampling. *Appl. Opt.*, 42(20):4166–4175, 2003.

J. S. Yedidia. Constructing free energy approximations and generalized belief propagation algorithms. Technical Report TR-2004-40, Mitsubishi Electric Research Laboratories, December 2004.

J. S. Yedidia, W. T. Freeman, and Y. Weiss. Generalized belief propagation. In *NIPS*, pages 689–695, June 2000.

J. S. Yedidia, W. T. Freeman, and Y. Weiss. Understanding belief propagation and its generalizations. Technical Report TR-2001-22, Mitsubishi Electric Research Laboratories, January 2001.

K. Zapién, J. Fehr, and H. Burkhardt. Support vector machine classification using linear svms. In *ICPR Hong Kong*, pages 366–369, 2006.

G. Zhao and M. Pietikäinen. Dynamic texture recognition using volume local binary patterns. In *Proc. ECCV 2006 Workshop on Dynamical Vision*, page 12 pp, Graz, Austria, 2006.

G. Zhao and M. Pietikäinen. Improving rotation invariance of the volume local binary pattern operator. In *Proc. IAPR Conference on Machine Vision Applications*, pages 327–330, Tokyo, Japan, 2007a.

G. Zhao and M. Pietikäinen. Dynamic texture recognition using local binary patterns with an application to facial expressions. *IEEE Transactions on Pattern Analysis and Machine Intelligence*, 29(6, in press.), 2007b.

Bibliography

254

Index

VDM Verlagsservicegesellschaft mbH

Die VDM Verlagsservicegesellschaft sucht für wissen-
schaftliche Verlage abgeschlossene und herausragende

Dissertationen, Habilitationen, Diplomarbeiten, Master Theses, Magisterarbeiten usw.

für die kostenlose Publikation als Fachbuch.

Sie verfügen über eine Arbeit, die hohen inhaltlichen und for-
malen Ansprüchen genügt, und haben Interesse an einer hono-
rarvergüteten Publikation?

Dann senden Sie bitte erste Informationen über sich und Ihre
Arbeit per Email an *info@vdm-vsg.de*.

Sie erhalten kurzfristig unser Feedback!

VDM Verlagsservicegesellschaft mbH
Dudweiler Landstr. 99
D - 66123 Saarbrücken

Telefon +49 681 3720 174
Fax +49 681 3720 1749

www.vdm-vsg.de

Die VDM Verlagsservicegesellschaft mbH vertritt

MIX
Papier aus verantwortungsvollen Quellen
Paper from responsible sources
FSC® C105338

Printed by Books on Demand GmbH, Norderstedt / Germany